THE BEST OF
IT HAPPENED IN
HOCKEY

BRIAN
McFARLANE

Stoddart

Published in 1997 by
Stoddart Publishing Co. Limited

Distributed in Canada by
General Distribution Services Inc.
30 Lesmill Road
Toronto, Canada M3B 2T6
Tel. (416) 445-3333
Fax (416) 445-5967
E-mail Customer.Service@ccmailgw.genpub.com

Distributed in the United States by
General Distribution Services Inc.
85 River Rock Drive, Suite 202
Buffalo, New York 14207
Toll-free Tel. 1-800-805-1083
Toll-free Fax 1-800-481-6207
E-mail gdsinc@genpub.com

01 00 99 98 97 1 2 3 4 5

The material in this book has previously appeared
in Brian McFarlane's *It Happened in Hockey,*
More It Happened in Hockey, and *Still More It*
Happened in Hockey, all published by Stoddart Publishing.

Cataloging in Publication Data

McFarlane, Brian, 1931–
The best of it happened in hockey

ISBN 0-7737-3046-X

1. Hockey – Canada. I. Title.
GV848.4.C3M33 1997   796.962'0971   97-931380-5

Jacket design: Bill Douglas @ The Bang

Printed and bound in Canada

We acknowledge the Canada Council for the Arts and the
Ontario Arts Council for their support of our publishing program.

Contents

1

Icons of the Ice

2

Guardians of the Nets

3

Amazing Achievements

4

Tough Guys

5

On-Ice Oddities

Playoff Heroics and Cup Capers

7

Behind the Scenes

Legends and Lore

ICONS OF THE ICE

How the Habs Got Beliveau

WHEN I WAS A JUNIOR HOCKEY PLAYER for an Ottawa Valley team called the Inkerman Rockets, we sailed through the playoffs one year and had Memorial Cup hopes in mind — until we ran into a powerful team from Quebec named the Citadels.

The Citadels had a marvelous player called Jean Beliveau, and the coach said it was my job to stop him. That, as you may have guessed, was impossible. Our entire team couldn't stop the giant centre.

Beliveau was the best we'd ever seen, and we were certain he would become an instant star with the Montreal Canadiens when he joined them the following year. In that era, before the introduction of the entry draft, NHL teams acquired junior players by signing them to "C" forms or by placing their names on a negotiation list. While Beliveau had not signed a "C" form with the Canadiens, his name topped their negotiation list — in capital letters — and this meant he could play for no other professional club.

But Beliveau, to our consternation, spurned a chance to play for the Canadiens. He had been so well treated in Quebec, and so well paid, even as an amateur, that he felt an obligation to his Quebec City fans. Hadn't they filled the new arena in Quebec City to see him play? Hadn't they bought him a new car — a 1951 Nash — and presented it to him during one of the playoff games with Inkerman? Now he would repay them for their support by playing senior hockey for the Quebec City Aces for another year or two.

The Canadiens couldn't stop him because the Quebec Senior League was not a professional league; it was called semipro even though all the players were paid. Beliveau, of course, was paid more than anyone else. For two years he was the Quebec League's biggest star, filling arenas everywhere he played.

Finally, the desperate Canadiens made a bold move. They bought the entire Quebec Senior League and turned it professional. That gave Beliveau little choice but to sign with Montreal. The money he received — a $20,000 bonus and more than $100,000 for a five-year contract — was an enormous sum in those days.

Frank Selke, Sr., then general manager of the Canadiens, was asked what secret he used to land the big centreman. "No secret," he replied with a grin. "I simply opened the Forum vault and said, 'Help yourself, Jean.'"

Montreal fans agreed Beliveau was worth waiting for. He soon became the Habs' most prolific centre and team captain, and helped them win ten Stanley Cups in the next two decades.

Stardom Denied

HALF A CENTURY AGO, at 18, Herb Carnegie was a first-rate Junior A player in Toronto, one of the best centre-ice players in the nation. His career led him to the tough Quebec Senior League, then considered to be just one small step below the NHL.

In Quebec, Carnegie became a big star and won

three MVP awards. He hoped his hockey skills would lead him to hockey stardom with the New York Rangers — everybody said he had the talent — but the opportunity never came.

Why? Because Carnegie was black. Carnegie knew the odds were against him right from the beginning. As a teenager he'd been told that Conn Smythe, owner of the Leafs, had said of him, "I'd sign him in a minute — if I could only turn him white."

It wasn't until 1958, when the Boston Bruins introduced Willie O'Ree, a rookie from Fredericton, New Brunswick, that a black player cracked the lineup of an NHL team. O'Ree scored four goals in 45 games and was shunted back to the minor leagues.

Shack Loads His Gun, Shoots, and Scores

FORMER BUFFALO SABRE MIKE BYERS recalls playing on a line with Eddie "The Entertainer" Shack one night in Buffalo. "We were waiting for the face-off in the other team's zone, and just before the official dropped the puck, Shack yells, 'Hold on a minute!' We all look over at him, and he's taking his hockey stick, turning it around, and cocking it like a rifle. Then he put the stick back in its original position and nodded, indicating he was ready for the face-off.

"Wouldn't you know, when the puck was dropped, it came right back to Shack and he snapped it into the net for a goal. Later I heard him tell reporters he stopped the game because his

Buffalo Sabre Eddie Shack hitches a ride on California Seals' Gerry Ehman. (Robert B. Shaver)

'gun' was out of bullets. I'll say this, he picked a great time to reload."

The Strange Twist That Brought Tony McKegney to the NHL

THE FIRST BLACK PLAYER to reach the NHL was Willie O'Ree, who enjoyed a brief stint with the Boston Bruins, joining them for a two-game trial in 1957–58. He rejoined them in 1960–61, scored four goals in 45 games, went back to the minors, and never resurfaced in the NHL. Mike Marson and Bill Riley joined the Washington Capitals in the seventies, but they, too, didn't stay around long. Marson scored 24 goals in 196 NHL games, Riley 31 in 139 games.

Clearly Tony McKegney from Sarnia, Ontario, stands out as the first black player to become a prolific NHL scorer — collecting 320 goals in a career that embraced 912 NHL games and saw him perform with eight different teams, including the Buffalo Sabres where he began his NHL career in October 1978.

But prior to that, in the spring of 1978, he became the first hockey player to be released from a pro contract — for racial reasons. It happened when John Bassett, owner of the Birmingham Bulls of the World Hockey Association, persuaded McKegney, a blue-chip prospect in junior hockey, to sign a contract with his Bulls. Bassett promised McKegney he wouldn't have to spend any time in the minor leagues and that he would play on a line with Ken Linesman, his centerman from junior hockey days in Kingston, Ontario. The deal appealed to McKegney. Deciding not to wait for the NHL draft to find out which club would select him, he signed a lucrative contract with Bassett.

A few days later, to McKegney's consternation, Bassett announced that he was releasing the young star from his Birmingham contract. The announcement of McKegney's signing had triggered an angry reaction from racists in Birmingham. Several season ticket holders threatened to cancel their tickets to Bulls games if a black player joined the team. Bassett reluctantly let McKegney go, and when the NHL draft was held that June, the Buffalo Sabres made McKegney their number one choice.

Bassett later apologized to the citizens of Birmingham, claiming he had "overreacted" to a very few complaints.

"The Birmingham situation came as a major surprise to me," McKegney told hockey writer Frank Orr of the *Toronto Star.* "I'd never run into anything like that in my life."

Another oddity in McKegney's background is that he had two hockey playing brothers — one white and one black. His parents, Larry and Cathy McKegney of Sarnia, had six children, three of whom were adopted. Tony's brother Ian, who is white, played in the Chicago chain, and his brother Mike, who is black, played in the American Hockey League and in Europe.

Blood in Boston

IT HAPPENED on December 12, 1933 at the Boston Garden. The Bruins were playing the Leafs that night and the Leafs, in the second period, were two men short.

Eddie Shore, the Bruins' great defenceman, dashed up the ice and was bowled over in the Leaf zone by King Clancy. Clancy led a return rush, and when he took off, Ace Bailey, one of Toronto's best forwards, stepped around the fallen Shore and took Clancy's place on the Leaf blue line.

Just then, Shore jumped up and charged Bailey from behind, sending the Leaf player flying with a vicious check. Bailey's head hit the ice with a crack that could be heard throughout the arena.

Red Horner of the Leafs retaliated at once. He smashed Shore in the face and knocked him out with one punch. Now there were two bodies on the ice, two heads oozing blood.

When Bailey was carried off the ice on a stretcher, a Bruin fan taunted Leaf owner Conn Smythe. Smythe lashed out, struck the fan and more blood flowed. Smythe was arrested by Boston police and thrown in jail.

With his skull fractured in two places, Bailey was rushed to hospital, where a team of brain surgeons tried desperately to save his life. Somehow he survived two major operations, but his hockey career ended that night.

Bailey's father, who had been listening to the game on radio back in Toronto, left hurriedly for Boston, packing a gun. He had every intention of shooting the player who had ended his son's career. Luckily he was intercepted in Boston by Leaf officials, who spiked his drink and placed the groggy father of the stricken star on a train back to Toronto.

Shore was vilified in the press and suspended for a month. But one man who never berated Shore was Bailey, the victim of his attack. Later that season, a benefit game was held for Bailey in Toronto — the first all-star game in NHL history — and when the two stars, Bailey and Shore, shook hands at centre ice, they received a deafening ovation.

Kelly Joins the Leafs

LIKABLE RED KELLY was an outstanding defenceman with the Detroit Red Wings in the 1950s. He skated on eight championship teams and four Stanley Cup winners. He won the Lady Byng Trophy for gentlemanly play four times and was a six-time all-star. Kelly was so good and so popular, it looked as if he'd spend his entire career in a Detroit uniform.

But during the 1959–60 season, his 13th as a Red Wing, Kelly heard rumors that Detroit manager Jack Adams thought he was all washed up. A few days later, Adams shocked the hockey establishment by trading Kelly — along with Billy McNeill — to the Rangers, in return for Bill Gadsby and Eddie Shack.

What Adams didn't count on was a huge stubborn streak in Kelly's Irish makeup. The redhead talked things over with his wife, Andra, then called Adams and politely told him the deal was unacceptable. He had no intention of reporting to New York. In fact, if need be, he'd retire from hockey before joining the Rangers. So the deal with New York was called off.

League President Clarence Campbell, disturbed at Kelly's attitude, advised the defenceman he had five days to report to New York or his name would be placed on the retirement list. "You'll be blackballed from hockey forever," warned Campbell. Two days before Campbell's deadline, Kelly received a call from King Clancy in Toronto.

"Red, how'd you like to play for Toronto?" asked Clancy, a fellow Irishman. Leaf manager Punch Imlach believed in veteran players, and Kelly, at 32, would fit right into Imlach's system. Kelly was swayed by Clancy's persuasive blarney and said he would be happy to wind down his career in Toronto. Imlach got on the phone to Adams, and dispatched a journeyman defenceman, Marc Reaume, to Detroit in return for a player who was far from washed up. In fact, some of Kelly's greatest seasons were still ahead of him.

When Kelly joined the Leafs there was another surprise in store for him. Imlach said, "Forget about defence. You're going to be my number one centreman." Imlach gave him two big wingers, Frank Mahovlich and Bob Nevin, and the trio clicked immediately.

With Kelly at centre, the Leafs won four Stanley Cups in the next seven years. The defenceman-turned-forward not only won championships, he combined hockey with politics and served as a member of Parliament while he played for the Leafs. Eventually, he even became their coach.

Death in Minnesota

NHL EXPANSION IN 1967 made it possible for dozens of players to fulfill their dreams of playing hockey at the highest level. One of these players was Bill Masterton, a Winnipeg native.

In the early sixties, Masterton had played with Cleveland in the American League. But he decided to quit pro hockey and return to university when none of the six NHL teams showed much interest in him. After graduating from Denver University with a master's degree he was hired by the Honeywell Corporation in Minneapolis. He considered pro hockey part of his past, and his future looked bright in the corporate world. From now on, he figured, he'd just play hockey on weekends — for fun.

Then came NHL expansion and a doubling of the league from six to twelve teams. The new clubs looked everywhere for talent, and someone in the Minnesota organization recommended Masterton. He hadn't been out of the game very long, he was still fairly young and he'd kept himself in top condition.

The North Stars contacted Masterton and suggested he give hockey one more whirl. Masterton couldn't resist. He agreed to a tryout and easily made the team. That was the end of his career with Honeywell.

On January 13, 1968, the 29-year-old rookie was playing against the Oakland Seals when he was checked by two tough defencemen, Ron Harris and Larry Cahan. Off balance, Masterton tumbled to the ice, struck his head and was knocked unconscious. He was rushed to hospital, but died two days later of massive brain damage.

Bill Masterton was the first and only player to die of an on-ice injury since the league was formed in 1917.

Big Earner, Big Spender

LAWYER BOB WOOLF, who at one time represented several famous athletes, once said, "Getting big money for hockey players isn't difficult. Getting them to hang on to their money is the big problem." Woolf knows from experience. One of his clients, Derek Sanderson, ranks as the all-time money spender in hockey history.

In 1972, the Philadelphia Blazers of the WHA lured Sanderson away from the Boston Bruins with a five-year $2.65 million-dollar contract. At $500,000 a year, Sanderson was regarded as the most highly paid athlete in the world.

But after the first few games of the 1972 season, and a series of injuries that kept their star out of the lineup, the Blazers wanted out of the contract. They paid Sanderson another million to forget the whole deal.

What happened to that money? Sanderson told me once he doesn't remember. "But there are a lot of things I don't remember from that time in my life," he added.

Someone once estimated Sanderson earned over $333,000 for each goal he scored in Philadelphia. During his ten-year career he grossed almost $2 million. But he spent the money as fast as it came in. On wine and women. On a trip to Hawaii, a Rolls-Royce. He'd buy new golf clubs, and after a single round, give them to the caddy. He'd lend money to friends and forget to ask for it back. He figures he may simply have blown $600,000 while drifting from team to team.

When his playing days were over, there was no money left.

Today, Sanderson has his life in order. He works as a commentator on Boston Bruins game broadcasts, and he's respected as a hardworking, clean-living individual who always has time to speak against drug and alcohol abuse to impressionable teenagers.

Phil Esposito's Wild Ride

IN THE SPRING OF 1973, the Boston Bruins were knocked out of the Stanley Cup playoffs by the New York Rangers. During the series, Bruins' star Phil Esposito was nailed by a Ron Harris check and taken to a Boston hospital, where doctors diagnosed torn knee ligaments. The star centreman's leg was encased in a cast to protect the injury.

When the Boston players decided to hold a postseason farewell party, one of them suggested that the affair "just wouldn't be the same without Esposito, our team leader." The others agreed. The NHL scoring champ had to be present, even if he made only a token appearance. So they went to the hospital to get him.

While two of the Bruins, posing as security men, distracted hospital personnel, several other players stealthily wheeled Esposito, still in his hospital bed, along a corridor, down an elevator and through an exit. Unfortunately, in the haste of their daring departure, they broke a metal railing.

The bed and its famous occupant flew down the avenue while car horns honked and pedestrians gawked. The Bruins, led by Wayne Cashman and Bobby Orr, wheeled their leader to a restaurant not far from the hospital. At one busy corner, Orr yelled, "Signal a left, Phil," and Espo's arm shot out from under the sheets.

After the party, Espo was wheeled back to the hospital. But officials there were not amused at the kidnapping of their famous patient. The Bruins were not only chastised for their behavior, they were presented with a bill charging them $400 for damage to hospital property.

They dealt with the bill in a predictable manner. While Espo slept, his mates quietly slipped the invoice under his pillow.

Flight to Freedom

IT WAS AUGUST OF 1980. Two officials of the Quebec Nordiques, Marcel Aubut and Gilles Leger, were in Austria, ostensibly to scout hockey players in the European Cup Tournament. But during the tourney, a secret meeting was arranged between the two Quebecers and the famous Stastny brothers of Czechoslovakia, three of the best hockey players in the world.

What transpired at the meeting has never been fully disclosed, but it's certain the Czech stars were offered huge salaries if they would defect from their homeland and leave immediately for Canada. Marian Stastny, the oldest brother, decided against the move, but he urged his younger brothers to jump to the NHL. The following day, after the final game of the tournament, Peter and Anton Stastny mysteriously disappeared.

Aubut and Leger had arranged for the Stastnys, accompanied by Peter's pregnant wife, Darina, to be spirited to Vienna. The two hockey stars traveled in fear that the Czech secret police would overtake them and force them to return to Czechosloviakia, where they would face severe punishment.

From Vienna the Stastnys flew to Amsterdam, then on to Montreal, and finally to Quebec City.

When reporters asked Aubut if he'd landed the

Czech stars at a bargain price because of their lack of knowledge of NHL contracts, he laughed and said, "No way. Someone in Montreal had been sending the boys the *Hockey News* every week. They knew all about the salary structure in the league."

The investment in the two brothers paid off handsomely for the Nordiques. Peter Stastny scored 109 points in his rookie season and won the Calder Trophy. Anton played well, too. The following year, in a dash to freedom almost as dramatic as that of his brothers, Marian joined the Nordiques and became an immediate star.

The Ultimate Free Agent

ANDRE LACROIX, the youngest of 14 children from Lauzon, Quebec, always negotiated his own hockey contracts, both in the NHL and the WHA. And he never made a bad deal. Sitting in the stands at the Hartford Civic Center one day, he told me this fascinating story.

"Let's begin in Philadelphia when I signed with the WHA Blazers in 1973. I negotiated a five-year contract worth $65,000 a year. The previous season I'd played for Chicago in the WHA — for $30,000 a year. The Blazers had to give me what I wanted because the team had called a press conference for the next day to announce the signing of their new coach — Fred Creighton. But Fred backed out at the last minute. They were really stuck for a news story and they looked to me to become the story. So I asked for a big contract and got it. They really needed me at that press conference. And I made

Wheeler dealer Andre Lacroix as a Hartford Whaler, one of many teams he played for in the NHL and WHA.
(Hockey Hall of Fame)

sure there was a clause in the contract that stated if the team was sold or moved I would become a free agent. Also, I demanded a car of my choice — a Mark IV — and I put in a lot of bonus clauses. Well, I won the scoring title that season, made the first All-Star team, and the Blazers had to pay me $40,000 in bonuses.

"Then the team moved to Vancouver, but I didn't have to move there because I was a free agent. I moved to New York instead and negotiated another fat contract with the team there. The next thing I asked for was a new Cadillac, and they said, 'No problem.' So I drove around in my new Cadillac until I got a phone call from the dealer. He said, 'Bring the car in, Mr. Lacroix. The team can't make the payments on it.'

"Within days the New York team moved to New

Jersey, and the minute they did I became a free agent again. The New Jersey team was owned by a construction man — Mr. Joe Schwartz. He said to me, 'Andre, we're going to move the team to San Diego.' I said, 'That's fine, but I may not go because I'm a free agent.' So he took me to Las Vegas for three days. I stayed in a big suite while we negotiated a new contract. As usual I was my own agent and I signed a new five-year contract with Joe with all the money guaranteed. And I told Joe I'd like to drive a Porsche as part of the deal. He said, 'No problem.' So I drove a big Porsche until Joe Schwartz ran out of money after a couple of years.

"That's when Ray Kroc [then the owner of McDonald's] came in and bought the club. He hired a big-name baseball man, Buzzy Bavasi, as club president. When Bavasi talked to me about signing, he told me, 'You know, Andre, baseball players, when they make so much money, don't have bonus clauses.' I told him, 'Look, I'm a hockey player, not a baseball player. I want bonus clauses.' I also told him I wanted a Rolls-Royce to drive, one of those $95,000 ones, not a cheap one. Mr. Bavasi said, 'No problem.'

"Kroc and Bavasi offered me $150,000 a year for five years. I said, 'No, I don't want to sign for that. I think I'll go back to the NHL.' And I got up to leave. But Kroc called me back and said, "Andre, I'm prepared to give you $175,000 a year for six years with the money guaranteed personally by me.' I said that sounds okay with me. So I signed a personal services contract with Ray Kroc, not the team or the league.

"It wasn't long before Kroc decided he didn't like hockey, after all, so he sold the team. Once again I became a free agent and I decided to go to Houston. And if Houston at any time didn't pay me, Kroc was still responsible for my contract. When Houston folded and several of the players went to Winnipeg, I didn't go. I was a free agent again, so I went to Hartford. The Whalers promised to honor my contract. If they didn't pay me, Kroc was still responsible.

"When I retired from Hartford, I still had two years left on my contract. I told the Whalers, 'Look, you'll owe me about $400,000 if I continue to play. And I'm not going to retire unless I get my money. So why not do this. You can have the advantage of using that money if you'll pay me over a period of time with interest. And they said fine. So I agreed to be paid over a period of seven years. When I quit in 1980, I knew there would still be plenty of money coming in. What's more, I'd have some time to look around and see what I wanted to do with the rest of my life. And I didn't have to work for the team to earn any of that money. I thought it was a pretty good deal.

"I never had an agent. Never felt I needed one. I made all my own deals and had good relations with all the owners, general managers, and coaches I ever played for — except for Vic Stasiuk in Philadelphia. I never liked him after he ordered the French-speaking players on our team to speak English only."

The Kid Could Always Score

WAYNE GRETZKY'S ACCOMPLISHMENTS as a professional hockey player are well documented and mind-boggling. But some of the records he set as a pint-size player in minor hockey are equally astonishing.

Wayne's first season of organized hockey was nothing special. In fact, as a five-year-old playing on a team of nine- and ten-year-olds, he scored just one goal for his Brantford, Ontario team. His father Walter, an amateur photographer, managed to snap a photo of his big moment. After the season, Wayne's coach told him not to worry, there'd be lots more goals to come. "You're just a little fellow but you've got lots of talent," he said. How right he was.

In his second season, Wayne scored 27 goals and in his third, 104. Then as a nine-year-old he scored 196 goals — plus 120 assists. No one in minor-hockey circles could recall a player ever being so prolific.

But Wayne had more surprises in store. By the time he reached peewee level, he was phenomenal. He scored 378 goals in 82 games, even though he was checked closely by opposing teams.

"And he wasn't a puck hog, either," states former teammate Greg Stefan, who went on to become an NHL goaltender. "He was always setting up his teammates with unbelievable plays."

The unbeaten Toronto Cedar Hill team played in Brantford one day and lost 6–0 when Gretzky scored four goals and added two assists. In a return match in Toronto, Cedar Hill was leading 8–0 when Gretzky sparked a miraculous comeback in the third period, leading his team to an 11–10 triumph.

In one tournament, he scored 50 goals in nine games, and by the time he was 13 he'd already scored the incredible total of 1000 goals. At the Quebec City Peewee Tournament one year, his dazzling play earned him the nickname White Tornado. He acquired two more nicknames in junior hockey — Ink for all the press attention he attracted and Pencil because he was so thin.

He even scored 158 goals one season in another sport — lacrosse!

At age 17, Wayne signed his first pro contract with the Indianapolis Racers of the WHA, after drawing up the contract himself in longhand. It was for four years and $875,000.

Even in minor hockey, Wayne had the right side of his hockey sweater tucked into his pants because his sweaters were always too big for him. He still keeps his sweater tucked in, but now it's become a habit or superstition. He even uses Velcro to make sure the sweater stays that way.

There Was Nobody Like Number Nine

BACK IN 1980 hockey's most famous player decided he couldn't play the game forever after all. So at the age of 52, Gordie Howe put away his skates and stick and said goodbye to the sport he loved.

It marked the end of a fabulous career. Howe is the only NHL player who remained a scoring threat well into his fifties. He's the only grandfather to play in the NHL, and he's the only player whose amazing career spanned 35 seasons and five decades.

In his time, Howe established an awesome list of records. He scored more than 1,000 goals, counting service in two pro leagues. He was the NHL's leading scorer and MVP six different times and an all-star 21 times. In the WHA, he was an all-star twice and MVP once.

Gordie's initial retirement from the game was in 1971, at the age of 43 and after a quarter of a century in a Detroit uniform. He took a front-office job with the Red Wings but was bored with the few assignments he was asked to handle.

Two years later, he was lured out of retirement by the Houston Aeros of the WHA. Not only for the money — he received a million dollars spread over four years, more than he had ever earned in the NHL — but because it gave him a chance to play on the same team with his sons Mark and Marty. It was a "first" for hockey, and it didn't take long for Gordie to prove he hadn't lost his touch. He scored 100 points in his comeback season and led Houston to the WHA championship. Later, he served as president of the Aeros and became hockey's only playing team president. Later still, when Mark's wife had a baby, he became pro hockey's only playing grandfather. During his stint in the WHA, Gordie added 218 WHA goals to his Hall of Fame totals.

Soviet fans watching the final four games of an eight-game Summit Series in 1974 were spellbound by Howe's performance in a losing cause. Gordie starred for Team Canada (WHA version) in the rough series. The Soviets said it was incredible that a man in his late forties could be such a huge factor in such a fast-paced international matchup.

At age 48, Howe kidded reporters by saying, "I'm going to play another year of two but my sons are going to retire." After four seasons in Houston, the Howes moved on to Hartford, and with the merger of the two leagues in 1979, Gordie found himself back in the NHL. He scored his final

NHL goal (his 801st) in his final game against Detroit in 1980. He was 51 years old.

Incidentally, Gordie Howe was a hockey Hall of Famer long before his playing career was over, another hockey "first." He was inducted in 1972, a year after he retired from Detroit and a year *before* he returned with Houston.

Wayne Gretzky has surpassed Gordie Howe as hockey's greatest scorer, but no one, says Gretzky, can top number nine when it comes to durability. "To play so well and for so long is simply incredible," says Wayne. "No player will ever do the things in hockey that Gordie did."

Harry Neale Gets a Message from Gordie Howe

WHEN HARRY NEALE FIRST COACHED Gordie Howe, the hockey superstar was almost in his fifties, the oldest player in pro hockey. Harry had difficulty treating Howe like all the other players on the Hartford Whalers, some of whom were young enough to be Howe's sons. Hell, two of them were his sons.

Neale would set a curfew at 11:00 p.m. and tell his players, "You better be in your rooms, because I'll be checking on you."

At 11:00 p.m. he would make his rounds, and when he came to Howe's room, he would see the light under the door and hear the TV set. So he would say to himself, Gordie's obviously in there. I'm not going to disturb a hockey legend. I'll pass on to the next room.

One morning Howe took him aside and asked, "Harry, am I on this team or not?"

"Of course you're on the team. What do you mean?"

"You set a curfew and said you were going to check our rooms. I usually go to sleep about 10:30, and I keep waiting up for you, sometimes until 11:30, but you don't show up. You never do."

"Well, I . . ."

"Never mind that," Howe said. "If I'm on this team, I want to be treated like everybody else. Don't ever do that again."

Bruins and Rangers Swap All Stars

WHEN DON CHERRY coached the Boston Bruins in the 1970s, three of his best players were Bobby Orr, Phil Esposito and Carol Vadnais. Cherry was particularly happy to have Esposito in his lineup because the big centreman had just turned down an offer from the WHA that would have paid him two and a half times as much as he was earning with the Bruins.

But the 1975–76 season began badly for Boston. With Orr out of the lineup with knee problems, the team stumbled from the gate.

In Vancouver in the middle of a long road trip, Cherry took a call one night from Bruin general manager Harry Sinden. "I've just traded Esposito and Vadnais to New York for Brad Park and Jean Ratelle," Cherry was told. It was a blockbuster of a trade, and Cherry was instructed not to tell anyone about it until morning.

At sunrise, Cherry hurried to Esposito's room

and broke the news. Espo was in tears when he found out he was going to New York. "Grapes, I hate New York," he said. "I told Harry I wouldn't hold out for a no-trade clause in my contract if he'd promise never to send me there. We shook on it. Now look what's happened." As it turned out, Esposito discovered he loved New York. Later he said Sinden did him a big favor by sending him there.

Cherry moved on to Carol Vadnais's room. When told of the deal, Vadnais said calmly, "Harry can't do that to me, Don. I've got a no-trade clause in my contract."

Cherry was stunned. How could that be? He called Sinden and Sinden hastily looked up the contract. Sure enough, Vadnais could not be traded without his permission. But there was no way the two clubs could back out now; the deal must go through. Did the Bruins offer Vadnais a lot of cash to let them off the hook? No. The Rangers, who wanted him badly, came through with a bundle of money, and Vadnais was on his way.

The Legendary Frank McGee

AT THE TURN OF THE CENTURY a young Ottawa forward named Frank McGee established himself as one of the finest hockey players in the world. To many fans of the era he was the greatest stickhandler who ever carried a puck down the ice.

Young McGee began playing hockey against his family's wishes. He started his career as a student at the University of Ottawa, and before long he was the star of the fabled Ottawa Silver Seven, Stanley Cup champions.

One night, early in his career, McGee's team tangled with the rowdy Montreal Wanderers. Toughest of the Wanderers was the hard-rock Pokey Leahy, and before the game was a few minutes old Leahy caught McGee by surprise and smashed into him, sending him crashing to the ice. McGee was carried off, bleeding from a head wound, and later, as a result of that check, he lost the sight in his left eye.

McGee recovered in time, and despite the urging of his friends and parents to give up the game, he returned to hockey. Just as fast and as dangerous with the puck as ever, he seldom talked about his accident, although he did threaten to catch up to Pokey Leahy one day and pay him back for the check that almost ended his career.

In the following years McGee set some amazing records. During one Stanley Cup game against Dawson City, he scored 14 goals, a mark no player has ever tied or topped. He once scored four goals in one minute and four seconds. In 1905, wearing tape to protect a broken wrist, he scored the tying and winning goals for Ottawa in a Stanley Cup–clinching game. That night McGee wore tape around both wrists to confuse opposing players who would certainly have slashed him on the broken one.

Then came the night when Frank McGee's path again crossed that of Pokey Leahy. When the teams lined up for the opening face-off, McGee told Leahy he was out to settle an old score. Leahy snarled back, "You try it, Frankie, and I'll knock your other eye out."

But McGee was determined to try it. He came

roaring down the ice and crashed into Leahy. They both went down, but Leahy was unable to get up. He was badly hurt and had to be carried off on a stretcher. Never again did he lace on skates to play hockey.

The collision with Leahy was one of the few times McGee deliberately tried to hurt another player. Normally he was a clean player who was idolized for his stylish play and good looks. His hockey pants were always freshly laundered and creased with an iron. An immaculately groomed man, McGee never failed to comb his blond hair neatly to one side.

He was a born leader, and when the First World War broke out, he was able to serve in the infantry despite the loss of his eye. To get around the handicap, he simply had a friend enlist in his name. Once in the army, he quickly rose from private to captain. In the winter of 1916, though, during one of the war's fiercest battles in France, an enemy shell ended the life of Frank McGee, one of hockey's greatest heroes.

A Scorer's Mistake Cost Bobby Hull the Record

IN THE SPRING OF 1962 Chicago's Bobby Hull was in hot pursuit of a goal-scoring record shared by two Montreal Canadiens — Rocket Richard and Boom Boom Geoffrion. They were the only two players ever to score 50 goals in 50 games. Hull had a remarkable second half in 1962. He scored 35 goals in 31 games, which allowed him to tie Richard and Geoffrion's formidable record.

The Golden Jet's second-half surge also vaulted him into a tie with the Rangers' Andy Bathgate for the individual scoring title and the Art Ross Trophy. Both men finished with 84 points, but it was Hull who captured the Ross award because of his greater number of goals (50 to 28).

All but forgotten was a goal Hull scored early in the season, a goal that would have given him a record-breaking 51 in 50 games and would have made him a clear-cut winner of the scoring crown. In a game against Detroit a few weeks into the season, Hull blasted a shot at Red Wing goalie Terry Sawchuk. His shot was deflected by a stick in front of Sawchuk's crease, and the official scorer awarded the goal to Hull's linemate Ab McDonald.

After the game, McDonald told the referee he hadn't touched the puck. He claimed that it had gone in off the stick of a Red Wing defenseman and that Hull should have received credit for the goal. But McDonald had waited too long to point out the mistake. The official report of the game had already been filed with the league office and nothing could be done to change the verdict. The mistake didn't bother Hull at the time. He just shrugged it off. On the final day of the season, however, someone reminded him that the goal given to McDonald had cost him the 51-goal record.

Bobby Hull in
Hair-raising Encounter

DAVE HANSON IS MORE FAMOUS for a role he played in the movie *Slapshot* than for anything he did on the ice in the NHL or the WHA. But he does recall an encounter with Bobby Hull in Winnipeg one night that brought him instant notoriety. Here is how Hanson remembers it.

"When I was in the WHA with Birmingham, I didn't have a lot of talent, but I wanted to impress some people. We were playing Winnipeg one night and I was on defense. I figured the fastest way to make a name for myself was to step into Bobby Hull and put him on his back.

"Well, Bobby came flying down the wing and I stepped into him and he flattened me. He knocked me right on my ass and skated over my face, leaving me gasping and humiliated. My pride was hurt and I made up my mind that the next time he came in on me I was going to be better prepared. I'd really get him.

"He came down again and I got my elbows up and roughed him, which he didn't take kindly to. So we dropped the gloves and started flailing away at each other. Then, to my amazement, I felt something soft. I had a full head of hair in my hands! I looked down and discovered I was holding Bobby's wig. I said, 'Oh, shit!' and threw the hairpiece out in the middle of the ice. Bobby just stood there completely bald, and the fans were as stunned as he was. It was as if the air had been sucked out of the building. You could hear a pin drop. I got fifteen minutes in penalties, and Bobby didn't get anything.

"The next day in the paper there was a huge picture of Ulf Nilsson, Bobby's linemate, looking down at this wig on the ice. You should have seen the headlines. All the Hull fans wanted to kill me. Reporters wrote things like: 'Some idiot out of nowhere embarrassed the Golden Jet' and 'Is nothing sacred? It's like painting a mustache on the *Mona Lisa*.' Radio stations started calling me for open-line interviews, asking things like 'Why would you do such a thing?' I must say Bobby Hull took it well. After it happened, he skated off to the dressing room and put on a helmet. When he came back, I went over to him and apologized. I really felt terrible. He said, 'Aw, don't worry about it, kid.' He took it in stride."

The Bizarre Tragedy of Spinner Spencer

THOSE OF US WHO have been associated with *Hockey Night in Canada* for a quarter century or more will never forget a Saturday night telecast during the 1969–70 season. Toronto Maple Leaf rookie Brian "Spinner" Spencer, an exciting addition to the Leaf roster, a kid with wavy blond hair, choirboy looks, and an irresistible personality, was to be host Ward Cornell's guest during the intermission of the Toronto game with Chicago.

While we looked forward to seeing Spencer's television debut, there was much greater anticipation of the event in far-off Fort St. James, British Columbia, Spencer's hometown. Brian's father, Roy Spencer, was bursting with pride that night. Not

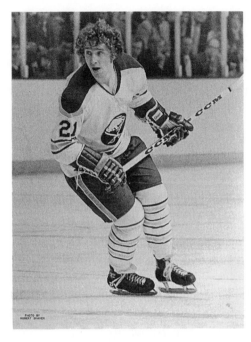

*Hockey bad boy
Brian Spencer as
a Buffalo Sabre.*
(Robert B. Shaver)

only had Brian's wife given birth to a baby girl two days earlier, but his son had made it all the way from the backyard rink to the mammoth ice surfaces of the NHL, and now millions of fans would get to see him — up close and personal, as they say.

But Roy Spencer was suddenly denied the opportunity to see his boy trade quips with Ward Cornell. He listened in disbelief as a CBC announcer informed him that the network affiliate in Prince George was switching from the Toronto–Chicago game to the Vancouver Canucks–Oakland Seals contest. Roy Spencer roared with frustration and outrage. How could the CBC do this do him?

He grabbed a rifle, stormed out of the house, and jumped into his truck. At high speed he drove the 90 miles to the CBC station in Prince George and skidded to a halt in the parking lot. Barging into the station and waving his rifle, he ordered the staff to line up against the wall. He demanded that one of them switch the channel to the Toronto game. When told by terrified staffers that it couldn't be done, Spencer ran back to the parking lot where, brandishing his rifle at approaching police officers, he met a tragic end. He was felled by three RCMP bullets fired from close range. Spencer dropped dead in his tracks. Meanwhile, in many parts of Canada, a million hockey fans were absorbed in his son's conversation with Ward Cornell.

From that point on, trouble seemed to stalk Brian Spencer relentlessly. Colorful, tough, and fearless, he had a tremendous physique. He played for four NHL clubs — the Leafs, Sabres, Islanders, and Penguins — but scored only 80 goals in 10 NHL seasons, hardly the stats of the star he wanted to be.

Martin O'Malley, who detailed his life story in *Gross Misconduct: The Life of Spinner Spencer,* once said of him, "To me he personified Canadian hockey in ways that Orr and Gretzky never did. He showed what you can do with sheer hard work and never-quit perseverance. And he loved the press . . . loved to tell stories."

In time, long after he hung up his skates, Brian Spencer became the story. And it wasn't a pretty one.

He was arrested by Florida police in 1987 and taken in handcuffs from a rundown trailer in a backwater swamp where he lived with a hooker. The charge was murder. He was accused, five years after the fact, of shooting to death Michael Dalfo, a man who had abused the prostitute who shared Spencer's trailer.

Evidence was provided by Spencer's former girlfriend Diane Fialco, who said she went to Dalfo's house on February 2, 1982, as a "professional escort." She left when Dalfo appeared to be high on cocaine, she testified. Later that night she and Spencer returned to the Dalfo house. Spencer forced Dalfo into their car, took him to a deserted area, and allegedly shot him to death.

But the prosecution had difficulty building a strong case against Spencer. In less than an hour, on October 16, a Palm Beach jury found him not guilty of first-degree murder. Had the seven-man, five-woman jury found him guilty, he would have faced a possible 25-year prison term without parole — or even death in the electric chair.

But tragedy, like a persistent checker in hockey, kept hounding Spencer. Despite the urging of friends to leave Florida, the former hockey player said he "didn't like the cold and couldn't afford the housing."

On the night of June 2, 1988, he told a new lady friend, Monica Jarboe, "See you in half an hour." He left their apartment and never returned. A few minutes later he was gunned down, the victim of an unknown killer.

Spencer was murdered while driving with his friend Greg Cook through a dangerous section of Riviera Beach, Florida. Cook, after stopping to buy $10 worth of crack cocaine, stopped again farther down the road for cigarettes. While he was looking for his money, an armed assailant approached the car and put a gun to Cook's head. Cook produced a few bills, but Spencer told the gunman he had no money. The mugger shot Spencer, and the bullet traveled through his arm and crashed into his chest. He died almost instantly.

It was not a contract killing, as many at first believed, but simply a case of Spencer being in the wrong place at the wrong time. Months later a man with a criminal record was arrested and confessed to Spencer's murder. He was subsequently sentenced to life in prison.

Unbelievable! A Defenseman Wins the Scoring Crown

IN THE LATE SIXTIES and early seventies Boston's Bobby Orr was the most electrifying player in hockey. Before Orr came along hockey people thought it was impossible for a defenseman to win the individual scoring title in the NHL.

Orr changed their thinking in a hurry. In 1969–70 he amazed everyone by finishing on top of the scoring race with 120 points, 21 more than teammate Phil Esposito. No defenseman had ever come close to winning a scoring title. It was unthinkable.

To prove it was no fluke Orr finished on top again five years later, this time with 135 points. In between he finished second three times and third once (all four times behind Esposito). What made his accomplishments even more remarkable was that he played for most of his career on aching knees that required numerous operations.

And while Orr's scoring titles have been well publicized, one of his most amazing marks hasn't been — his career plus-minus rating. For his 657-game career Bobby was a plus 597. That means he was on the ice for 1,188 even-strength goals and on for only 591 goals against.

Why Coffey Missed Orr's Record

IT WAS THE FINAL GAME OF THE 1985–86 NHL season and Paul Coffey of the Edmonton Oilers was awfully close to tying or breaking Bobby Orr's remarkable record for a defenseman — 139 points in a season. Trailing by a point in the season finale against Vancouver, it figured that Coffey would be a shoo-in to establish a new mark. But he soon discovered there were factors involved that might prevent him from reaching his goal. Bob McCammon, then an Oiler assistant coach, revealed the reason for Coffey's failure to displace Orr months after the incident, when he joined the Canucks as head coach.

"In that final game with Vancouver, Glen Sather wanted to keep the score down, win the game, and avoid meeting Calgary in the first round of the playoffs. Paul began rushing with the puck, looking for points, and taking chances. Finally Sather benched him."

The benching was the start of a rift between Coffey and his coach. Coffey finished the game pointless and wound up with 138 points to Orr's 139.

Fortunately Coffey was able to take some satisfaction in smashing another of Orr's long-standing records — 47 goals in a season for a defenseman. Coffey finished with 48.

Rags to Riches

IN THE EARLY SEVENTIES Charlie Simmer was just another minor leaguer. Too slow for the NHL, all the experts said, although they liked his size and his attitude. Charlie had played a few games as a checking centerman with the California Seals and a few more with the same club when they became the Cleveland Barons. When he was released by the Barons, he signed a minor league contract with the Los Angeles Kings organization, but his future looked bleak.

"Poor Charlie doesn't have NHL speed" was the verdict of two Kings coaches, Ron Stewart and Bob Berry, "especially for a centerman."

"Why don't you fellows play him at left wing, his natural position?" Kings general manager George McGuire asked.

"I'll keep it in mind," Berry replied. Meanwhile Simmer languished in the minors and rode the buses from city to city. It was a depressing existence, and Charlie decided that if he didn't get a break soon, he'd give up hockey and find a nine-to-five job somewhere.

His break came midway through the 1978–79 season. A series of injuries hit the Kings, and Berry called on Simmer. This time he played him at left wing, with Marcel Dionne at center and Dave Taylor on the right side, forming the Triple Crown Line. For the next few seasons it was the most feared line in hockey.

Simmer's scoring touch delighted Kings fans, and he closed out the season by scoring goals in five straight games. When the 1979–80 season got under way, he potted goals in the first six games. That amounted to a streak of eleven straight goal-scoring games, surpassing a league record of 10, held jointly by Andy Bathgate and Mike Bossy.

But the NHL refused to recognize Simmer's streak because it spanned two seasons. There was only one thing to do — start another streak. In game after game Charlie pumped in goals from far out and in close. He scored on breakaways, rebounds, and tip-ins. And he wasn't stopped until he'd scored 17 goals in 13 consecutive games — a modern-day NHL record.

Despite spending most of the first five years of his career in the minors, Charlie Simmer went on to play 711 NHL games. He recorded back-to-back 56-goal seasons, made the All-Star team, and won the Bill Masterton Trophy for his qualities of perseverance (he had that in abundance), sportsmanship, and dedication to hockey. He even married a *Playboy* playmate of the year. Not a bad career turnaround for a player who "couldn't skate."

Credit Morenz for Big League Hockey in New York

MENTION THE NAME Howie Morenz to hockey old-timers and the superlatives fall like water over Niagara. King Clancy, who played against him, once said, "Morenz was the greatest I ever saw. He was as fast as a bullet and had a shot to match. He could stop on a dime and give you five cents change. The first time I played against him he sifted right through the Ottawa defense and scored. I said to him, 'Kid, you do that again and I'll cut your legs off.' He said to me, 'Clancy, I'll be right back.' Seconds later, there he was again, cutting right between my partner and me and scoring again. I couldn't believe the little bugger could move that fast."

Morenz was to hockey what Babe Ruth was to baseball. But in New York, North America's sporting capital in the twenties, neither hockey nor its biggest star figured prominently in America's sports future. Promoter Tex Rickard was building Madison Square Garden, but he saw no reason to install machinery for making artificial ice.

Then another entrepreneur, Tom Duggan, a hockey fanatic who had finagled three franchises from the NHL for a mere $7,000, became involved. Duggan knew that a New York franchise was critical for the success of hockey in the U.S., but Rickard had to be sold on the merits of the ice game.

Duggan persuaded Rickard to journey to Montreal with him and see the great Morenz in action. Rickard, accompanied by the famous columnist and sports fan Damon Runyon, made the trip north, and both visitors were thrilled by the play of Morenz and the Canadiens. Rickard returned to Broadway and ordered his architects to make some changes. An ice-making facility must be added to the plans for his new arena.

When the New York Americans, in their star-spangled uniforms, hosted the Montreal Canadiens in their NHL debut at the new Madison Square Garden in 1925, fans were thrilled by the speed and finesse of the players, especially the flamboyant superstar Howie Morenz. It was a game that might never have been played — if Morenz had not been equally spectacular on the night Rickard and Runyon saw him play a few months earlier.

The Day Howie Morenz Quit Hockey

WHEN I TALK with hockey old-timers, men who remember the early stars of the game, invariably they speak of Howie Morenz. They talk of his lightning speed and his incredible rushes and how he ranks among the top ten players ever to put on skates.

But Morenz's career almost ended before it began. The Morenz family was from Mitchell, Ontario, but when Howie was a teenager the family moved to nearby Stratford. The Stratford hockey team, having heard that young Howie had shown some promise as a high school player in Mitchell, invited him to try out for the local team.

When he arrived at the rink, Howie had only his skates and a stick because his family was too poor to provide him with any additional equipment. In the scrimmage that followed, Howie was roughly handled by the fully equipped Stratford boys. In the dressing room he showed the manager his bruised and bleeding hands. "The other boys hacked at my hands because I have no gloves," he protested. "You won't see me out for your team again." And he walked out into the night.

Morenz was all but forgotten until later in the season when the Stratford club took a beating from archrival Kitchener. The manager, seeking ways to strengthen his team, remembered the kid with no equipment and gave Morenz a call. Would he come and help them out in their return match with Kitchener? The club would even scrape up some gloves, pants, and shin pads for him. Morenz agreed and turned in an outstanding game, beginning a career that would take him right to the peak of professional hockey with the Montreal Canadiens.

Playboy Seeks Hockey Player for Nude Layout

WHO WOULD HAVE THOUGHT that *Playboy*, the men's magazine, would offer a hockey player $75,000 to appear nude in the publication? Yet it happened in 1992.

The hockey player is the young female player Manon Rheaume, who made headlines by playing in goal with the Trois-Rivières Draveurs, a Junior A team in the Province of Quebec. Manon became the first woman to play as high as the Junior A level. In November 1991 she was called off the bench in the second period of a game between Trois-Rivières and the Granby Bisons. She played 20 minutes, allowed three goals on 10 shots, and left the game when she was cut for three stitches by a slapshot to the face mask.

Rheaume used a different dressing room and showered away from the other players. "When the players first saw me at tryout camp, they were amused," she said. "But in no time they stopped treating me like a girl."

A few weeks later she turned down a $75,000 offer from *Playboy* to pose nude in a future issue of the magazine. "I wouldn't do that for a million dollars," the attractive young goaltender insisted.

Rheaume went on to become the first female player to play for a professional hockey team, signing with the Atlanta Knights of the International Hockey League. Prior to the 1992–93 season she also tended goal briefly in an exhibition game for the Tampa Bay Lightning.

Lafleur Was Fast Off the Ice

WHEN THE MONTREAL CANADIENS were winning four consecutive Stanley Cups from 1976 to 1979, their fastest skater and most prolific scorer was Guy (Flower) Lafleur. One night the superstar's fast pace off the ice almost cost him his life.

Postgame partying was something Lafleur enjoyed, and there were always friends and teammates willing to share his penchant for liquor, rock music, and endless cigarettes. When the partying was over, he would race home at dizzying speeds in his Cadillac Seville. But in the early-morning hours of March 25, 1981, Lafleur fell asleep behind the wheel and near disaster followed. His powerful vehicle roared off the highway and plunged down an embankment, smashing into a metal post that shattered the windshield. Part of the post, twisted into something resembling a knight's lance, missed Lafleur's head by a fraction of an inch and sliced off part of his right ear. He was lucky to come out of the accident alive.

Lafleur had already established a reputation for high-speed driving. In 1978, according to *The*

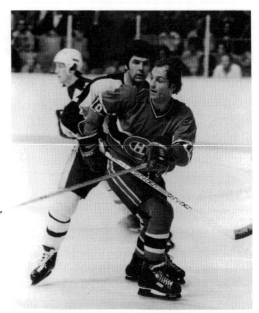

When the Montreal Canadiens swept to four straight Stanley Cups from 1976 to 1979, Guy Lafleur was their ace scorer, winning three consecutive scoring titles.
(Robert B. Shaver)

Hockey News, he reached speeds of 177 miles per hour while driving his Ferrari the 150-mile distance from Montreal to Quebec City.

After his brush with death in 1981, Lafleur promised to change his lifestyle. "I decided to slow down after that," he said. "I realized that my family was more important to me than downtown nightlife."

The Unlikely Hockey Hero

HE PLAYS A MAJOR ROLE in every game, but he can't skate, has never scored a goal, doesn't know the rules, and doesn't care who wins or loses. Hockey players say they admire the way he works his way around the ice, and they scatter in all directions when they see him coming.

He is, if you haven't already guessed, the world-famous Zamboni, the incredible ice-resurfacing machine, a rugged, reliable performer in arenas around the world since the forties.

The Zamboni, a household name wherever hockey is played, is the invention of the late Frank Zamboni of Paramount, California. Zamboni's odd-looking machine revolutionized hockey and made the game easier to play and more pleasurable to watch for millions of players and fans.

Zamboni, a native of Utah, moved to California as a young man to work in his brother's garage. Later he and his brother set up an ice-making plant, which turned out 50 tons of ice per day. Then, when millions of electric refrigerators killed the ice-making business, the brothers decided to erect a skating rink, using the old plant to make the artificial ice that covered the floor. But when the arena opened, the Zambonis found that resurfacing the ice became a problem. It required a lot of time and manpower.

In 1942 Frank Zamboni began to experiment with vehicles to do the job, and the first machine he built was pulled on a sled towed by a tractor. However, this primitive model didn't produce a smooth surface because it didn't pick up the snow adequately. In 1947 Zamboni tried again but without much more success. By 1949 he had a machine that gave good results. It would consistently create a good sheet of ice.

One day his strange machine caught the eye of the famous figure skater Sonja Henie, who was practicing at the Zamboni rink for her ice show. Henie ordered a second machine and used it on her nationwide tour. Wherever she appeared rink operators made inquiries, and soon Frank Zamboni was getting phone calls and letters from all over North America. Since those early days, his unique ice machines have been in demand from rink operators in dozens of countries around the globe.

For a time his machine was known simply as "the ice resurfacer." Then one night at a hockey game some leather-lunged fan yelled out: "Get the damn Zamboni out and make some new ice!" The man didn't know it at the time, but he gave hockey a new name.

Hockey's Biggest Practical Joker

WHEN FUN-LOVING NICK FOTIU retired from hockey, his teammates breathed a sigh of relief. No longer would they have to be on guard against the game's biggest practical joker.

Many of Fotiu's most notorious pranks took place when he played for the New York Rangers. He learned, for example, that teammate Phil Esposito abhored bugs, especially cockroaches. So Fotiu delighted in swatting roaches — just enough to stun them — and depositing the ugly little insects in with Espo's hockey equipment. When Espo reached for a jock strap or an elbow pad, he was apt to be greeted by a creepy-crawly that would drive him berserk. On another occasion, when Esposito carelessly left a brand-new pair of white golf shoes in the Ranger dressing room, Fotiu painted them bright orange.

Fotiu was known to substitute shaving cream for whipped cream on the dessert tray in restaurants, to put talcum powder in the dressing room hair dryers, and to swab black shoe polish on the earpiece of telephone receivers. Once he placed a live lobster on the chest of his sleeping roommate Bill Goldsworthy, whose screams on awakening could be heard for miles. Another time Fotiu hid in a hotel room closet and waited there until his roommate woke up and started to get dressed. When the roomie reached in the closet for his shirt and jacket, Fotiu grabbed him around the throat, scaring the tar out of him.

If Fotiu happened to rise in the morning before his roommate, he would turn on the shower, close the bathroom door, and go down for breakfast. The unsuspecting roommate would eventually get up, hear the shower sounds, and wait patiently for his turn under the spray — and wait and wait and wait.

From time to time teammates exacted revenge on the impish Fotiu. Goalie John Davidson, often a victim of Fotiu's elaborate pranks, recalls the time he pilfered Fotiu's truck keys out of a pocket, started the vehicle, and turned on the lights, the heater, the radio, the windshield wipers — everything. Then he left the keys inside and locked the doors.

One night Davidson led a Ranger attack force to Fotiu's house where they toilet-papered everything in sight. Trees, the family car, the house itself — everything was covered in toilet paper. Then Davidson called the police, told them a man was trapped in a house, and gave them Fotiu's address. When the police arrived and pounded on Fotiu's door, the astonished hockey player was at a loss to explain his papered property.

Davidson recalls how upset he was the day he caught Fotiu red-handed in the middle of a practical joke. He happened to look out a restaurant window to see Fotiu filling Davidson's car with garbage from cans on the street corner.

The goalie also recalls the time Fotiu discovered that most of the Rangers had traveling bags with little keys attached — keys that were seldom if ever used. When the trainers piled the luggage onto the team bus one day, Fotiu unobtrusively locked all the bags and pocketed the keys. When the players checked into their hotel rooms and tried to open their bags, there was enough cursing and shouting to bring a hotel detective running.

Fotiu might have come running, too, for angry epithets were always music to his ears. But he was too busy laughing.

Pass the Damn Puck, Regan!

WHEN I WAS A KID playing endless games of shinny on an Ottawa playground rink, whenever Larry Regan showed up to play, the rest of us groaned. He was too good for most of us, an extremely talented stickhandler and scorer. Maybe that was why he seldom passed the puck.

After playing Junior A hockey with the Toronto Marlboros and kicking around the minors for a few seasons, Regan joined the Boston Bruins at the ripe old age of 26 and won the Calder Trophy as rookie of the year. Regan enjoyed five NHL seasons with two clubs — Boston and Toronto — and in 1968 he turned up as a coach and general manager of the Los Angeles Kings of the expanded NHL. By the time he reached the NHL he had rid himself of his puck-hogging habits.

Perhaps it was in Pembroke, Ontario (one of his minor league stops), that he learned a lesson about making better use of his linemates. One night Regan was stickhandling all over the ice and completely ignoring his wingers. One of his mates, Rheal Savard, kept rapping his stick on the ice in frustration, calling for a pass. When Regan finally spotted Savard in the clear and whipped the puck in his direction, the winger had grown weary of waiting. He snared the pass, flipped the puck from his stick to his glove, and skated over to his team's bench. He handed the disk to trainer Bill Higginson and said, "Here, Bill, get this damn thing mounted. It's the first bloody pass I've got from Regan all season."

Cory Gurnsey Finds a Big League Pal

ON A WINTER DAY IN 1980 Cory Gurnsey, a nine-year-old Calgary boy, was walking home from school when he was brutally assaulted and stabbed several times. Destroyed in the attack was Cory's beloved hockey jersey, a Montreal Canadiens sweater with Guy Lafleur's number 10 sewn on the back.

It wasn't long before the Montreal Canadiens heard about Cory's plight, and within a day or two a brand-new Guy Lafleur sweater was delivered to his hospital room. Guy himself phoned the hospital to talk with Cory and to wish him a speedy recovery. He even promised to score a goal for Cory in an upcoming game between Montreal and Toronto. Of course, he kept his promise. Then he had the puck mounted on a plaque, autographed it, and mailed it to Cory.

But there was an even bigger surprise in store for Cory. When the young man recovered sufficiently to travel, he was flown to Montreal to see his hockey hero in action — as a guest of the Canadiens and Guy Lafleur. Against Vancouver that night Lafleur scored another goal, once again keeping a promise to his young friend. In the weeks ahead, whenever the Canadiens visited Calgary, Cory could rely on at least a phone call and sometimes a luncheon invitation from the man who had taken such an interest in his well-being.

Of the 518 goals Lafleur scored in his career, two will never be forgotten by Cory Gurnsey of Calgary. Those were the two dedicated to him — by one of the greatest goal scorers of all time.

Bossy Had a Backer

THE DAY BEFORE THE 1977 entry draft meetings got under way, New York Islander scout Henry Saraceno walked into general manager Bill Torrey's office, took a picture off the wall, and replaced it with a large color portrait of Mike Bossy. The message was clear — Saraceno was pleading with Torrey to select Bossy in the upcoming draft. For weeks Saraceno had been trying to convince Torrey to grab the teenage sniper from the Laval Nationals of the Quebec Major Junior League. He told his boss repeatedly that if he signed Bossy he would never regret it.

But Torrey had heard some disturbing things about the shooter from Laval. There was no doubt he could score goals, but he was a skinny kid and prone to injuries. Even more, his defensive play was suspect and he disliked fighting with a passion. Those raps had to be considered.

Saraceno reminded Torrey that he had been Bossy's coach one year in Peewee hockey and the kid had once scored 15 goals in a single period. He talked of Bossy's 309 goals in his Junior career — only five fewer than Guy Lafleur.

"Take him, Bill. He'll burn up the league."

"I don't know, Henry. It's a tough decision. Besides, he may not be around when I get to draft. Remember, we're number 15 on the list."

On draft day 14 Juniors were selected — among them six right wingers — and Bossy was still available. Obviously the other clubs had scouted him well and were concerned about his deficiencies.

Torrey took a deep breath, made up his mind, and announced, "The New York Islanders select Mike Bossy, right winger with Laval."

No one in hockey — not even Bossy himself — was more elated than Saraceno when Torrey made his choice.

"I'm sure it was the happiest day of Henry Saraceno's life," Torrey would say at his scout's funeral two years later. "Others doubted Mike, but Henry never did. He had absolute faith that Mike would become one of hockey's greatest scorers."

Bossy, too, had confidence in his ability to put the puck in the net. When Torrey signed him to a contract, the GM asked the 20-year-old rookie how many goals he planned to score.

"I should get 50" was the reply.

"Fifty!" Torrey exclaimed. "No rookie has ever scored 50."

"Well, I think I will."

And he did. He pumped home 20 goals in his first 22 games and established a rookie record for goal scoring with 53. The previous record holder was Buffalo's Richard Martin with 44.

Fifty-goal seasons became Bossy's trademark. In nine seasons as an Islander he never scored fewer than 50 — a feat no other player, not even Wayne Gretzky, has achieved. He would easily have completed a 10th 50-goal season had not a back injury hampered his play and forced him into early retirement.

His rookie record of 53 goals lasted until 1992–93 when Teemu Selanne of the Winnipeg Jets established a new mark of 76. But 50 goals or more for nine consecutive years? That record should stand for a long time.

If Henry Saraceno were around to comment, he would no doubt say, "I'm so proud of Michael and his accomplishments. All the records he set, the All-Star teams, the four Stanley Cups, the Hall of Fame. But then I knew he could do it all the time. I'm glad Bill Torrey listened to me."

A Night for Johnny — Halfway Through His Career

IN 1968 THE BOSTON BRUINS held a night for veteran left winger Johnny Bucyk, one of their most popular players. Bucyk had served the Bruins well for a dozen seasons, but his goal production had slipped to 18 the previous year and retirement seemed imminent. Bucyk accepted the new car, the outboard motor, and the other gifts, as well as the plaudits for serving the Bruins so well for so long.

There was just one hitch. At age 32 Bucyk had no intention of retiring. To prove he hadn't lost his scoring touch, he recorded a 30-goal season. Then, like a kid starting all over again, he scored 24 goals, 31 goals and, incredibly, 51 goals. At age 35 he had become the only player of that vintage to score 50 goals or more in a season.

Bucyk still gave no thought to retirement. Five years later, at age 40, he potted 36 goals. Only when he turned 43 did he decide it was time to step aside . . . after a "disappointing" 20-goal season.

More than 10 years had passed since he had been honored on Johnny Bucyk Night at the Boston Garden. The car and the outboard had long since worn out. But not John. He had stayed around for two Stanley Cup victories plus several individual honors, including a pair of Lady Byng trophies. He had scored another 319 goals since his "retirement" party and had become the fourth-leading scorer of all time with 556 markers.

No wonder he was swiftly inducted into the Hockey Hall of Fame in 1981.

Milt Schmidt Signs with Boston

WHEN MILT SCHMIDT FIRST ATTRACTED the attention of the Boston Bruins, he was a naive 17-year-old from Kitchener, Ontario. Invited to the Boston training camp, he wrote Bruin manager Art Ross and told him he would get a summer job immediately so that he could pay his way to the team's training quarters in Hershey. Ross chuckled about that letter in later years. "Miltie was so green," he said, "he didn't know the team picked up all travel expenses."

"Oh, I was green, all right," Schmidt told me recently. "Especially when Ross called me in to sign my first contract with the Bruins. He offered me something like $3,000, and I told him I'd like $3,500. Well, he raised his eyebrows and said that was more than he'd been authorized to give me. He said he'd have to go down the hall and discuss my request with the team owner, Mr. Adams. So I waited patiently while he went to see Mr. Adams. In a few minutes he was back, and he had a grim look on his

Boston's celebrated Kraut Line: Bobby Bauer (left), Milt Schmidt, and Woody Dumart. (National Archives of Canada)

face. 'Sorry, Milt,' he said, 'I fought for you, but Mr. Adams wouldn't budge on the $3,000 offer. He told me you could take it or leave it.'

"So I reached for a pen and signed the contract. On my way out of the building I passed Mr. Adams's office. I said to myself, I think I'll go in there and ask Mr. Adams why he wouldn't give me the extra 500 bucks I requested. So I entered the office and encountered Mr. Adams's secretary.

"'Yes? Can I help you?' she asked.

"'Hi. I'm Milt Schmidt. I just signed with the Bruins and I'd like to see Mr. Adams, please.'

"She smiled and said, 'I'm sorry, but Mr. Adams isn't in today. He won't be in all week.'"

Milt turned to me. "Brian," he said, "they lied to me from day one, and they've been lying to me ever since."

The Bear Wrestler

WHEN JOE LOUIS first retired as the heavyweight champion of the world in 1949, he left without much money. So he took a job with the Barnum and Bailey Circus to make ends meet. His job was to referee wrestling matches between a mean-looking circus bear and anyone brave or foolish enough to try to put the furry creature down.

Sometimes it was difficult to persuade local strongmen to climb into the ring with an animal that looked so ferocious. But not in Joliette, Quebec, where a 16-year-old hockey player named Marcel Bonin leaped fearlessly over the ropes.

"Mr. Louis, I'll wrestle this bear. Let's see how tough he really is," Bonin said.

The ensuing struggle is still talked about by old-timers in Joliette. Young Bonin, they say, fought the muzzled monster to a draw. *Mais oui,* he failed to put the mangy bruin down, but the citizens of Joliette cheered young Bonin, anyway, when the match was over.

Only recently, when I chatted with Bonin at the Montreal Forum, did he confess there was a reason for his bravado that day. "Sure, the bear had a muzzle and he'd been declawed, but still, he was a very big, tough old bear. Must have weighed 400 pounds. But Marcel Bonin is not crazy. I went to see that bear in the morning, before the match, and I fed him and played with him until we were pretty good friends. He was glad to see me when I jumped into the ring.

"I wrestled that same bear many times in the small towns in Quebec. Nobody else wanted to take a chance with him. I think we put on a pretty good show for the people.

"My friend Marcel Pronovost was playing with Detroit in those days, and when I came up to play hockey with the Red Wings, he told everybody I was a tough little bear wrestler from Joliette. The papers made a big thing of that."

Bonin was later traded to the Montreal Canadiens where he played on four Stanley Cup-winning teams. One year, hoping to change his scoring luck, he borrowed a pair of Rocket Richard's old gloves. "Maybe they'll help me get out of my slump," he told Richard. In the next eight games Bonin scored eight goals.

Why Stemmer Got Traded

PETE STEMKOWSKI WAS a key member of the last Toronto Maple Leaf team to win the Stanley Cup — the Leafs of 1967. He was a popular Leaf and a happy Leaf. He was even naive enough to figure he would be with the Toronto organization forever.

That was why it came as such a shock when he was traded to Detroit a year after celebrating the Leafs' Stanley Cup victory. But he put past triumphs behind him and concentrated on having some big seasons with his new club. His first season in a Red Wing uniform was excellent — he doubled the number of goals he had scored as a Leaf in 1967. And the next year was even better — a 25-goal season, an impressive total for the sixties. Why then was he suddenly sent packing from the Red Wings in 1969?

Well, it seems his off-ice sense of humor wasn't appreciated by Ned Harkness, who was the team's coach and general manager back then. Harkness had been a highly successful coach in U.S. college hockey at Cornell, but he had never been with a pro team in his life.

The first time he met Stemkowski he told him to get a haircut. Stemmer made a date with the barber, but not enough hair was clipped to please the coach. Stemkowski got a second haircut and mailed the hair clippings to Harkness to prove he was following orders.

Then came the fateful day when Stemkowski entered the Red Wing dressing room wearing the coach's beloved Cornell windbreaker and baseball cap. The jacket and cap had become a Ned Harkness trademark in college. Stemmer blew a whistle and began to put on a show for his grinning teammates.

"Gimme a C!" he shouted. "Gimme an O, gimme an R, gimme an N!"

But before he could finish spelling out Cornell in his best cheerleader fashion, the door popped open and in walked Harkness. Stemkowski never got to finish his routine. His performance was cut short and so was his stint in Detroit. A few days later he was traded to New York for Larry Brown.

Thirty Minutes for Talking

HALL OF FAMER Frank Frederickson, who once scored 41 goals in 30 games for the Victoria club of the old Pacific Coast Hockey league, was as fine a player as ever laced up skates. His only problem was his penchant for talking. He voiced opinions on everything, to the dismay of his family and friends and, of course, to every player, penalty timekeeper, and referee in organized hockey.

One day Lester Patrick, Frederickson's coach and manager, came up with a brilliant solution for dealing with his star player's gift for the gab. He allowed Frederickson 30 minutes a day for nonstop chatter. In Patrick's office each morning Lester would pull out his watch and tell Fredrickson to spout off on any subject. Exactly half an hour later Patrick would call a halt.

It seemed to work as Frederickson poured out his comments and opinions each day across the desk from Patrick, his one-man audience. In time Patrick began to look forward to these daily monologues. That pleased his players. They, in turn, could look forward to half an hour each day without having to listen to a compulsive chatterbox.

A Rocky Day for Perry Turnbull

THE WINNIPEG JETS JOURNEYED to New York a few seasons back, and in this shopping mecca of North America, Jets forward Perry Turnbull spotted a bargain. On a street corner he saw a man selling videotape recorders at what appeared to be a reasonable price. The man was willing to bargain, and Turnbull, pleading limited funds, soon had the price down to $150.

The man hesitated. "Make up your mind," Turnbull said. "I'm with a hockey team and I've got a bus to catch to the airport."

"Sold," the man said, pocketing the cash. "Here's one that's already boxed. It's the same as the model you've been looking at."

Turnbull took his purchase and hurried off to catch the team bus. En route to the airport he told his mates about the bargain price he had paid for a quality VCR.

"Open the box," someone said. "Let's have a look at it."

Turnbull obliged. Inside the box, wrapped in newspapers, was a large stone.

When he reported for practice the next morning, someone had placed two rocks inside his locker. On one the word BETA was printed in bold letters, on the other VHS.

2

GUARDIANS OF THE NETS

Goalies Are Different

GOALIES AREN'T AT ALL LIKE the other players on a hockey team. They not only use different skates, pads and sticks but they act differently.

Look at one of the all-time best — Georges Vezina, after whom the Vezina Trophy is named. Vezina enjoyed playing goal in his street shoes until he was in his late teens. He'd probably have played in the NHL that way if the Montreal Canadiens had let him.

Another early-day goalie was Percy LeSueur from Ottawa. He used the same goal stick for every league and playoff game for five straight seasons. There was fat Billy Nicholson, too, a 300-pounder who astonished everyone early in the century by rambling up the ice and attempting to score goals. Fred Brophy of Montreal Westmount became the first goalie to race down the ice and score a goal in 1905.

Goalie Fred Chittick, an Ottawa star in 1898, refused to play in a Stanley Cup playoff game because management wouldn't cough up a "fair number" of complimentary tickets to a big game.

In the NHL, Montreal's Bill Durnan was amazingly ambidextrous. He often switched his big goal stick from hand to hand, thoroughly confusing opposing forwards.

Gary "Suitcase" Smith, who played with eight different NHL teams, used to strip off his uniform between periods of each game. Teammates marveled at the energy he put into taking off 30 pounds of gear, then putting it all back on again. Early in his career, Smith wore as many as 13 pairs of socks under his goal skates. Smith also developed a unique habit of drop-kicking the puck a hundred feet down the ice after making a save.

Ken Dryden quit the Montreal Canadiens one year to earn $135 a week with a Toronto law firm. Boston's Gerry Cheevers painted stitch marks on his goal mask as a reminder of what might have happened to his face if the mask hadn't been there. Jacques Plante, who introduced the face mask to NHL hockey, was an excellent knitter and used to knit toques and other garments to pass the time on road trips.

Gilles Gratton had some interesting quirks. He once streaked across the ice naked and was a firm believer in reincarnation. "In Biblical days I stoned people to death," he would say. "Now they are repaying me by hurling pucks at my head."

In 1987, Philadelphia's Ron Hextall duplicated Brophy's turn-of-the-century feat and fulfilled a lifelong ambition by scoring a goal — from goal line to goal line against the Boston Bruins. Later, he scored another in a playoff game.

Who says goalies are just like the other players on a team?

A Dummy in Goal

SOME HOCKEY PEOPLE, including several prominent players who chose the position, say a fellow has to be crazy to play in goal. Either that or he has to be a real dummy. But only once in NHL history has a dummy been between the pipes.

Many decades ago the Chicago Blackhawks' ec-

Chicago goalie Charlie Gardiner. Certainly no dummy. (Hockey Hall of Fame)

centric owner Major Frederic McLaughlin decided his team needed a second goaltender, one who would be good company for All-Star netminder Charlie Gardiner. McLaughlin wanted a practice goalie only, one who had no fear of shooting drills, one who never complained, and best of all, one who never had to be paid. Presto! He invented hockey's first dummy.

McLaughlin had a member of his staff stuff bags full of straw into a scarecrow-shaped figure roughly resembling a goalie. When the job was done, the dummy was hauled across the ice and strung up in the center of the goal net. While All-Star goalie Charlie Gardiner tended goal in practice at one end of the ice, the dummy defended the opposite goal. Chicago players took their hardest shots at the chunky figure, hoping to knock the stuffing out of the latest addition to their roster.

For the next few days Gardiner heard comments in the dressing room like: "That dummy's lookin' better every day. He never complains about us shootin' high or yaps at us for not clearin' the puck. He's a lot smarter than our other guy and better lookin', too. He deserves a start, don't you think? In fact, I hear the owner's signed the dummy long-term and wants to send our other guy to the minors."

The other guy — Gardiner — took the ribbing in stride for a few days. Then he ended the dummy experiment once and for all. After practice one day, he hauled the dummy into the dressing room, flopped him onto the rubbing table, and said to the trainer, "Give this poor kid a rubdown, will you? He's falling to pieces out there. Then find some clothes for him, give him a few bucks for a beer and a sandwich, and get him the hell out of here."

Fournier the Fireman

ONE NIGHT BACK IN 1906, fans filled the tiny arena in Buckingham, Quebec for the big game with arch-rival Vankleek Hill. The 400 hometown fans anticipated a victory, perhaps an easy one. Their optimism was based on the play of young Guy Fournier, a local lad who was enjoying an outstanding season in goal.

The fans chanted Fournier's name and jeered the opposing players as the teams skated through the warm-up period. Then, just as the referee was ready to drop the puck, the lights in the arena went out and a cry of "Fire" was heard.

The arena doors were thrown open and the fans rushed into the street. Fortunately, no one was injured in the dash to the exits. A block away, flames could be seen leaping into the sky, consuming the town's only department store. Several fans rushed off to help the fire brigade battle the blaze.

When the fire was finally out, the fans returned to the arena. Some had grimy faces and their clothes smelled of smoke. The hockey players, meanwhile, had been resting in the dark in their dressing rooms, and when electricity was restored, they returned to the ice.

All but one. Goalkeeper Guy Fournier of Buckingham was missing. On learning of the blaze, Fournier, whose father was the town engineer, had raced from the arena still wearing his skates and goal pads. He skated down the snow-packed street to the pump house to help his father keep water flowing to douse the flames. He was gone for more than an hour. He even offered to help get power restored, but his father said, "I'll look after that. You've got a hockey game to play."

It was 9:30 when Fournier arrived back at the rink. The fans gave him a huge ovation. When the referee was finally able to start the match, young Fournier proved he was just as quick in goal as he was in getting to the pump house. He was the number-one star as Buckingham won the game 4–1.

Brimsek's Brilliance

NO ROOKIE GOALIE ever got off to a better start in the NHL than a kid from Minnesota named Frankie Brimsek.

On December 1, 1938, the Boston Bruins started Brimsek in goal against the Montreal Canadiens at the Forum. The Bruins claimed Brimsek would make everyone forget their former netminder, the great Tiny Thompson, who'd been sold to Detroit for $15,000. The Boston players doubted it, for Thompson, a ten-year veteran, had won four Vezina trophies and was extremely popular. Dit Clapper, Thompson's roommate, was so upset at the goalie's departure he threatened to quit hockey.

Brimsek, aware he was replacing a Bruin immortal, was cool, quick and unflappable in his debut against Montreal. Still, the Bruins lost 2–0.

But in the next seven games Brimsek played his way out from under Thompson's huge shadow and into a spotlight of his own creation. He went into Chicago and shut out the Black Hawks 4–0. Two nights later, he shut them out again, this time 2–0. He followed up with a third straight shutout, a 3–0 whitewashing of the Rangers. In game five he broke Thompson's Boston record for shutout minutes as the Bruins edged Montreal 3–2. Until Montreal scored, Brimsek had gone 231 minutes and 54 seconds without allowing a goal.

In his next three games, he was perfect again. He blanked the Canadiens 1–0, the Red Wings 2–0 and the New York Americans 2–0 — three more shutouts for the Bruin rookie, who was already being called Mr. Zero.

It couldn't last forever. The Rangers finally snapped his second shutout streak with a 1–0 victory. But what a start for rookie Brimsek! Six shutouts in his first eight games. No wonder he went on to win the rookie award (with ten shutouts and a 1.59 goals-against average), the Vezina Trophy and a berth on the first all-star team.

Thanks to Brimsek's sensational netminding, the Bruins swept to the Stanley Cup finals against Toronto. Mr. Zero gave up a mere six goals to the

Leafs in the final series, and the Bruins captured the Cup four games to one.

The Stingiest Goalie

GEORGE HAINSWORTH of the Montreal Canadiens set a remarkable NHL record during the 1928–29 season. He recorded 22 shutouts in 44 games. What's more, he allowed only 43 goals in the 44 games he played.

An Unbeatable Goaltending Streak

IN MODERN-DAY HOCKEY, when NHL teams use two, three, four or even five goalies in a season, it's hard to believe that just a few years ago teams relied on one man, and one man only, to guard their nets.

And no team relied on a netminder more than Chicago in the sixties when Glenn Hall toiled for the Windy City club. Game in and game out, Hall was always there. He played three, four, five hundred games in a row. Remember, this was in the era before the face mask, when all goaltenders suffered frequent cuts and concussions.

On the night of November 7, 1962, Chicago was at home to Boston. And Hall wasn't feeling well. Of course, nobody expected him to feel well; his penchant for throwing up before games and between periods was widely publicized. Similarly his habit of wrestling with the team trainer for several minutes in an effort to settle his pregame nerves had become a familiar ritual.

But on this night there was no wrestling in the dressing room. Hall's physical problems wouldn't allow it, for they were far worse than a nervous stomach. The pain in his lower back was excruciating. A lesser athlete wouldn't have thought of suiting up for the game. But when the Hawks took the ice that night, Hall was standing calmly between the pipes as usual. It was his 503rd consecutive game, or his 552nd counting playoffs.

The game was only a few minutes old when Boston's Murray Oliver shot the puck at Hall and it flew right between his legs. Hall's back pain was so intense that he simply hadn't been able to bend over to block the puck the way he normally would have. It was impossible for him to carry on in goal.

Hall skated slowly to the Hawk bench, said a few words to his coach and then moved on to the dressing room, ending more than 33,000 consecutive minutes of goaltending in his 503rd game.

The most fantastic iron-man streak in professional sport was finally over.

The Last Goalie to Do It

THE LAST GOALTENDER TO PLAY in every one of his team's games in a single season was Boston's Ed Johnston in 1963–64. The NHL schedule encompassed 70 games in that era.

We all know that Jacques Plante popularized the goalie face mask in 1959. The last goaltender to play in the NHL without wearing a mask was Andy Brown, who toiled for Pittsburgh and Detroit from 1971 to 1974.

The last goaltender to play an entire All-Star

game was Chicago's Glenn Hall, who led his All-Star mates to a victory over the Montreal Canadiens, the defending Cup champions, in 1965.

The last non-goalie to stand in goal during an NHL game, substituting for an injured goaltender, was Boston's Jerry Toppazzini. He took over for Don Simmons in the dying seconds of a game on October 6, 1960. Boston lost the match 4–1.

Battle of the Bulge

IN THE LATE 1940S AND EARLY 1950S fat and funny Turk Broda of the Toronto Maple Leafs was one of the most popular players in the NHL. He led the Leafs to four Stanley Cups in the '40s and another in 1951. Old-timers say he was one of the greatest "money" goalies in hockey.

But none of Broda's countless fans will ever forget a week in November 1949 when Leaf owner Conn Smythe demanded that the goalie reduce his waistline . . . or else. Broda weighed 197 pounds at the time, and Smythe decreed publicly, "My goalie's too fat. He'd better lose seven pounds before the next game or I'll be looking for another goalie."

To show he meant business, Smythe recalled goalie Gilles Mayer from the Leaf farm club in Pittsburgh, where Mayer, a skinny kid, was drinking milkshakes trying to gain weight.

So began the famous Battle of the Bulge. Broda went on a crash diet and lost four pounds the very first day. All of Canada got caught up in the story. Papers carried photos of Broda emerging from a steam room, Broda nibbling on celery sticks, Broda lifting weights in the Leaf dressing room.

The weigh-in was set for Saturday afternoon, just before a big game with the New York Rangers. When Broda stepped on the scales, the needle settled just under 190. He'd made it! Canadians from coast to coast breathed a little easier, and the grinning goaltender accepted congratulations from friends and teammates.

When the slimmed-down netminder skated onto the ice that night, he received a tremendous ovation from his fans. The regimental band at the Gardens played "Happy Days Are Here Again" and followed up with a chorus of "She's Too Fat For Me."

Broda rewarded his supporters in the best possible way, by chalking up a shutout over the visiting Rangers.

Brother against Brother

ON MARCH 20, 1971 I was fortunate to witness a unique bit of hockey history at the Montreal Forum. I was hosting a *Hockey Night in Canada* game between the Canadiens and the Buffalo Sabres, and our telecast crew gave the contest a lot of extra hype because, for the first time in history, we anticipated that two brothers — both goaltenders — would be facing each other.

The brothers were Ken and Dave Dryden.

Then just before game time came disappointing news. The brother against brother matchup wouldn't happen after all. While Buffalo coach Punch Imlach announced that Dave Dryden would be his starting netminder in the game, Montreal coach Al MacNeil turned spoilsport and named Rogie Vachon as the Canadiens' starter. It didn't seem to bother MacNeil that he was depriving the fans of being witness to a history-making event. They showed their displeasure when the starting lineups were announced.

The possibility of the two Drydens facing each other became even more remote when Imlach changed his mind at the last minute and started goalie Joe Daley in the Sabres' net.

Then in the second period, Rogie Vachon went down with an injury. He was unable to stay in the game, and off the Montreal bench to replace him came the tall rookie, Ken Dryden. Now it was up to Imlach to make a move. Sure enough, he pulled Daley off the ice and sent Dave Dryden in to guard the Buffalo goal. The fans went wild.

Both brothers admitted later that they were very nervous as they stared at each other across 180 feet of ice. When he wrote his best-selling book *The Game* in 1983, Ken recalled that encounter. "I didn't enjoy that game very much," he wrote. "I had played only two previous NHL games, and seeing Dave in the other goal was a distraction I didn't want or need."

Dave was just as conscious of the unique situation. Obviously, he was distracted, too, because he fanned on the first shot he faced, a hummer off the stick of Jacques Lemaire from 70 feet out.

Montreal won the game 5–2, but those in attendance talked more about witnessing a hockey "first" than about the final outcome. At the siren, the two brothers skated to centre ice, smiled and shook hands. Both received a prolonged ovation.

Ken Dryden's Remarkable Debut

THE KID HAD BEEN A STAR in college hockey at Cornell. He had played well with the Montreal farm team in Halifax. He was tall, wore glasses, and was said to be very bright, an intellectual. That was about all we knew about rookie netminder Ken Dryden back in 1971 when he was called up to the Canadiens. That and the fact his brother Dave was also a goalie.

It was late in the season and the Habs were on their way to a third-place finish when they gave Dryden a half-dozen starts in goal. He surprised everybody by winning every game.

When the Canadiens opened the playoffs against Boston, they were said to be in too deep. The Bruins

Ken Dryden stood tall in the Montreal Canadiens' net during the battling seventies. (Robert B. Shaver)

had smashed a handful of records on their way to a first-place finish. They had Bobby Orr, Phil Esposito, Wayne Cashman, Ken Hodge, and Johnny Bucyk, plus home ice advantage in the series.

The Bruins were pleased to see Dryden start in goal for Montreal. They'd soon show him what playoff pressure was all about. As expected, Boston took the opener 3–1, while in game two the Bruins raced out to a 5–1 lead.

Suddenly the Canadiens found a groove and fought back. They scored a goal, then another, then four more to take a 7–5 lead. The Bruins were rattled by the second-period barrage, but they weren't about to concede. They regrouped for a third-period attack on Dryden.

But the lanky goaltender turned aside shot after shot. Some of his saves were truly magnificent. And when the final buzzer sounded, he almost fainted from the constant pressure he had been under.

His confidence bolstered by the comeback in game two, Dryden continued to give Montreal spectacular goaltending, and the Canadiens eventually eliminated the frustrated Bruins in seven games. Phil Esposito, who had scored a record 76 goals during the regular season, couldn't believe "the big giraffe" in the Montreal net had held him to just three goals in the series.

The Canadiens went on to eliminate the Chicago Blackhawks in the final series, with Dryden again playing a key role in the victory. At season's end he was awarded the Conn Smythe Trophy as MVP of the playoffs, a remarkable achievement for an inexperienced newcomer with only six regular season games under his big pads.

The following season he continued to play brilliantly and skated off with the Calder Trophy as the league's top freshman. No player in history had been a playoff MVP one season and a rookie award winner the next. It happened to Dryden. It may never happen again.

Rookie Swede Stops Habs' Amazing Streak

IT WAS FEBRUARY 23, 1978, and the New York Rangers faced almost certain defeat as they prepared for a game at the Montreal Forum. After all, they were mired in last place in their division and they hadn't won a game at the Forum in six years. As for the hometown Habs . . . well, the Canadiens were too hot for anyone to handle. They hadn't lost in 28 games, winning 23 and tying five. It was an NHL record, surpassing a 23-game undefeated mark shared by the 1940–41 Boston Bruins and the 1976 Philadelphia Flyers.

"We are determined to keep the streak going," Guy Lafleur told reporters. "We don't want any other team to break our record." (In time another team would — the Philadelphia Flyers.)

One of the attractions of hockey is that upsets can occur at any time. Perhaps the Rangers took to the ice that night feeling they had nothing to lose. Coach Jean-Guy Talbot must have felt that way. Otherwise why would he have plucked a nervous Swedish goaltender from the American League to face the mighty Canadiens?

Fans were stunned when 26-year-old Hardy Astrom, who would later play for Don Cherry in Colorado and be called "my Swedish sieve" among other things, was announced as the Rangers' starting goalie. Astrom had never played in an NHL game. When asked about his startling choice of goaltenders, Talbot shrugged and said, "Listen, when you play a hot team like Montreal, a coach will try anything."

It was hardly a vote of confidence, but the rookie Swede played like an All-Star. His mates, bolstered by his solid performance, checked with unfamiliar gusto, and New York skated off with a 6–3 victory. Hockey's longest undefeated streak was over — snapped by the team least likely to break it.

It was a spectacular debut for Astrom, but his finest 60 minutes of NHL play were never to be duplicated. He played another 82 games in the NHL, with the Rangers and the Rockies, and compiled a dismal 17–44–12 mark.

It's Raining Rubber

WHEN THE QUEBEC NORDIQUES faced the Boston Bruins at the Boston Garden on March 21, 1991, Quebec goalie Ron Tugnutt knew he was in for a busy evening. He would be facing renowned shooters like Cam Neely and Ray Bourque and he expected a heavy work load. But he didn't expect to be worn to a frazzle.

The 155-pound Tugnutt was pelted at the rate of more than a shot every minute, most of them sizzlers. But time and again the nimble netminder denied the Bruins of glorious opportunities. With the game knotted at 3–3, Tugnutt put on a display of overtime goaltending that brought the Bruin faithful to their feet in a seldom seen tribute to a gallant opponent.

With seconds left to play in the overtime frame, Tugnutt robbed both Bourque and Neely of near-certain goals to salvage a tie and a single point for his team. When the final buzzer sounded, the young man had stopped 70 of 73 shots to earn the respect and admiration of everyone in the building.

As the crowd stood and roared, Cam Neely skated up to the exhausted Tugnutt and said, "Take a bow. It's you they're applauding."

Most of the fans assumed the 73 shots on Tugnutt set a league record. Not so. The mark for most shots in a game is held by a former Chicago netminder, Sam LoPresti, who was bombarded by 83 Boston shots in a game played at the Garden 50 years earlier, almost to the day. Incredibly LoPresti almost stole a win for the Hawks that night, finally losing 3–2.

The patriotic LoPresti joined the U.S. Navy shortly afterward, saying, "It may be safer facing Nazi U-boats in the Atlantic than dodging hockey pucks in the NHL." Ironically he had plenty of time to consider that sentiment when his ship was torpedoed and he managed to survive for 45 days adrift on a life raft.

A Big Star, but Not an All-Star

GOALIE AL ROLLINS HAD a terrific season for the Chicago Blackhawks in 1954, and even though his team finished dead last in the standings, at season's end Rollins was awarded the Hart Trophy as the NHL's most valuable player. Amazingly Rollins was overlooked by the All-Star selectors that season. They placed Toronto's Harry Lumley on the first team and Terry Sawchuk on the second, which raises the question, how can a player be voted best in the league and not be an All-Star? But Rollins was accustomed to being snubbed by hockey's award voters. In 1951 he captured the Vezina Trophy as top NHL goaltender. He was passed over in the All-Star balloting that season, too. Detroit's Sawchuk was voted number one and Chuck Rayner of New York was the second-team choice.

Bruins Seek Goalie: Aging Rookie Gets the Job

IN 1971 ROSS BROOKS, a 34-year-old goalie with 13 dreary winters of playing in hockey's minor leagues behind him, was almost ready to give up his dream of making the NHL. It was not only a personal disappointment, but it was unfortunate for another reason: Brooks would have provided the answer to a wonderful new question for trivia buffs. Who was the only Jewish netminder in NHL history?

After all, he had spent the past seven years as a backup goaltender in Providence, playing only when Marcel Paille, the Reds' number one man, was extremely weary or incapacitated. Then, to his consternation, midway through the 1971–72 season, Brooks was handed his outright release by Providence management.

"I was stunned," he said. "I thought about buying a lunch bucket and finding a job, but I still wanted to play hockey more than anything. My wife and I decided to sit down and write a letter to every general manager in every league. It cost us all of eight bucks for paper and stamps and the message was simple — I was out of work and wanted to play.

"Talk about luck. My letter reached Milt Schmidt of the Bruins just when he was seeking a goalie. He called me and signed me and sent me to Oklahoma City. Then it was on to the Boston Braves [a Bruin farm team in the American League] where I shared goalie of the year honors with Dan Bouchard. When Bouchard was drafted by Atlanta, an expansion team, and when Gerry Cheevers, Boston's number one goalie, bolted to the WHA, I got a call from the Bruins and finally found myself in the NHL. I was 36, one of the oldest rookies ever, and while it was no big deal, I became the first Jewish goaltender in league history."

After a decade of playing in the shadow of other netminders, Brooks was determined to make the most of his opportunity. For the next three seasons he played the best hockey of his career. During one stretch, he won 14 consecutive games to equal a team mark set by the legendary Tiny Thompson in 1929–30. By the end of his rookie season he'd compiled an extraordinary record of 16–3–0 with a goals-against average of 2.36. For two more seasons, playing backup to Gilles Gilbert, he was always ready and always reliable. When he retired in 1974, his big league stats were 37–7–6. His career goals-against average was 2.64 — lower than that of two Bruin Hall of Famers, Gerry Cheevers (2.89) and Frankie Brimsek (2.70).

"A lot of people, especially young people, could look at my story and learn something from it," Brooks said after he bowed from the scene with no regrets. "After so many years of people doubting I could play well, so many years of people not knowing I was alive out there, after a lot of perseverance and hard work, I finally achieved my goal and proved myself with the greatest team in hockey."

The Goalie's Release Was Forged

IN 1906 GOALIE HENRI MENARD of the Montreal Wanderers filled his daytime hours enrolled as a student at the University of Laval. One day a stranger handed him a letter. It read: "Dear Mr. Menard. As the Wanderers have been able to obtain a goalie with outstanding credentials, we will not require your services in the game tonight against the Shamrocks. Thank you for your past efforts on our behalf. [Signed] James Strachan, President."

That evening the young netminder entered the arena moments before game time and was surprised to find an anxious band of Wanderers relieved to see him. "Get dressed!" they demanded. "Why are you so late? Where have you been?"

"But I'm not playing tonight," he told them. "I was released today. I have the letter of dismissal in my pocket."

Mr. Strachan, the club president, stepped forward.

"Let me see this letter," he demanded. After scanning the document, he cried, "This is a forgery. That's not my signature. Some despicable rascal, obviously a Shamrock supporter, tried to keep you out of the game tonight."

Menard hastily suited up and played a solid game for the Wanderers in their victory over the Shamrocks. Meanwhile news of the forged letter swept through Montreal hockey circles. A reporter wrote: "Great indignation was expressed over the meanness of the artifice. Two detectives have been hired to investigate the forgery."

But the culprit was never discovered, even though a reward of $25 was posted for his arrest and conviction.

Journalist in Goal

IN THE FALL OF 1977 George Plimpton, a noted American journalist and sports fan, asked the Boston Bruins if he could play goal for them in a big league hockey game. He had never played goal before, but he wondered what an NHL goalie's life was like. He wanted to write about it. What better way to find out than to stand in the net, wearing the goaltender's armor, and face sizzling slapshots?

Bruins coach Don Cherry vetoed any notion of Plimpton playing in a regular season game but consented to let him represent the Bruins in a brief five-minute trial during a preseason game. Plimpton was also required to sign a "no-fault" contract, releasing the Bruins and the NHL from any responsibility for injuries he might suffer, including death.

Plimpton attended the Bruins' fall training camp

and roomed with minor league goalie Jim Pettie, who instructed him in the fundamentals of netminding.

Cherry didn't make it easy for the literary volunteer. He decided to start Plimpton in a game against the Philadelphia Flyers at the Spectrum. In the dressing room prior to the game Gerry Cheevers, Boston's number one goalie, approached Plimpton with some last-minute advice. "Stand up! Stand up!" he said, meaning to remind him to stay upright on the ice. Plimpton misunderstood and thought Cheevers was commanding him to stand up in the dressing room. So he shot to his feet. While the other players laughed Cheevers said, "Not in here, George. Out on the ice." He turned to his mates and muttered, "What a basket case this guy is."

When the game began, Plimpton had no problems for the first two minutes, for the Bruins went on the attack and kept the puck in the Flyer zone. Then the tide turned and a wave of Flyers surged into the Boston zone, and Plimpton had only a fleeting glimpse of "that awful black puck, sailing elusively between sticks and skates, as shifty as a rat in a hedgerow."

The first shot the Flyers took went in, a zinger from the point tipped in by Orest Kindrachuk. Plimpton yelled loudly in dismay and beat the side of his helmet with his blocking pad as Flyer fans, showing no sympathy, laughed at his plight.

Then Boston's Bobby Schmautz took a penalty, and Plimpton found himself facing the Flyer power play. One shot ricocheted off the crossbar. Another just missed the far corner as Plimpton sprawled awkwardly onto the ice. In an effort to get back onto his feet he grabbed a defenseman around the leg and hauled himself upright, using his surprised teammate the way a drunk might use a lamppost.

Six Flyer shots were drilled in his direction and, amazingly, none went in. One bounced off his mask. The rest hit various parts of his body. At one point during the barrage he turned completely away from the play to peer into his net, thinking a puck had eluded him. A photographer jumped up and snapped a shot of him, staring into the depths of the goal, like a man looking for an escape route, while the action raged furiously in front of his crease.

Later, writing about his NHL debut in *Sports Illustrated,* Plimpton would take no credit for any of the saves. He was, he said, "somewhat akin to a tree in the line of flight of a golf ball."

With the author's five-minute stint just about over, Boston's Mike Milbury threw a stick at an incoming Flyer forward and a penalty shot was called. Reg Leach, who had once scored 61 goals in a season, was the shooter. Leach raced in from center ice. Plimpton moved out to cut down the shooting angle and collapsed like a house of cards just as Leach fired. Eyes closed, Plimpton felt the shot graze his goal skate and deflect high into the crowd.

The Bruins surged off the bench and hauled George upright. They cuffed him with their gloves and dragged him over to the bench. "They handled me like a sack of potatoes," he later wrote. "Of course, they told me Leach was a psychological ruin after he failed to beat me. And they said I'd made 30 or 40 saves at least in my brief appearance."

After his ordeal on the ice, Plimpton knew he "belonged as a Bruin" when he began to get dressed. His tie was chopped in half, the toes had been snipped from his socks, and the seat was gone from his underwear.

Cherry said to him, "George, you should feel honored. And lucky, too. When my guys initiate someone, usually the hair goes, too."

The Goalie Was a Golfer

IN THE EARLY SEVENTIES goalie Ed Johnston of the Boston Bruins was seeking a raise. He told Boston executive vice president Charles Mulcahy he wanted a modest increase, enough to bring his salary to $20,000 a year. Mulcahy, in reply, said he didn't think Johnston's work in goal merited that amount. When the two men failed to reach an agreement, Mulcahy, who was a scratch golfer, challenged Johnston to a golf match — three holes at Mulcahy's course. If Johnston won, he would get his raise. The odds appeared to favor Mulcahy because he had won several golf tournaments and had even represented the U.S. internationally at one point in his career.

But Johnston was a capable golfer, too, and had lots of experience wrestling with par. "Let's make the stakes double or nothing," he suggested. "If I win, you pay me $40,000 a year. If I lose, there'll be no raise."

Mulcahy laughed. "You're on. See you on the tee."

On the day of the match Johnston's drives were long and straight, his putting superb, and he beat

*Goalie Ed Johnston
when he played for
the Toronto Maple
Leafs.*

his boss over the three holes they played. Only after
he signed the check that doubled Johnston's salary
did Mulcahy learn that his goaltender had already
established himself as one of the finest golfers ever
to play professional hockey.

Johnston went on to become a successful general
manager in the NHL, first with Pittsburgh, then with
Hartford. In Pittsburgh he signed Mario Lemieux to
one of the richest contracts in hockey history. But
Johnston never once suggested a golf match to
determine Mario's salary. For Lemieux's golfing
prowess is awesome, and he would be more than a
match for any general manager.

But, Coach, I Was Watching the Replay

FORMER NHL GOALTENDER John Garrett, now a *Hockey Night in Canada* broadcaster, will never forget the most embarrassing moment in his career. He was the starting goalie for the Hartford Whalers one night in Washington. One of the things that fascinated Garrett about the Washington arena was the huge screen on the scoreboard over center ice, a screen that enabled fans to watch video replays of goals and other exciting plays.

Garrett was pleased with his performance that night, and by the midway point of the hockey game he had robbed the Caps of several goal-scoring opportunities. But suddenly he had to deal with a two-on-one situation. Two Cap players skated into the Hartford zone. The lone Whaler defenseman fell down while trying to intercept a pass, and one of the Caps slipped the puck through Garrett's pads into the net.

Recalling the incident, Garrett says, "I couldn't believe they'd beaten me on the play. I was sure the puck didn't quite cross the goal line. So I looked up at the big screen to watch the replay. Perhaps it would confirm I was right.

"While I was watching the replay the referee dropped the puck and play resumed. The Washington centerman won the draw and slipped the puck over to hard-shooting Mike Gartner. He stepped over the blue line and rifled a shot in my direction. But I didn't see the puck coming because I was still watching the replay on the giant screen.

"That's when I heard my teammates screaming at

me to wake up, and suddenly I knew I'd made a terrible faux pas. I tried to recover and focus on the slapshot headed straight for my net, but it was too late. The puck zipped past me and the Caps scored a second goal — all in a matter of seconds. It was almost a record for the two fastest goals.

"Coach Don Blackburn waved me over to the bench and told me to sit down. 'You can watch the next replay from the end of the bench,' he snapped as he made a goaltending change. My face was so red I wouldn't even take my goal mask off."

Wayne Gretzky Stole My Car

MIDWAY THROUGH THE THIRD PERIOD of the 1983 All-Star game on Long Island, the Campbell Conference All-Stars held a 5–2 lead over their Wales Conference rivals. It was an exciting moment for Campbell Conference goalie John Garrett, then with the Vancouver Canucks. Garrett was an emergency replacement for the Canucks' number one netminder Richard Brodeur, who was sidelined with an injury.

"I was probably the only player ever to appear in an All-Star game without ever acquiring any votes to help get me there," Garrett said later. "Anyway, as the game progressed shots kept hitting me and I made some good saves and Lanny McDonald kept reminding me I was in line to win a new car as the game's MVP. Hey, wouldn't that be a thrill?

"After I made a particularly good save, Lanny skated over to me and said, 'Great stop, John. That gets you the tires and the license plate.' After another save he said, 'Now you've got the engine and the frame.' And after a third save he said, 'They'll have to give you the keys to it now, John.'

"The car was a new Camaro Z-28, and I was beginning to think it would look very pretty sitting in my garage. I was told later that the sportswriters who did the voting were leaning heavily in my direction. Midway through the final period the name Garrett was on all of their ballots.

"Then, just as the ballots were about to be collected, Wayne Gretzky scored a goal for the Campbells. Lanny skated right over to me and said, 'I don't know, John. There goes the trunk.' A few minutes later Gretzky scored again and Lanny said, 'There goes the steering wheel, John.' When Gretzky popped in a third goal, Lanny shrugged and said, 'I think Wayne just found the keys, Johnny.' And when Gretzky scored a record fourth goal in the period, Lanny shook his head and said, 'John, I think he just stole the damn car right out of your driveway.'

"Meanwhile, up in the press box, the writers were busy erasing my name from their ballots and writing in Gretzky's." Garrett smiled. "Aw, but he deserved to win it, even if it was the 13th car he'd won in hockey."

Be My Guest

HALL OF FAME GOALTENDER Bill Durnan played for the Montreal Canadiens in the forties and captured the Vezina Trophy six times in seven seasons. Long after his career was over, Durnan confessed he had one lingering regret:

he hadn't had the courage to emulate a stunt perpetrated by another pro goalie — Alec Woods.

Woods toiled throughout his career in the American Hockey League and performed in only one NHL game, with the New York Americans in 1937. "Alec was born in Falkirk, Scotland," Durnan recalled, "and he had a reputation for being thrifty. That's why I was surprised at his amazing display of generosity one night. Woods's team failed to give him much support in the game I'm talking about, and goal after goal sailed into his net. Finally the score reached 8–0 and there were only a few seconds left to play.

"Suddenly Woods braced himself for yet another challenge as an opposing forward raced toward him, cradling the puck. The player looked for an opening and prepared to shoot. That's when Alec did something completely unheard of, something I later wanted to try in the NHL but didn't dare. Just as the player wound up for his shot, Alec grinned at him and stepped aside. He waved his goal stick at the empty net and said, 'Be my guest.'

"The startled shooter laughed and said, 'Thanks, goalie,' as he slipped the disk into the goal. I'd never heard of such a thing happening in professional hockey. I don't think anything like it has happened since."

Vezina Was a Remarkable Man

GEORGES VEZINA, WHOSE MEMORY is perpetuated in the Vezina Trophy, enjoyed a brilliant 15-year career in professional hockey. The Montreal Canadiens discovered him one night in 1910 when they played an exhibition game in Chicoutimi, Vezina's hometown. Vezina, already nicknamed the Chicoutimi Cucumber for his coolness under fire, stopped the mighty Habs without a goal in that game. By the time the next season rolled around, he had signed a professional contract with Montreal.

For the next decade and a half Vezina served as the Canadiens' regular netminder. Incredibly, though, he didn't learn how to skate until he was in his late teens. Until then he preferred to tend goal wearing his everyday shoes or boots. It was only two years prior to his pro debut with Montreal that he appeared on the ice wearing skates.

Vezina married young, at age 20, and then raised a whopping big family of 22 children. One of his offspring was born on the night the Montreal Canadiens won the Stanley Cup in 1916. To mark the occasion, the infant was named Stanley. Fortunately it was a baby boy.

On November 28, 1925, in Montreal's home opener, Vezina took his place in goal for a game against Pittsburgh. He had been feeling poorly for some time, but on this night he was gravely ill. Before the game his temperature reached 105 degrees. But he insisted on playing and managed to get through one period before collapsing on the ice. He was carried off, never to return. Doctors told him he was suffering from an advanced case of tuberculosis. The great goaltender died four months later in Chicoutimi, the town he loved and had made famous.

Fan Claims Vezina Wore No Gloves

BACK IN 1968 J. TUDOR, an elderly hockey fan from Perth, Ontario, wrote me a letter in which he described early-day hockey at Dey's Arena in Ottawa. Here is an interesting excerpt:

I could tell you some amusing stories about those oldtimers. For example, I saw Cyclone Taylor score that famous goal while he was skating backwards. My brother and I used to go to all the games played at Dey's Arena. Believe me, it was worse than a barn. The wind would whistle through the cracks in the boards and I'm sure it must have been warmer standing out in the middle of the Rideau Canal. My brother and I would stand in behind the wire netting back of the goal when the Montreal team was playing the Ottawas. We'd bring pea-shooters to the game and we fired peas at Georges Vezina's head whenever an Ottawa player came in to take a shot on goal.

Vezina couldn't speak English but he sure knew how to curse in French. After a time he got wise and pulled a small cap over his head. He would pull the cap around with the peak at the back to deflect the peas we'd shoot, aiming for the back of his neck. That cap robbed us of a lovely target.

Vezina wore no gloves. He had a great pair of hands. The players today are sissies compared to the oldtimers. They are only on the ice a minute or two. In the old days, a man would play the full sixty minutes without relief. And sometimes overtime.

I remember a great player named Ching Johnston, a defenseman. He used to stop plays by stretching out full length on the ice. The only way to get around him was to flip the puck in, leap over him and go after it. He was tough and rugged. I saw him play once with his face completely covered by bandages. I mean covered. Only his eyes and mouth could be seen. Those were the good old days when they had better players and games than they have today.

In those days the rush end seats cost only fifteen cents. The goal judge stood on a board on the ice right behind the goal. Many times a player, usually the rover, would dash in and send him flying, especially if the puck was being shot at the Ottawa goal. This prevented the goal judge from seeing whether the puck went in or not.

I should point out that the game in which Cyclone Taylor was alleged to have scored a goal while skating backward took place in Renfrew, not Dey's Arena in Ottawa. I still find it difficult to believe that Georges Vezina ever played without gloves but will accept the testimony of an eyewitness.

Jacques Plante's Amazing Comeback

AFTER THE 1964–65 NHL SEASON, Jacques Plante, one of the NHL's greatest goaltenders, decided to retire from hockey. He was 37 years old and he had lost his starting position with the New York Rangers — first to Marcel Paille and then to Gilles Villemure. A proud man, Plante had even been sent to the minors, and that enraged him.

There were other problems facing Plante. A bad knee required surgery and his wife was quite ill. Her weight had dropped from 128 to 98 pounds, and the doctors feared she was on the verge of a nervous breakdown. Plante's two boys, aged 10 and 14, had grown up virtually without a father because of his frequent long absences from home.

So Plante quit hockey and began working for the Molson brewery in Montreal. He also did part-time work for the CBC and for a newspaper. Each week he chipped in $2.50 to play pickup hockey with a group of old-timers.

Then, on December 16, 1965, he was invited by coach Scotty Bowman to tend goal in an exhibition game at the Montreal Forum, playing for a Junior team against the vaunted Soviet national squad. Plante was superb in the contest. Veteran columnist Andy O'Brien called his performance "the greatest single display of skilled goaling I have ever seen."

Three seasons passed and Bowman, now coach and general manager of the St. Louis Blues, was looking for an experienced goaltender. He had never forgotten the game in which Plante had stunned the Soviets. At the 1968 NHL draft meetings in Montreal, Bowman shocked the hockey world by selecting Plante, the 40-year-old has-been. Bowman had no concerns about Plante's age. In the previous season, 37-year-old Glenn Hall had taken the Blues to the Stanley Cup finals, and Hall had capped his season by winning the Conn Smythe Trophy as playoff MVP.

After being drafted, Plante decided to have arthroscopic surgery on his wonky knee. Then he

Jacques Plante stands tough minus stick, ready for all comers.

(National Archives of Canada)

started his comeback. In his first game as a St. Louis Blue he shut out Los Angeles 6–0. He and Hall went on to win the Vezina Trophy and to produce the lowest goals-against average record of a Vezina winner in 13 years. Plante's average was 1.96, Hall's 2.17. Their combined total was 2.07.

Plante Calls for a Tape Measure

SHORTLY AFTER HE WAS TRADED from the Montreal Canadiens to the New York Rangers in 1963, All-Star goaltender Jacques Plante told his general manager there was something wrong with the goal nets at Madison Square Garden.

"Wrong, Jacques?" was the reply. "What could possibly be wrong?"

"I don't know," Plante admitted. "But I think they may not be the right size. Maybe they're too high or too wide."

"But that's impossible, Jacques. They're all made to standard specifications."

"Let's check them out," Plante said. "I know I'm right."

They took a tape measure out onto the ice and measured the opening. The standard opening for a goal was four feet by six feet, but the nets in New York were bigger by an inch and a half. The manager was astounded. He discovered that certain manufacturers of goal nets placed the crossbar directly on top of the two upright posts, while others welded it in between the posts, accounting for the inch-and-a-half discrepancy. Plante had been the only goalie to wonder about it, the only one to complain.

"What difference does it make?" a reporter asked. "It all evens out over a season."

"No, it doesn't," Plante argued. "If I play 40 home games in front of a bigger net than the one Glenn Hall protects over 40 games in Chicago, and Hall and I are in the Vezina Trophy race, who do you think has a better chance of winning it? That little extra space may mean as much as 20 goals against in a season. Maybe more."

NHL officials agreed, and immediate steps were taken to measure all the nets used by every team. Several had to be replaced.

Benedict's Brilliance Still Doesn't Bring Him the Cup

IN THE 1928 STANLEY CUP PLAYOFFS, goalie Clint Benedict of the Montreal Maroons played the best hockey of his career. Game after game he was sensational. In the first round, a two-game series against Ottawa, he shut out the Senators 1–0 in game one and was almost as stingy in game two, winning 2–1. Then he faced the first-place Montreal Canadiens in another two-game series. His Maroons tied the first game 2–2 and won the second 1–0. In the final series against the Rangers, Benedict racked up his third playoff shutout in the opener, winning 1–0. Game two, a 2–1 Ranger triumph, will long be remembered as the game in which 44-year-old Lester Patrick, the Ranger coach, took over in goal when his regular goaltender was injured. The Rangers beat Benedict and the Maroons in overtime that night by 2–1. Benedict bounced back with his fourth playoff shutout (2–0) in game three, but the Rangers, with Miller in goal, returned the compliment and shut down the Maroons 1–0 in game four. New York captured game five 2–1 and skated off with the Stanley Cup.

Nobody blamed Clint Benedict for the Maroons' defeat. He had compiled four shutouts in nine games and allowed a mere eight goals. His near-perfect netminding was reflected in his goals-against average — a minuscule 0.89.

It was a brilliant record. Unfortunately, not brilliant enough to get his name on the Stanley Cup.

The Stingy Scot

CHARLIE GARDINER SHOULD BE HIGH on the list of hockey's best all-time goaltenders. He was born in Scotland and learned to play hockey in Winnipeg. In the NHL he toiled for the woeful Chicago Blackhawks in the late twenties and early thirties. It wasn't Charlie's fault his team won only seven games each season during his first two years on the job. In seven seasons he won the Vezina Trophy twice and was named to the first All-Star team three times.

Year after year Gardiner was the best of a sorry lot, and when the 1933–34 season rolled around, Charlie had almost given up his dream of playing in the Stanley Cup spotlight. The Chicago scorers were pitiful that season, totaling only 88 goals, the lowest production in the NHL.

But somehow the Blackhawks found themselves in the playoffs, and that was when Gardiner decided he better come up with some of his best efforts. Playoff action was heady stuff for Chicago. It might be his one and only chance for hockey glory. In the days ahead his play was truly spectacular as he guided his team past the Canadiens and then the Maroons.

Only the Detroit Red Wings stood between the Hawks and Lord Stanley's old mug. Most hockey men didn't give the upstarts from Chicago a chance against the Red Wings. After all, they hadn't won a game in Detroit in four years, and the first two games of the final series were scheduled for the Olympia.

Even Roger Jenkins, one of Gardiner's teammates, downgraded his own team's chances. He bet Gardiner no goalie could stop the Wings. "If you do,

I'll wheel you around the Loop in Chicago in a wheelbarrow," he promised.

Another teammate, Alex Levinsky, had lost faith earlier than that. He put his wife on a train for Toronto when the playoffs began and packed all his clothes in his car. "See you in a few days, hon," he told her. For the next month he kept dragging a change of clothes out of the trunk of his car.

Gardiner turned in an outstanding performance in the opener of the best-of-five final series as the Hawks won 2–1. He added another solid effort two nights later, winning 4–1. The Red Wings fought back on Chicago ice and beat him 5–2, while the fourth game in this best-of-five final required more than 30 minutes of overtime before Chicago's Mush March connected for the Stanley Cup-winning goal.

The low-scoring Hawks had captured their first Cup, and Charlie Gardiner, the stingy Scot, had realized his dream. Two days later he climbed aboard a wheelbarrow and enjoyed a bumpy ride around the Loop, with Roger Jenkins providing the horsepower.

Two months later the cheering stopped. Back home in Winnipeg the popular 30-year-old netminder suffered a brain hemorrhage and died shortly after being admitted to hospital.

He Wore Double Zero

WHEN BERNIE PARENT JOINED the Philadelphia Blazers of the World Hockey Association (he was originally signed by the Miami Screaming Eagles, a team that never materialized), he wore jersey number 00. If a curious member of the media asked him why he chose those numerals, he would reply, "Every time a puck gets past me and I look back in my net, I say 'Oh, oh.'"

Speaking of Strange Numerals

GOALIE ROYDON GUNN of the Saskatoon River Kings of the Central Hockey League wore .45 on his jersey during the 1993–94 season as a pun on his name and on the .45-caliber revolver. "It's such an oddity," said Craig Campbell of the Hockey Hall of Fame in Toronto, "that we'd like Gunn's jersey to add to our collection."

Meanwhile a hockey player in England decided to wear 102.1 on his back to help publicize the team sponsor, an FM radio station.

Women Goalies Create History in Same Season

ON OCTOBER 30, 1993, a 22-year-old goalie from Glens Falls, New York, became the first woman in professional hockey history to be credited with a goaltending victory. Erin Whitten, playing for the Toledo Storm of the East Coast Hockey League, was the winning netminder when her team defeated the Dayton Bombers 6–5. The five-foot-five goalie began playing hockey at the age of eight and spent two years on the varsity team in high school. She went on to star for the New Hampshire Wildcats in women's college hockey before joining the Storm.

Whitten won her second pro game a couple of days later, and this time she may have set some kind of record, for she gave up 10 goals while her teammates were scoring 11. Nobody seemed to know if a goaltender had ever given up so many goals before and still been credited with a win. It is very unlikely.

Just one week after Whitten made her way into the history books, 21-year-old Manon Rheaume, a more-publicized woman goaltender playing in the same league, stopped 32 of 38 shots to help the Knoxville Cherokees to a 9–6 victory over the visiting Johnstown Chiefs. Knoxville fans booed when Rheaume wasn't announced as one of the three stars.

Then, early in 1994, goalie Kelly Dyer became the third woman to play a regular season game in professional hockey when she donned the pads for the West Palm Beach Blaze of the Sunshine League in Florida. The 27-year-old netminder played only 10 minutes against the Daytona Beach Sun Devils and stopped all seven shots she faced in a 6–2 win. The following day she played again, this time for 26 minutes, as the Blaze won 8–4. Dyer stopped 16 of 18 shots and shared the victory with regular netminder Scott Hopkins. Dyer was Tom Barrasso's backup goalie in high school hockey in Massachusetts and gained international recognition when she backstopped the U.S. women's team in two world championships.

Language Ban Led to Bernie Parent Trade

FORMER PRO ANDRE LACROIX says a gag order led to Bernie Parent being traded from the Philadelphia Flyers. Lacroix, who led the Flyers in scoring in 1969 and 1970, recalls the events leading up to the deal.

"Vic Stasiuk was coaching the Flyers at that time. He was the worst coach I ever had. One day he called all the French-Canadian players on the team together — there was myself, Jean-Guy Gendron, Simon Nolet, Serge Bernier, and Bernie Parent — and he told us, 'Guys, from now on, no more speaking French. Speak English only.'

"We were very upset. Who was Vic Stasiuk to tell us we couldn't speak our language? It wasn't as if we were a clique. We didn't hang around together. We all mixed in with our English teammates.

"What's more, we'd been losing games, and it was almost as if he was blaming the French-speaking players for the losses. So we were disturbed. And we were told not to tell anybody about this edict from Stasiuk.

"But somebody told. And it made all the papers, especially in Quebec where it was front-page news. Stasiuk was called before [NHL president] Clarence Campbell, and he denied he told us we couldn't speak French.

"It was Bernie Parent who leaked the story to the

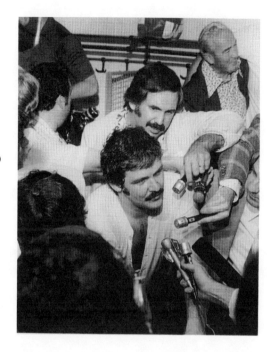

Philadelphia Flyer Bernie Parent being interviewed after Stanley Cup victory in 1974.

(Robert B. Shaver)

Montreal press. And the Flyers were mad at Bernie for that. It was one of the biggest reasons they traded him to Toronto in January 1971."

The Flyers didn't stay angry with Bernie very long. They reacquired him in a 1973 trade with the Leafs, and he promptly led Philadelphia to back-to-back Stanley Cups. His jersey number (1) has been retired by the Flyers.

AMAZING
ACHIEVEMENTS

Bucko the Bodychecker

IT'S AN NHL record you'll never find in any record book — Bucko McDonald's feat of knocking 37 opponents to the ice in one NHL game.

It happened in the Montreal Forum in the 1936 playoffs, in the first game of a series between the Detroit Red Wings and the Montreal Maroons. The Red Wings were relying on their bashing defenceman, Bucko McDonald, a second-year man in the league, to punish the Maroons. The former lacrosse star from Fergus, Ontario loved to hit, and the Maroons were advised to keep their heads up.

Bucko McDonald's pregame meal was a single boiled egg and a dish of ice cream. He'd have eaten a lot more if he'd known he was about to perform in the longest game in NHL history, one that would go into a sixth overtime period. The game began on March 24 and finished in the wee small hours of March 25.

Before the game, a Detroit fan approached Bucko and offered him five dollars for every Maroon he bodychecked to the ice. Of course, the fan never dreamed Bucko would have almost nine periods of hockey — the equivalent of three games — in which to do his body work on the Maroons.

The fan kept score and witnessed 37 crunching checks that sent Maroon forwards sprawling before Bucko's gleeful bashing came to an end. Mud Bruneteau of the Wings scored a dramatic winning goal for Detroit at 2:25 a.m. to end the marathon contest. Bucko collected $185 in "hit" money that night.

"The Maroons became easier to hit as the long overtime wore on," recalls Bucko. "The ice got soft and slushy. They lost their speed, they found it difficult to stay out of my way so I just kept knocking them down."

Bucko McDonald became a member of Parliament after his playing days and a highly regarded coach. In Parry Sound one year, he helped tutor a young phenom named Bobby Orr. It was Bucko who advised Orr's father to let his son play defence. Bucko insisted young Orr was the finest defence prospect he'd ever seen. How right he was. Even though Orr set many records during his NHL career, one he could never top was Bucko's mark — 37 bodychecks in a single game.

A Fast Start

SITTING ACROSS THE NHL Oldtimers' dressing room from me, Gus Bodnar stopped lacing his skates and took a minute to tell me about the fall of 1943 when, as an 18-year-old rookie, he journeyed from his home in Thunder Bay (then Fort William) to try out with the Leafs.

"When I arrived at training camp, Bucko McDonald, a veteran defenceman, took me aside and gave me two bits of advice. 'Keep your head up, kid, and get your hair cut.'

"Well, I got the haircut and I managed to keep my head up often enough to score a few goals in the scrimmages, and coach Hap Day decided I was good enough to play on his hockey club. There I was in the Leaf starting lineup on opening night. I remember it was October 30, 1943. Naturally I was anxious to play, but I hadn't expected the coach to send me out to take the opening faceoff against the New York Rangers.

"Everything was a blur after that. Seconds after the puck was dropped I found myself going in all alone on Ranger goalie Ken McAuley, who was also a rookie. Somehow I shot the puck past him. I'd scored after just 15 seconds of play, on my first shift, on my very first NHL shot. That's a record that has lasted almost 50 years. And poor McAuley, in the same time span, gave up his first NHL goal, which may have been a record, too.

"Even today, half a century later, I can hardly believe I scored that goal. But I know I did because my name is still in the NHL record book. It says: Fastest goal by a rookie, Gus Bodnar of Toronto, in 15 seconds. The closest anyone ever came to matching my mark was when Danny Gare of Buffalo scored after 18 seconds in his first shift. That was in 1974.

"The day after I scored the goal in 15 seconds, the lady who owned the boardinghouse I was staying in baked a big cake for me in recognition of my achievement. My teammates and I demolished that cake in minutes, even though our coach had strict rules about eating too much rich heavy food.

"I went on to play 12 seasons in the NHL with three different teams, but of all the exciting things that happened to me over those years, few can top my first 15 seconds on the ice."

Darryl Sittler's Biggest Night

WHEN TORONTO HOSTED BOSTON in a game at Maple Leaf Gardens on February 7, 1976, the fans anticipated some sparkling performances . . . especially from the Bruins. Coached by colorful Don Cherry, the Bruins were looking for their eighth straight win and veteran centre Jean Ratelle was looking for a milestone goal — his 350th. Forty-year-old left-winger Johnny Bucyk was on the verge of moving into second place on the all-time point-scoring list, and there was even a chance that goalie Gerry Cheevers, lured back to Boston from the WHA a day or two earlier, would be the Bruins' starting goaltender.

What the fans didn't anticipate was a record-smashing performance from a Leaf — captain Darryl Sittler who embarked on a scoring rampage unequaled in the more than 13,000 games played in the NHL up to that night.

Moments before our *Hockey Night in Canada* telecast on the CBC that night, play-by-play announcer Bill Hewitt and I were surprised to learn that Cheevers would not be the Bruins' goaltender. Don Cherry handed the starting assignment to a kid out of college, rookie netminder Dave Reece.

During the game, Ratelle succeeded in scoring his milestone goal, and Bucyk, with two points, moved ahead of Alex Delvecchio and into second place (behind Gordie Howe) on the list of all-time career-point scorers.

But by then, any Bruin scoring feats had been completely overshadowed by Darryl Sittler's incredible performance. The Leaf captain demolished Reece and the Bruins, collecting a record ten points in Toronto's 11–4 romp. He broke by two points the previous record held by a pair of Canadiens, Rocket Richard and Bert Olmstead.

Sittler, then at the peak of his playing career, scored three goals against Reece in the second period and three more in the third to become the first in the NHL to score three goals in each of consecutive periods and the eighth to score six times in a game. His six-goal total was one short of the all-time record of seven, held by Joe Malone of Quebec, a mark set in 1920. Half a dozen goals, plus four assists, added up to the greatest individual-scoring performance in NHL history.

Sittler not only set two league records and tied a third, he shattered four team marks. He also shattered the big-league dreams of young Dave Reece, for the Boston goalie was dispatched to the minors and never played another NHL game.

"The record-tying (sixth) goal was a lucky one," Sittler told reporters. "I tried a pass from behind the net and it hit Brad Park's skate and went in. But the thing I'll always remember about that game was the ovation I received when I broke the record with my ninth point. It was unbelievable."

Before the next home game, Sittler received an unexpected reward from Leaf owner Harold Ballard, a silver tea service worth several thousand dollars.

Berenson's Six Goals
Still a Record

HE WAS A GOOD-LOOKING redheaded centerman, a Michigan graduate who wanted to play pro hockey. Nobody thought he would, not at the NHL level. No American college grad had ever jumped to the NHL. Why should Red Berenson be any different?

But he was different. He was a shade faster and a bit smarter with the puck than his college confreres. And he did crack the lineup of the Montreal Canadiens in 1961. He stayed around to play on a Montreal Stanley Cup–winning team in 1965, one of the big thrills of his NHL career.

Berenson moved on to play with the Rangers and the Blues, and it was after he donned a St. Louis uniform that he blossomed into one of the top scorers in hockey. One unforgettable game took place on November 7, 1968. It was a road game against the Philadelphia Flyers, and Berenson was in the middle of a slump. The season was a month old and he had scored just one goal.

But there was magic in his hands and stick that night against goalie Doug Favell and the Flyers. Every time Berenson touched the puck the red light flashed behind Favell. The redheaded centerman scored six goals in the game, a record for a road game, as the Blues shut out the Flyers 8–0.

"The odd thing is, I might have scored two or three more in the game," Berenson said later. "I hit one goalpost and missed on a couple of other good chances. It was a great confidence booster after my dismal start that year. And what really amazes me is that neither Lemieux nor Gretzky have tied or beaten my mark. I never thought it would stand for 25 years."

Berenson was presented with a new station wagon by the Blues' owners in recognition of his feat. When he sold the vehicle to broadcaster Dan Kelly a few days later, he angered team management, and it wasn't long before he was traded to Detroit as part of a deal for Garry Unger. In a career that spanned 17 NHL seasons, Red scored 261 goals.

Fast Start, Fast Finish

NO PLAYER HAS EVER MADE as spectacular a debut in the NHL as Don Murdoch, the New York Rangers' number-one draft choice in 1976. Murdoch scored eight goals in the first three games, including five in one game, to tie a rookie record.

Halfway through his rookie season he had 32 goals. He was well on his way to a record number of goals by a rookie. Then ankle injuries kept him sidelined for several games, costing him the record and rookie-of-the-year honors. However, his fast start made him an instant celebrity in Manhattan. Ranger fans called him "Murder" Murdoch, and at the bars and discos people bought him drinks and offered him other temptations. It wasn't long before he became a kid with a drinking problem and, in time, a kid with a drug problem.

Later Murdoch would say, "I was in the limelight and my life was moving so fast I didn't even know where I was going. I fell in with the wrong crowd and that was a big mistake."

After Murdoch's second season, on his way

home to Cranbrook, B.C., a small amount of cocaine was found in his suitcase by customs agents in Toronto. Murdoch was arrested and charged with possession. In court, he was given a suspended sentence and fined $400. But NHL President John Ziegler wanted to make an example of Murdoch, as a warning to other players to stay clear of drugs. He suspended the Ranger sniper for a year.

Eventually, Murdoch's case came up for review, and Ziegler lifted the suspension after 40 games. Ziegler said he hoped Murdoch had put his past difficulties behind him and that he would resume his career, one that showed so much promise.

Murdoch was delighted to get a second chance and couldn't wait to show his fans that his off-ice problems were behind him. But he never recaptured the form that had made him a rookie sensation and the toast of New York. After the Rangers cooled on him, he had stops in Detroit and Edmonton before drifting off to the minors.

Goalie Hextall's Long-shot Goals

IN 1979 GOALTENDER BILLY SMITH of the Islanders received credit for scoring a goal against the Colorado Rockies, a "first" in the NHL. But Smith's goal was tainted. He didn't actually shoot the puck into the Colorado net that night. He was simply the last Islander to touch the puck before an opposing player accidentally scored on his own team.

But on December 8, 1987 in Philadelphia, goalie Ron Hextall did what no other goalie had done in 71 years of NHL play. With the Flyers leading

Boston 4–2, and the Boston goalie on the bench with time running out, Gord Kluzak flipped the puck into the Flyer zone. Hextall stopped the disk and wristed it high in the air down the ice. It landed on the Bruin blue line and slid the rest of the way into the empty net.

Hextall, who can shoot the puck better than any goalie in history, took the achievement in stride. "I don't mean to sound cocky," he said, "but I knew I could do it. I knew it was just a matter of time before I flipped one in. It'll be something to talk about when I'm finished with hockey. And by then, maybe I'll have scored another one."

Just 122 games later, in a playoff series between Philadelphia and Washington, Hextall did score another — the first goal by a goalie in Stanley Cup history. With the Caps trailing 7–5 late in the third period, and the Washington goalie replaced by an extra shooter, Hextall trapped the puck behind his net, saw an opening and flipped it high in the air. The puck skipped once inside the Caps' blue line and skidded into the empty net. It was almost a carbon copy of his regular season goal.

Washington general manager David Poile, who witnessed the historic goal that helped send his team to defeat, told reporters after the game, "Bobby Orr, Wayne Gretzky, Mario Lemieux, they all changed the game. Now Hextall's changing it, too."

In the Flyers' dressing room, one of Hextall's teammates quipped, "Some of the teams will have to start shadowing him now."

Goal of the Century

IF HOCKEY FANS were asked to pick the greatest goal ever scored they'd have no trouble coming up with an answer. It would be Paul Henderson's famous goal that sank the Soviets and won the Series of the Century back in September 1972.

It happened in Moscow in the deciding game of the incredibly exciting eight-game series between Team Canada and the Soviets. Henderson's goal was a fitting climax to the most fascinating series ever played.

What many people don't know about that goal is that Paul Henderson almost wasn't around to score it. He almost sat out the most important game of his life.

In the previous game, in which he also scored the game-winning goal, he had fallen heavily into the boards, striking his head. Fortunately, Henderson was one of the few pros of the time who believed in wearing a helmet, and the helmet probably saved him from a concussion and a trip to the hospital. He was still feeling the effects of his injury before game eight, and the team doctor suggested he let somebody else take his place. But Henderson said no. There was no way he was going to miss what might be the most important game of his entire career.

It was a decision he would never regret. In the third period of the game, Team Canada fought back with three goals to tie the score at five. Then, in the final few seconds, Phil Esposito whirled and shot. Vladislav Tretiak, the Soviet goaltender, made the save, but the rebound came right to Henderson, who was all alone in front. Paul shot once. Another rebound. He shot again, and this time the puck slid past Tretiak into the net. Team Canada won the game and the series. No one who saw that final game or even listened to it on the radio will ever forget Paul Henderson's goal. It was the goal of the century.

Recently, I asked Tretiak about his feelings when the puck went in. He said, "I think the Lord himself gave that goal to Henderson. It was a beautiful goal and a great surprise. Seconds earlier, Paul had fallen down behind the net, and I didn't even notice him. Do I dream about that goal? I can say with a smile, 'I think about it every day of my life.'"

The Flyers' Famous Undefeated Streak

IN AMATEUR SPORTS there have been many impressive undefeated streaks. For example, in college basketball UCLA won 88 straight games many years ago, and the Oklahoma football team once won 47 in a row. But in all of the pro sports, the longest undefeated streak belongs to hockey — and the Philadelphia Flyers.

The streak the Flyers topped belonged to Montreal. In 1977–78 the Canadiens went 28 games without a loss, winning 23 and tying 5 before Boston spoiled their fun.

Just two seasons later, the Flyers took off on a streak that would soon draw the attention of everyone. After losing the second game of the season to Atlanta, the Flyers topped Toronto 4–3, and that was the beginning of a remarkable romp around the NHL.

Coach Pat Quinn deserves much of the credit for the streak. He changed the Philadelphia style that year, emphasizing speed and quick passes and eliminating much of the brawling that was a Flyers trademark in the early seventies. During the streak, the Flyers averaged only 17 minutes in penalties per game. When they were known as the Broad Street Bullies, some said they accumulated that much penalty time during the playing of the national anthem.

The Flyers were a little nervous in game 28 when they tied the Canadiens' record and even more uptight in game 29 when they broke the record with a win over the tough Boston Bruins. By then, hordes of reporters and television crews were following their every move.

In December they went beyond the mark of 33 games established by basketball's Los Angeles Lakers with a 5–3 win over the Rangers. As the new record-holders for pro sports teams, their next goal was to stretch their unblemished mark into the New Year. They did — but only for a week.

All good things must end, and the end came for the Flyers on January 7, 1978, in Minnesota. In game number 36, the Flyers were zapped 7–1 by the Minnesota North Stars, and hockey's most famous undefeated streak (25 wins and 10 ties) was finally over.

"It was great fun while it lasted," said Flyer captain Mel Bridgman. "We couldn't believe we went for so long without a loss."

Miracle on Main Street

NO ONE IN HOCKEY could have predicted that the 1980 Winter Olympic Games in Lake Placid, New York, would produce one of the greatest upsets in hockey history, a triumph so incredible it's often referred to as the Miracle on Main Street.

Main Street was the site of the Olympic Arena in Lake Placid. There, on February 22, 1980, Herb Brooks, coach of the U.S. Olympic team, gave his players a pep talk before their big game with the Soviet Union.

"You were born to be hockey players," said Brooks. "You were meant to be here. This is your moment."

Despite their unbeaten record in the tournament, nobody gave the Americans a chance against the Soviets. Hadn't the Soviets skated off with every Olympic gold medal in the past 20 years? Didn't everyone say they were invincible? Hadn't the young American team — average age 22 — been seeded only seventh before the Olympics began?

But on this day against the experienced Soviets, U.S. goalie Jim Craig was spectacular, far steadier than his more famous counterpart, Vladislav Tretiak. After the U.S. scored a pair of goals against Tretiak, he was replaced by Vladimir Myshkin. The Americans fell behind 3–2 in the second period, but they fought back to tie the score at 3–3 in the third on a Mark Johnston goal. Moments later, U.S. team captain Mike Eruzione slammed a screened 30-footer through the pads of Myshkin for what proved to be the winning goal. At the final buzzer, all of North America celebrated the thrilling victory.

It was a stunning upset. Mark Johnston, a two-goal scorer for the victors, kept repeating, "I can't believe we beat them. I can't believe we beat them. Now we're just 60 minutes away from the gold medal. I simply can't believe it."

And two days later, before millions watching worldwide on television, the young Americans captured the coveted gold medal by beating Finland 4–2 and completing the saga known as the Miracle on Main Street.

Following the Olympics, the gold-medal winners were flown to Washington where they were guests at the White House and where each team member was congratulated personally by President Jimmy Carter.

"Your victory was one of the most breathtaking upsets, not only in Olympic history but in the entire history of sports," the President told his guests.

The Best-Ever Canada Cup

ALAN EAGLESON has often claimed that the Canada Cup tournament features the best hockey in the world. Millions of fans who witnessed the finals of the 1987 event would be quick to agree with him.

The '87 Canada Cup — featuring a three-game final for the first time in history — produced another classic confrontation between the best of the Soviets and the best players in the NHL. It also made teammates of two of hockey's greatest players, Wayne Gretzky and Mario Lemieux.

In the best-of-three final series, played in Hamilton, the Soviets took game one, 6–5. Then, in game two, Mario Lemieux scored three times as Team Canada won 6–5 in the second period of overtime.

The final game was simply one of the most exciting games ever played. Team Canada coach Mike Keenan played Gretzky and Lemieux on the same line in this crucial match — he'd placed them with other teammates throughout the rest of the tournament — and they clicked immediately. They were marvelous. Gretzky collected five assists, and Lemieux came through with his second straight hat trick — after Team Canada fell behind 3–0.

The goal everybody remembers was Lemieux's game winner. The score was tied 5–5 with time running out in the third period. He took a pass from Gretzky, who had carried it deep into the Soviet zone, and blasted a shot past goalie Sergei Mylnikov. It was Lemieux's eleventh goal of the series, a tournament record, and it came with 1.24 minutes remaining.

Team Canada held on to win the game 6–5 and the tournament, a tournament credited with making a complete player of Mario Lemieux. Prior to the Canada Cup, he had been labeled a floater by some hockey experts, notably Don Cherry.

In the Team Canada dressing room after the game, Mario said quietly, "I think I've answered a few questions about myself in this tournament."

Clancy Did It All

IN MARCH 1923, the Ottawa Senators of the NHL traveled to the West Coast, where, after beating Vancouver in one Stanley Cup playoff series, they were challenged by Edmonton in another.

It was a two-game total-point series, and when Ottawa won the first game 2–1, the stage was set for a performance unmatched in professional hockey history.

In game two, when both the Senators' star defencemen were injured, off the bench came 19-year-old King Clancy to replace one, then the other. When Ottawa centreman Frank Nighbor went down, Clancy moved to centre ice. Later, Clancy played on right wing, subbing for the regular winger who had gone off to have a cut stitched up. After that, the versatile Clancy gave the left-winger a rest.

But Clancy's versatility was put to the ultimate test when the Ottawa goalie, Clint Benedict, drew a minor penalty. Off he went to the box, for in those days goalies were required to serve their own penalty time. Benedict casually handed Clancy his goal stick and said, "Here kid, take care of my net till I get back." For the next two minutes, Clancy bravely guarded the Ottawa goal and was not scored upon.

Years later he told me, "The story of my brief stint in goal was embellished by sportswriters later on. One of them described a number of spectacular saves I made. Another wrote that I not only made a remarkable stop of a breakaway but that I took the puck and raced up the ice with it, firing a hard shot at the Edmonton goaltender. It would be nice if these things were true but none of it happened. I didn't make a single save in those two minutes. Oh, I did fall on the puck once when it came close to my net, and Mickey Ion, the referee, said to me, 'Do that again, kid, and you're going off.' I said, 'Yes, sir, Mr. Ion.' "

Ottawa won the game, the series and the Stanley Cup, and Clancy made history. He was the only player in the NHL to play every position for his team in a Stanley Cup playoff game.

Three Stars for the Rocket

IN THE SPRING of 1944 Maurice "Rocket" Richard of the Montreal Canadiens put on one of the greatest offensive displays in Stanley Cup history. The Canadiens played the Toronto Maple Leafs in a semifinal series that year and Richard, a second-year man who had scored 32 goals during the regular season, was being closely shadowed by big Bob Davidson, a tenacious checker.

After his Canadiens lost by a 3–1 score in the opener, Richard predicted a different outcome in game two. After all, his team had captured the regular season championship, finishing 33 points ahead of the third-place Leafs. But the Leafs kept Richard and the Habs off the score sheet in the first period of game two, and Montreal fans were concerned. Would their favorites ever break out and score a few goals?

Richard relieved their anxiety early in the second period. Two minutes into the period he raced in to beat Paul Bibeault for the game's first goal. Seventeen seconds later he returned and scored again. Toronto fought back with a goal midway through the period, but before the buzzer sounded, Richard took a pass from Toe Blake and scored once more. It was his third goal of the period — a Stanley Cup hat trick.

By then Montreal coach Dick Irvin was shifting Richard from line to line, which confused the Leafs and enabled the Rocket to escape the persistent checking of Davidson. In the third period Richard stayed hot. He scored his fourth goal early in the frame and added a fifth at 8:34. Final score: Richard 5, Toronto 1. The last time a player had scored five or more goals in a playoff game was back in 1917 when Bernie Morris of Seattle scored six against the Canadiens.

There is now, and was then, a popular tradition of selecting three stars after each NHL game, with the third star being introduced first. Fans at the Forum that night roared with anger when the public address announcer intoned, "Tonight's third star — Rocket Richard!" How could that be? How could the Rocket score all five goals and be a lowly third star?

The announcer continued over the howling of the fans. "Star number two — Rocket Richard!"

Now the fans began to catch on. Cheers and applause erupted throughout the Forum, and fans threw hats and programs into the air even before the announcer made his dramatic third announcement. "And tonight's first star — Maurice 'Rocket' Richard!"

The fans treated Richard to one of the greatest ovations ever. It was the only time an NHL player was awarded all three stars.

Did Cyclone Score While Skating Backward?

FOR DECADES AFTER HE STARRED for the Renfrew Creamery Kings in the 1910–11 season, Cyclone Taylor refused to confirm that he once scored a goal while skating backward. But he didn't deny it, either. When I asked him about it — he was in his nineties then — he chuckled and said, "Why don't you ask someone who was at the game?" Well, it was somewhat difficult to locate a living survivor among the 3,000 or so fans who attended that long-ago game in Renfrew, but newspaper accounts of the contest appear to confirm that such a goal was scored.

That season a bitter rivalry existed between Ottawa and Renfrew, and Taylor, in conversation with his friend Ottawa goalie Percy Lesueur one day, stated that it might be "no trouble at all to take a pass in full flight, spin around, and score a goal against Ottawa while skating backward." Taylor said later that he was only joking, but when his comment was printed in an Ottawa newspaper, the Capital City fans were furious. The next time he appeared for Renfrew on Ottawa ice they hurled bottles and rotten fruit at him.

He was unable to score in that game, but in a return match in Renfrew a few nights later, and with an arena full of fans urging him on, he made good his boast by spinning around in front of Lesueur, skating backward for several feet, and scoring with a hard shot to the upper corner.

But Taylor's unique goal wasn't the only reason that game became a memorable one. Renfrew owner

M. J. O'Brien, a multimillionaire, offered a team bonus of $100 for each goal scored in the game and a personal reward of $50 to every player who scored one. Spurred on by the owner's promise, Renfrew walloped Ottawa 17–2, and O'Brien cheerfully doled out $2,250 in bonus money, a fortune in that era.

Gretzky Catches Howe

IT WAS ONLY FITTING that it happened in Edmonton. On October 15, 1989, the former hometown hero, Wayne Gretzky, returned to smash one of hockey's longest-standing individual records — Gordie Howe's mark of 1,850 career points.

And he did it in typical Gretzky style, scoring a goal in the last minute of regulation time to tie the score 4–4. The goal was the Great One's 1,851st point, and it stopped the game for several minutes. Gordie Howe, who said he was "cheering like hell when the goal went in," came out of the stands to congratulate Wayne and present him with a gift. League president John Ziegler and Mark Messier, the Oiler captain and Gretzky's best friend, added their congratulations. Messier presented Gretzky with a bracelet fitted with 1.851 carats of diamonds spelling out "1,851."

The record-setting goal was produced by a short backhand shot, a technique Howe had told Gretzky years earlier to work on. Gretzky pumped the puck behind Bill Ranford for his 1,851st point in his 780th NHL game. It had taken Howe 26 years and 1,767 games with Detroit and Hartford to set the standard the Great One so easily eclipsed.

"Gordie is still the greatest in my mind and in the

minds of everyone else," Gretzky said. "Remember, his points were scored in a different era. The game was a lot different then. Players just weren't scoring 100 points per season."

"I don't know how he does these things so dramatically," Howe said of Gretzky's accomplishment. "There's no sense of loss. I held the record for a long time [almost 30 years] and I hope to be around when he scores 3,000 points."

Gretzky took a hammering in the game and was lucky to be around at the finish. After assisting on Bernie Nicholls' first-period goal, earning the point that tied the record, he took a hit from Jeff Beukeboom in the second and was in a daze for several minutes.

"He was very dizzy and I had to keep checking on him," Kings coach Tom Webster said. "But by the third period he was back to normal. He had his old jump back."

Indeed he did, enough to smash the record with time running out. And enough to add to his total and win the game 5–4 with a whirl-around-the-net move that saw him beat Ranford again at 3:24 into overtime.

When the Hockey Hall of Fame requested the helmet, gloves, and stick used in the historic game, Gretzky quickly obliged. He said another 13 sticks used in the game would go to his dad, Walter Gretzky, who would pass them along to various charities for fund-raising purposes.

The Day Grove Sutton Outshone Wayne Gretzky

WAYNE GRETZKY WILL REMEMBER the game as one of the most important of his career. He will recall the bitter disappointment in the dressing room and how he hung his head and cried after his team lost by five goals. Personally he had done well, scoring a goal and collecting three assists. But Grove Sutton, a star player on the opposing team, had done even better, scoring five goals in leading his team to a 9–4 victory.

Grove Sutton? Outscoring Gretzky? I must be kidding, you say. Where and when did this happen?

It was 1974, and there was more than the normal excitement and hype to the 15th Annual Quebec Peewee Hockey Tournament. Wayne Gretzky, the tiny tornado from Brantford, was the biggest story at the event. Everyone had heard reports about his amazing scoring exploits and how he had bagged 378 goals in one season alone when he was 10 years old and only four foot four. Children much bigger and older than he sought his autograph, and over 10,000 fans turned out to see him play in his first tournament game.

Brantford humiliated a terrified group of youngsters from Richardson, Texas, 25–0 in game one. The Americans were hockey novices. They had never seen slap shots before, never played at this level, and seldom played before more than a handful of people. Their goalie was so frightened he couldn't perform, and a teammate who had never worn goal pads before had to take his place in the net.

During the game, Gretzky scored seven goals and added four assists for 11 points, breaking Guy Lafleur's single-game tournament record by one. He followed up with two goals and three assists in Brantford's 9–1 victory over Beaconsfield, Quebec. Game three was against Verdun, Quebec, led by a flashy little centerman named Denis Savard. Fan interest was so high that Gretzky had to battle his way through the crowds to the dressing room. With a policeman's help he finally reached his destination and had to hurry into his uniform. Brantford won again 7–3 with Wayne notching three goals.

His next test — in the tournament semifinals — was against a team from Oshawa, Ontario, a solid club that had often spelled trouble for the Brantford boys in the past. Wayne played both defense and forward and collected a goal and three assists, but Oshawa had a swift-skating Peewee named Grove Sutton, a heads-up player who outshone Wayne with five goals in the 9–4 Oshawa victory. Sutton wasn't just a one-game wonder, either, for he collected 17 goals in the tournament, four more than Gretzky. And in the championship game Sutton led his team to the Peewee title with a victory over Peterborough.

At the time few could have foreseen that Wayne Gretzky, or "le Grand Gretzky" as he was called, would grow up to become hockey's greatest scorer. Just as no one could have predicted that Grove Sutton would soon fade from the hockey scene, only to be remembered by the fans who had witnessed his greatest week in hockey, the week he outscored Wayne Gretzky, the most talked-about young player in the game.

Pat Hughes Snapped a Gretzky Record

"**S**URE, RECORDS ARE MEANT to be broken — but not that quickly" is what Wayne Gretzky might have said to Pat Hughes the night Hughes did the impossible. Gretzky, you see, had just established another in his amazing collection of NHL scoring records, and it was one that made him proud. As an Edmonton Oiler one night, with his team shorthanded, the Great One had slipped through the opposing team's power play and scored. Not once but twice — on the same shift. Two goals in 27 seconds while playing shorthanded is an amazing feat. No player in NHL history had ever come close to such a mark. Even Gretzky conceded: "That's a record that should last a long, long time."

A few nights later the Oilers again found themselves shorthanded. Helping to kill the penalty was forward Pat Hughes, a decent scorer but hardly in Gretzky's class when it came to scoring short-handed goals or any other kind of goals. But Hughes broke away and lit the lamp with a surprise score. Moments later he did it again. To his and everyone else's astonishment, he had scored twice in 25 seconds while killing a penalty, and Gretzky's newly minted mark was shattered.

Wayne laughed about the oddity. "That's one of my records that didn't last too long," he told Hughes after the game.

But wait! Another Oiler, Essa Tikkanen, had a surprise up his sleeve. In the first period of a game against Toronto on November 12, 1988, he snapped in a pair of shorthanded goals in a mere 12 seconds, causing both Gretzky and Hughes to shake their heads in disbelief.

Does Anybody Remember Warren Young?

FROM 1980 THROUGH 1984 Warren Young's hockey career amounted to little more than a depressing bus ride through minor league cities such as Nashville, Oklahoma City, Birmingham, and Baltimore. He was thankful he had graduated from college (Michigan Tech) because his minor league stats hadn't attracted much interest from NHL clubs.

When he was invited to Pittsburgh's training camp prior to the 1984–85 season, he knew it was his last chance to make an impression. He was in his 29th year, a doddering old man by hockey standards.

For some reason, rookie sensation Mario Lemieux, then 19, liked Young's style and asked to be placed on the same line. Despite the ten-year age difference, the two fitted together like hand and glove. Young had never seen the kind of passes Mario deftly placed on his stick. He converted a large number of them into goals and finished the season with 40 lamplighters (only three fewer than Lemieux) and had 32 assists plus a berth on the rookie All-Star squad.

"They were a magic act," Jim Christie wrote in Toronto's *Globe and Mail,* "but it was Mario who was the magician."

He was indeed. Despite being called "the laziest player in the NHL" by TV commentator Don Cherry,

Lemieux helped convert Young from an unknown minor leaguer into a much-publicized big league celebrity. His teammates praised Young's accomplishments and kidded him about his late arrival, calling him Warren Old and Geritol. They decided not to initiate him with the traditional head shave when one of them pointed out, "At his age it may never grow back."

Good fortune smiled on Young again the following season. It was the year Detroit went on a spending spree, signing a number of free agents to million-dollar deals. Young was one of them. He signed a multiyear contract with the Wings that had him earning twice as much as Lemieux's base salary of $125,000.

But without Lemieux to set him up, Young found that goals were harder to score in Detroit. He would never again recapture the glory that was his in Pittsburgh. He would forever be known as the player who rode Mario's passes to a single unforgettable season. After a couple of mediocre years in a Red Wing uniform, Young faded from the scene.

Tom Reid's First Shift

TOM REID, A DEFENSEMAN with Chicago and Minnesota for 11 NHL seasons, vividly recalls his first game in the NHL. "I remember the game clearly, but my first shift in the game is a little fuzzy in my mind," he says. "I was brought up to Chicago, and coach Billy Reay sent me on the ice early in the game. We were playing against the Red Wings and Gordie Howe. Big Gordie was Detroit's star player at the time, and I made a mental note to beware of him.

"I'd been on the ice for a few seconds when the puck came to me and I cleared it out of our zone. That's when I was hit as hard as I'd ever been hit in my life. I don't know where he came from, but Gordie nailed me to the fence. I was knocked out for a few seconds, and when I opened my eyes and tried to get up, I fell down again. My knees were rubbery and my vision was blurred. My eyes were watering, and when I wobbled over to our bench, I began to panic because I couldn't see out of my right eye. I remember being near tears, thinking I'd been blinded and had my brains scrambled on my very first shift at the tender age of 19.

"When I reached the bench, coach Reay looked surprised. 'Reid, what the hell are you doing back here so soon?' he roared.

"'Coach,' I said, 'that old man with Detroit just blinded me. I can't see a thing out of my right eye.'

"Billy laughed and said, 'No wonder.' He grabbed my helmet and twisted it around until it was back on straight. Once he did that I could see again instantly. It was beautiful.

"I didn't think to ask him if he could do anything to fix my splitting headache."

Al Hill Makes Sensational Debut

IT IS STILL THERE in the NHL record book — Al Hill's impressive rookie scoring mark. In his first big league game, on February 14, 1977, Hill was called up from Springfield of the American Hockey League to play in his first NHL game with the Philadelphia Flyers. The six-foot-one left winger responded with two goals and three assists against the St. Louis Blues for a five-point night. The Flyers won the game 6–4 and Hill won the hearts of Flyer fans. They figured — after a debut like that — he would soon become a Flyer immortal, right up there with Bobby Clarke and Bill Barber. Hill scored 36 seconds into the nationally televised game and went on to make the game a miserable experience for Blues goalie Yves Belanger.

But Hill's moment in the spotlight was brief. Never again would he come even close to matching the magic of his big league debut. After a handful of games, he was returned to Springfield and had to wait two more years before getting a chance to score NHL goal number three.

Hill played parts of the next four seasons with Philadelphia, spent the following four years in the minors, and was recalled by the Flyers for a handful of games in 1986–87 and 1987–88. In 221 NHL games he collected 40 goals. But his first two — plus three assists — in his major league debut have kept his name in the record book since 1977.

Toronto Granites Wallop World's Best Amateurs at Chamonix

IN 1924 THE TORONTO GRANITES represented Canada at the Winter Olympic Games held in Chamonix, France. Old-timers say the Granites were absolutely the best amateur team ever to wear Canadian colors at the international level. The scores they compiled were truly extraordinary and will never be matched.

The Olympic ice surface in Chamonix was an open-air rink with boards measuring a scant 12 inches high. Spectators often tumbled into one another as they leaped to avoid flying pucks.

In the opening round the Granites walloped Czechoslovakia 30–0, then Sweden 22–0, and finally Switzerland 33–0. In a semifinal match the Granites humbled Great Britain 19–2, and in the final game with the United States the Canadians skated to an easy 6–1 triumph.

In five games played the Granites scored 110 goals and gave up a mere three. Top scorer in the tournament was Harry Watson, who collected 38 goals, an average of more than seven per game.

At one point early in the tournament Granite star defenseman Dunc Munro looked over his shoulder to find the Canadian net empty. Goaltender Jack Cameron, bored with so little work, had skated over to the side boards and was engaged in a lively conversation with two attractive young ladies.

Stranger to the Sin Bin

VAL FONTEYNE WAS A SKINNY LITTLE GUY, a dandy penalty killer for the Detroit Red Wings, the New York Rangers, and the Pittsburgh Penguins in the sixties and early seventies. Most penalty killers, because their sole objective is to stop the opposing team's top scorers, are often tenants of the penalty box themselves. They know all the obstruction tricks, like holding, hooking, and interference — infractions that seldom go unnoticed.

But Val Fonteyne avoided penalty boxes as if they

were snake pits. He played five consecutive years without ever being in one. In his 13-year career, which encompassed 820 regular season games, he served a mere 28 minutes in penalty time. He took a career high of eight minutes in 1964–65, which for him was akin to being a hardened criminal.

He Led Three Teams in Scoring . . . in Three Consecutive Seasons

NO PLAYER IN THE NHL had ever led three different teams in scoring in consecutive seasons . . . until Vincent Damphousse accomplished the unusual feat in 1992–93. Damphousse was the top scorer in Toronto's lineup in 1990–91 with 73 points. Then he was traded to Edmonton, where he collected a team-high 89 points the following season. Another trade sent him to the Montreal Canadiens, and once again he topped all his teammates with 97 points. The only other player to lead three different teams in scoring, but not in consecutive years, is retired pro Lanny McDonald, who was his team's scoring leader in Toronto, Colorado, and Calgary.

Dick Rondeau's Most Memorable Game

MOST PROLIFIC GOAL SCORERS, when you ask them to name their most memorable game, have difficulty confining the choice to one contest. Not former U.S. college star Dick

Rondeau, who was a top scorer for the Dartmouth College Indians many years ago. Dartmouth dominated college hockey during World War II, and in 1944 the Indians achieved their most one-sided victory, a 30–0 shellacking of Middlebury. Rondeau was unstoppable in this game, scoring 12 goals and adding 11 assists for 23 points — a once-in-a-lifetime performance. Incidentally, from 1942 to 1946, Dartmouth won 30 consecutive games, a U.S. college record that was snapped by Cornell (with Ken Dryden in goal) in 1969–70. Cornell set the new standard with 31 straight wins.

One Way to Beat the Russians

PAUL PROVOST, an Ottawa boy who played hockey in the forties and fifties, was too small for a pro career. So he opted for a career in European hockey where, at five foot seven and 125 pounds, he became a big man in the scoring summaries.

One year he signed on as player-coach of the Chamonix team in France and was impressed with the lengths his players would go to avoid a loss. Provost's team was involved in a close game with a touring Russian club one night. The contest was held at an outdoor ice rink during a blinding snowstorm. Late in the game the Chamonix club was trailing by a goal, and Provost urged his men to find a way to get the equalizer. Moments later one of them did. The goal judge signaled a goal and the score was tied.

Only later did Provost find out how the puck went in. "I was skating around in the snow," one of his players confessed, "and couldn't see three feet in front of me when the puck struck my foot. It bounced up, so I caught it and hid it in my glove. Then I skated in behind the Russian goalie and dropped it in the net. The referee saw it lying there and so did the goal judge. They decided to call it a goal. I guess I was the only one out there who knew what really happened. And I'm not telling anyone but you, Coach."

Gatecrasher Scores the Winner

FORWARD BILL SUTHERLAND was forced to become a gatecrasher and bull his way into the arena for the home opener of the Philadelphia Flyers the night they made their NHL debut. It was early in October 1967, and Sutherland was eager to suit up for the Flyers' first game in their new home — the Spectrum.

What a surprise when he arrived at the rink! Nobody knew him and nobody would let him in.

"But I'm playing tonight," he protested. "I'm a Flyer."

"Prove it," the man attending the gate snapped.

When Sutherland couldn't produce anything to show he was on the Flyer payroll, he was told to get lost. "Nobody gets in without a ticket," the man at the gate said.

When the attendant turned to look after some paying fans, Sutherland dashed through the gate and ran down the corridor to the Philadelphia dressing room. An hour later, when he skated out to face the Pittsburgh Penguins, he vowed to do something that night to make the fans — and gate attendants —

remember him. Early in the third period he scored the only goal of the game to give the Flyers a 1–0 victory.

Take Your Best Shot, Grandma!

IN WINNIPEG A FEW YEARS AGO a 48-year-old grandmother rivaled any pro player in the NHL for shooting accuracy. And in doing so she won a cool $58,000 in prize money.

Joan Palmer, a grandmother of four, was selected to try her shooting luck during the intermission of a Winnipeg Jet–Detroit Red Wing game at the Winnipeg Arena. Her challenge was to shoot a three-inch puck through a tiny three-and-a-quarter-inch opening 120 feet away.

Grandma Palmer was allowed just one shot, and she turned it into the shot of a lifetime. The puck slid straight toward the net and slipped through the hole. Her prize was $58,000 — five times her annual salary as a Pink Lady Courier.

But Joan Palmer wasn't the only female Winnipeg fan involved in such a competition. On another occasion a female shooter whacked the puck from center ice into the corner of the rink, missing the net by several feet. The crowd groaned. But her puck hit another puck on the ice, left there by a previous shooter. The crowd urged officials to give the woman another chance. What could they lose? So they called her back and gave her a second shot, a rare concession. This time her shot went straight toward the goal and slid through the narrow opening, making her the proud winner of two new automobiles.

The One-in-a-Million Shot

WHEN DAVE DUNCAN of Oshawa, Ontario, attempted to win $8,000 toward the purchase of a new car in one of those hockey Score-O competitions between periods, he wasn't given a chance. Aside from being legally blind, Duncan was faced with the near-impossible task of shooting a puck three-quarters of the way down the ice surface and through a slot just slightly wider than the puck itself. Duncan, 25, amazed onlookers by sending a perfectly aimed shot through the slot with a one-in-a-million shot.

TOUGH GUYS

Killer Dill's Comeuppance

DURING THE 1944–45 hockey season, Montreal's Rocket Richard was the most talked-about man in hockey. Although he was hampered by a sore knee. Richard was averaging a goal a game and fans were wondering how long he could keep up the pace. It was the season he would go on to score 50 goals in 50 games, a remarkable feat. Rival teams did everything in their power to keep him from reaching the 50-goal plateau.

One night in New York, the Rangers assigned tough guy Bob "Killer" Dill to stop Richard. Dill had quite a reputation. He was related to two famous prizefighters, and he had been banned from the American League because of his rough play. He was looking for trouble against Montreal, and when he taunted Richard, calling him a "cowardly frog," he got it.

Richard's fist shot out. He flattened Dill with one punch, which left the Killer a quivering mass on the ice. When Dill revived a few minutes later, he tried to salvage what was left of his tough-guy reputation. He challenged Richard a second time, this time while both players were in the penalty box. Richard unleashed a series of punches, one of which opened a large cut over Dill's eye. Dill had never been so badly beaten, or so humiliated, in his life.

Both players were given double majors, and when Richard came back to play, Dill wasn't around to hamper his style. He'd had quite enough. The Rocket rubbed it in a bit by scoring the game-tying goal, his 19th in 19 games.

After the game, Ranger coach Frank Boucher,

asked to comment on the fisticuffs, said: "That crazy Richard had better learn to control his temper. He's liable to kill someone one of these days."

The Rocket's kayo of Killer Dill served as a warning to other bullies in the league to beware of the Rocket's hot temper. He would not be intimidated, and anyone foolish enough to think he could be stopped with racial slurs or a raised fist was likely to end up as Dill had — flat on his back.

Dill, meanwhile, happened to run into the Rocket as they left the arena after the game that night. Through his puffed lips, Dill smiled and told the Rocket he'd never been in such a one-sided battle. When the Rocket said, "Let's have dinner sometime," the Killer said he'd love to.

Eddie Shore's Hazardous Journey

WHEN EDDIE SHORE, the Edmonton Express, moved from the Pacific Coast League to the NHL in 1926 he became an instant superstar with the Boston Bruins, a tough, fearless, indestructible defenseman who would win MVP honors four times. Art Ross, Boston's general manager, often held Shore back from the player introductions prior to a game. Then he would have the band play "Hail to the Chief" while Shore made a grand entrance wearing a gold dressing gown over his uniform. When Shore nodded that he was ready to play, a valet would remove the gown.

One day Shore missed the train carrying the Bruins from Boston to Montreal. He phoned a

Eddie Shore, the Edmonton Express, has some fun with the puck.
(Hockey Hall of Fame)

friend, a wealthy Boston fan, and borrowed the man's big limousine and his chauffeur. Then he took off in pursuit of his teammates.

When Shore reached the Green Mountains of Vermont, he found himself in the middle of a blizzard. The terrified chauffeur, after spinning his wheels on the slippery mountain roads, wanted to turn back. Shore pushed the man out of the driver's seat and took the wheel himself. He could barely see the highway, and four or five times he found himself sliding into the ditch. On one occasion he sought the help of a farmer who hitched up a team of horses to haul the limo out of a snowdrift.

Driving all night and all the next day, Shore arrived at the Montreal Forum just before game time. His hands were raw and frostbitten, and he looked so haggard and exhausted that his coach suggested he see a doctor and then go straight to his hotel room for a good night's sleep.

Shore refused and grabbed his skates and hockey gear. He played the full sixty minutes against the fast-moving Montreal Maroons and turned in a flawless defensive performance. He even made a few dashes into the offensive zone. In fact, on one of these forays he slammed in the game's only goal, which made the long, hazardous journey through the mountains worth the effort.

Eddie Shore's Quirks

When Hall-of-Famer Eddie Shore bought the Springfield hockey club many years ago, he became notorious for running the franchise on a shoestring.

Don Cherry, who played under Shore, tells some fascinating yarns about Shore's idiosyncrasies. For example, until just before game time Shore could be found outside the arena parking cars. Then he'd dash inside, suit up and play for his team.

Some other economies: he told his players fifteen cents should be a maximum tip to a cabdriver, and soon no cabbie would pick up a Springfield hockey player. If a player had a bonus clause for scoring 30 goals, invariably Shore would bench him when the player drew close to his target.

Shore had many other bizarre ideas.

As coach of the Springfield club, Shore insisted his players practice tap dancing in hotel lobbies and ballet moves on the ice. He told one player he'd score more often if he combed his hair in a different style. He told another his legs were too far apart when he skated. So he tied the kid's legs together, then told him to skate. In practice, he sometimes tied his goalie to the crossbar, a lesson in how to remain standing upright. At least once Shore locked a referee in the officials' dressing room because he thought the man had done a poor job.

He prescribed his own special treatments and home remedies to sick or injured players. He told them he'd cured himself of cancer and that he'd survived eight heart attacks. He delighted in displaying his chiropractic skills — he'd had no training, of course — until bones cracked and body parts were properly aligned. "You'd ache for a week after he finished working on you," says Cherry. "Some players were terrified to get on that medical table."

Once Shore invited all the players' wives to the arena. They dressed for the occasion, thinking he'd planned a surprise party for the players. When the ladies arrived he sat them down and lectured them, telling them that "too much sex" was the reason for the team's poor play. "Be celibate," he ordered the wives, "at least until the playoffs are over."

He destroyed the NHL hopes of many players, who quit the game rather than play for him. Others credit his tutoring with making them stars. But it was never easy playing in Springfield, then known as the Siberia of hockey.

Once Shore traded for a player named Smith. When Smith walked into the Springfield dressing room, Shore said, "Where are your goal pads?" The puzzled Smith said, "But I'm not a goalie. I'm a forward." Leave it to Shore to trade for the wrong Smith.

The Green–Maki Incident

FOR SOME UNKNOWN REASON the 1969–70 preseason NHL exhibition games were rampant with brawls. The most serious flare-up occurred on September 21 in Ottawa in a game between the Boston Bruins and the St. Louis Blues.

Derek Sanderson of the Bruins recalls talking to teammate Ted Green before the game and hearing him say, "You won't see me hitting anyone out there tonight. I'm still negotiating a new contract. When I'm signed, then I'll hit."

Sanderson, sidelined with a sore knee, watched from the stands as Wayne Maki, a swift but unspectacular winger with the Blues, moved around Green during the game. They bumped and suddenly Maki swung at Green with his stick. Green retaliated by throwing a punch at Maki, knocking him down. Maki jumped up and speared Green. Then Green slashed Maki on the arm, and for a split second that appeared to be the end of it. But as Green turned to skate away, headed for the penalty box, Maki hit the Bruin squarely over the head with his stick. Green collapsed and lay on the ice, unconscious and bleeding.

Bobby Orr leaped off the bench and smacked Maki. Then Ace Bailey belted him. But the sight of Green lying on the ice knocked the toughness out of all the players. The right side of Green's head was crushed and his left side was partially paralyzed. His speech was slurred. Sanderson recalls saying to himself, "Here's the toughest guy on skates and he's in big, big trouble."

Green was rushed to an Ottawa hospital and underwent a five-hour brain operation. A few days later other surgery followed, including the insertion of a metal plate in his skull.

The suspensions handed out seem ludicrous in retrospect. At the time they were called "the stiffest in league annals." Maki was suspended for 30 days and Green for 13 games if and when he returned to action. It was assumed he never would. Police laid charges against both players, the first of their kind in NHL history.

Weeks later both men were exonerated after testifying in an Ottawa courtroom. A year later Green made what was called "a miraculous comeback" and played effectively for the Bruins. The following year he was a key performer on Boston's 1970 Stanley Cup–winning team. After that he played a few years in the WHA and retired following the 1978–79 season. When he left the game, he spoke out against violence in hockey and asked owners to put an end to it.

Ironically Maki's NHL career was cut short by a brain tumor, discovered while he was playing for the Vancouver Canucks in 1972. He died in the spring of 1974.

Even though the Green injury shocked most NHL players, they still weren't prepared to adopt helmets as protection against similar incidents. The Bruins tried to force helmets on their players, issuing headgear to Bobby Orr and others. When coach Milt Schmidt saw his players at practice one day without their helmets, he ordered them to put them on or get off the ice. Orr looked at him, then slowly skated off the ice, followed by the rest of the Bruins. Schmidt decided not to make an issue of it and the helmets were stored away.

The Fight John Ferguson Waited For

WHEN JOHN FERGUSON was 14 years old, he was the envy of his hockey-playing pals. The teenager already had a position in professional hockey: he was the official stickboy for the Vancouver Canucks of the Western Hockey League.

Years later, when he was helping the Montreal Canadiens win Stanley Cups, when he was known as the NHL's most feared enforcer, fans wondered what motivated him to play the way he did. Why did he fiercely protect his teammates? Why was he willing to slug it out with the toughest players in the game?

Perhaps the pattern of his aggressive and sometimes violent approach to hockey was established one night in Vancouver, while he was filling water bottles and tending the team sticks during a game between Vancouver and the Edmonton Eskimos. At the time, one of John's idols on the Canucks was soft-spoken Phil Maloney, the WHL's leading scorer. During the game, there was a skirmish in front of the Canuck bench and Maloney was attacked by Larry Zeidel, a hard-nosed Eskimo defenseman. Right in front of the horrified stickboy, Zeidel dropped his gloves and clubbed Maloney with rights and lefts. When Maloney fell to the ice, Zeidel fell on him and administered a pummeling that left Maloney dazed and bleeding.

Then Zeidel stood and challenged the rest of the players on the Vancouver bench to do something about it. Nobody did. But Ferguson, the teenage stickboy, was left seething with rage. He was furious with Zeidel for beating up on his idol and furious with the Canucks for not coming off the bench to help a teammate in trouble. If Ferguson had been a little older and a little bigger, he would have leaped at the throat of the burly defenseman, no matter how foolish it might have been.

Ten years went by and Ferguson, now 24 years old, had found his own place in the game. He was a well-respected winger with Cleveland of the American Hockey League. In a game with Hershey one night he came face-to-face with veteran Larry Zeidel, the toughest player in the circuit.

"Suddenly that fight in Vancouver a decade earlier flashed through my mind," Ferguson would say later. "I could see poor Maloney sagging to the ice and Zeidel pounding him. I'm sure Zeidel had forgotten it, but I never would. Then I got the perfect opportunity to do something about it. Zeidel whacked me with his stick up around my head."

When Zeidel clubbed the Cleveland rookie, Fergie whirled, threw off his gloves, and slammed into Zeidel, who was taken by surprise. He didn't know Ferguson from a goalpost and had no idea the kid was seeking revenge for the Maloney beating long ago.

The bout was brief and brutal. Ferguson's big fists slammed into Zeidel's face and head. The veteran's knees buckled and he staggered. Another solid blow to the face knocked him out.

When the officials pulled Ferguson toward the penalty box, he snarled back at the unconscious Zeidel, "That's for Phil Maloney!"

Fergie Fought His Friends

WHEN JOHN FERGUSON TOILED for the Montreal Canadiens in the 1960s, he was hockey's toughest player. It took a brave man to challenge him. One who often did was pesky Bryan Watson of Detroit, even though he was one of Fergie's best friends. They had roomed together when both were rookies with the Canadiens, and a bond had been established. But it seemed to vanish when they met as rivals on the ice. Whenever Montreal played Detroit, it appeared as though they were trying to annihilate each other.

"That friendship stuff doesn't mean much to me in a game," Watson told the late Paul Rimstead one day. "Why, I'd run my stick through Fergie just as fast as I would any other guy. Naw, I guess I wouldn't. Maybe just halfway through 'cause he's such a nice fellow."

"The guy [Watson] charged me into the boards one time, so I gave him a good punch on the head," Fergie said. "He spun around and gave me a two-hander with his stick. A good thing it missed my skull."

It is understandable that good pals, in the heat of battle, while playing for opposing teams, might come to blows. But Fergie very nearly flattened one of his own teammates during a game one night.

In New York the Canadiens were being manhandled by the New York Rangers. On the bench Fergie was seething. When the Rangers continued to beat up on the Habs, Fergie leaped up and was about to jump into the battle when a teammate restrained him.

"Aw, it's not worth it," he said.

Fergie won't name the player. But he does admit the fellow will never know how close he came to being the first NHLer to be punched out by one of his own teammates in the middle of a game.

King Clancy Gets Starched

ONE OF HOCKEY'S greatest storytellers was the late Hall of Famer King Clancy, former star defenseman with the Toronto Maple Leafs and, prior to that, the Ottawa Senators. One day I asked Clancy to tell me about hockey's renowned tough guy of the twenties — Sprague Cleghorn.

"Sprague was an awesome competitor in the NHL," King said. "He broke his leg in a game one year and was so frustrated at being sidelined that he hauled off and struck his wife with his crutch. The story made all the papers when his wife took him to court. And he was always getting into disputes with his coaches and other players in the league — some of them on his own team.

"I remember in 1923 when he played for Montreal and cross-checked Boston's Lionel Hitchman dizzy in a playoff game. Cleghorn's manager, Leo Dandurand, was so repelled that he didn't wait for the league to discipline his star. He suspended Cleghorn himself because of his violent behavior on the ice. His own player!

"When I was a rookie with the Ottawa Senators, I got cute with Cleghorn one night, and boy, did I suffer the consequences. He was lugging the puck up the ice and I was right behind him, trying to catch up. When I realized I wasn't going to overtake him, I yelled, 'Sprague, drop the puck!' Well, he thought I was a teammate calling for a pass, and without looking back, he dropped the puck right onto my stick.

"As I wheeled around and led a return rush, the Ottawa fans howled with laughter. But Cleghorn did a slow burn and his cheeks turned beet red. No player likes being humiliated like that, especially by a rookie, and Cleghorn was no exception. He glared at me but did nothing at the time. But when the period ended and the players were leaving the ice — we all left by the same exit in those days — I heard someone behind me say, 'Oh, King!' I turned around, and that's when every light in the rink went out. Cleghorn had starched me. When I finally opened my eyes, the trainer was throwing water in my face and there was a priest bending over me.

"That gave me a start. I thought I was getting the last rites. I was told later that when my teammates tried to get at Sprague, he fended them off with his stick and insisted, 'Honest, fellows, all I said to King was that he had the makings of a great little hockey player. And then I gave him a friendly pat on the head.'

"I'll say this. It's the only pat on the head I ever heard of that required a bucket of water to revive a fellow and brought a Catholic priest on the run."

Ottawa Acquired an All-Star Player — For Nothing

TOMMY GORMAN, who once guided the Chicago Blackhawks and the Montreal Maroons to successive Stanley Cups, was managing the Ottawa club in 1919 and he needed defensive help. The player he coveted was rugged Sprague

Cleghorn, a star performer with the Montreal Wanderers.

When the league managers gathered in Montreal for a preseason meeting, Gorman took Wanderers manager Sam Lichtenhein aside and casually mentioned that he was somewhat interested in Cleghorn.

"You know he broke his leg in an auto accident last summer?" Lichtenhein asked.

"Yes, I know about that mishap," Gorman replied.

"And you know he more or less skipped out of the hospital and broke his other leg?" Lichtenhein added.

"My goodness, two broken legs," Gorman said. "That doesn't auger well."

"Then his wife swore out a warrant for his arrest. So he's got some personal problems, too."

"Oh, my," Gorman said.

"The guy is jinxed," Lichtenhein snorted. "He's a write-off. You want him, you can have him. He'll never play hockey again."

"I'm probably making a big mistake, but I'll take him," Gorman said. "How much?"

"Nothin'," Lichtenhein said. "I said you could have him. He's not worth anything."

So Sprague Cleghorn's name was quietly placed on the Ottawa reserve list.

Early in December, on the eve of the new NHL season, Gorman received a phone call from Montreal. It was Sprague Cleghorn.

"I think my legs have healed perfectly," he said. "My wife and I have solved our problems and I'm anxious to play hockey again, especially for you."

It cost Gorman only $8.50 — the price of two train tickets — to bring Cleghorn and his wife from Montreal to Ottawa. When Cleghorn stepped on the ice the next day, his legs were perfect. That season he went on to become the most brilliant defenseman in the NHL.

Smith Goes on Rampage in 1911 Game

STAR FORWARD HARRY SMITH'S last game in the Timiskaming League in Northern Ontario was a memorable one. A write-up in the Cobalt newspaper on Monday, January 16, 1911, featured the headline: "Harry Smith under Arrest. Cobalt Player Struck Opponents and Felled Referee. Smashed Teeth and Broke Noses in Haileybury Match."

Harry Smith, center of the Cobalt team, played his last game of hockey in this section last night when near the close of the first half of the game against Haileybury, two policemen walked onto the ice and nabbed him for deliberate rough work. Harry was escorted to the cells but was subsequently let out on bail.

In the first ten minutes of the game little rough work was done, but shortly afterwards Smith hit Johnston with the blade of his stick, breaking Johnston's nose, for which Smith spent five minutes on the fence. When he came back, he cut Morrison on the lip and loosened two teeth. He then struck at Skene Ronan and got another five minutes. He had just got on the ice again when Con

Corbeau started down with the puck and Harry chopped him.

George Gwynne of Liskeard, the referee, skated over and called Smith to the penalty box. While Gwynne was going to the side, Smith skated up behind him, and swinging his stick like an axe, struck the referee with the blade over the side of the face. This was too much for the crowd, and Chief Miller and PC Collins arrested Smith on the spot.

Referee Gwynne received two bad cuts on the face and above his eye as well as two broken teeth.

The executive of the league will probably forbid Smith from ever playing again.

During the following week, another write-up appeared:

Twenty-five dollars and costs was the fine meted out to Harry Smith, the Cobalt hockey player, by Magistrate Atkinson as a result of Smith's rampage during the hockey game on Friday night. In addition Smith received a severe lecture from the judge. The information was laid by Chief Miller, referee Gwynne not caring to lay information. The Magistrate told Smith that if Gwynne had laid the charge or even been present the defendant would have been given a lengthy prison term.

Just as the sentence was announced, the referee came rushing into the courtroom to lay the charge.

But it was too late. Smith was allowed to go free after paying his fine.

And they say modern hockey is violent.

A Former Goon Controls the Game

NHL REFEREE PAUL STEWART comes by his whistle-tooting honestly. His grandfather, Bill Stewart, was a big league referee and a major league umpire before he took a job in the NHL as rookie coach of the Chicago Blackhawks.

Big Bill may have lacked coaching experience, but he knew enough about handling athletes to astonish all the so-called experts. Stewart took the Blackhawks all the way to the Stanley Cup championship in 1938. And he did it with a team that won only 14 games during the regular season.

Paul Stewart speaks with pride of his grand-daddy's record. And if you ask, he'll show you the gold watch fob he inherited from his distinguished grandparent, a prized souvenir of that long-ago Cup victory.

As inheritor of the famous Stewart bloodlines, you might assume that Paul was a stickler for fair play growing up, a play-it-by-the-rules kind of guy in his own athletic endeavors. As a player, his approach was quite the opposite. His record as a goon and troublemaker in pro hockey, especially the World Hockey Association, is truly astonishing.

The native of Boston started his pro career in 1975 with the Binghamton Dusters in the North American Hockey League, where he quickly gained a reputation as a brawler. In his second season he punched a referee between periods of a game after being cut by a high stick. The offense drew an eight-game suspension. His pro career included a two-year stint in the WHA with the Cincinnati Stingers, and finally — a dream come true — 20 games with the Quebec Nordiques in the NHL. In five pro seasons he logged more than 1,200 penalty minutes.

He tried a normal job after retiring as a player but found he missed hockey. "I loved the action, the involvement, the travel," he says. "So I decided to make a comeback — this time as a referee."

Now 37, the popular arbiter explains his switch from pugilist to peacekeeper this way: "It's no different than a fellow who fought on one side during the war, then turns around and becomes an ally. I discovered years ago it's more fun to hand out penalties than to receive them — especially when I can earn more money refereeing than I ever did as a player."

Have Résumé, Will Travel

WHEN THE NHL DOUBLED its six teams in 1967, dozens of players were drafted by the new franchises. Young kids who were as green as grass and old pros who had toiled in the minors for years found themselves on big league rosters. Nobody was overlooked.

One was. For 17 years hard-rock defenseman Larry Zeidel had bulled his way through three minor leagues, leading all of them in penalty minutes. If any of the expansion teams considered him at all, their assessment was "too old" or "washed up." But Zeidel had absolute confidence in his ability and soon found a novel way to sell himself to the new owners.

He invested $150 and prepared a glossy résumé, extolling his virtues as a player and as a hockey executive. "Why not?" Zeidel asked. "That's the way you get a good job in the business world." The résumés were mailed to all six expansion teams, and most of them, predictably, found their way into the nearest wastebasket. But Keith Allen, general manager of the Philadelphia Flyers, read one through and was impressed. He contacted Zeidel and offered him a tryout.

"There's just one snag," Zeidel said. "I still belong to Cleveland of the American League. But let me deal with that."

The resourceful player quickly arranged a conference call with the Cleveland owner and talked the deal into completion. To that point in his career, Zeidel had spent nearly 2,500 minutes in the penalty box, time equal to more than 40 full games.

Even though he had been away from the NHL since 1954, Zeidel had no difficulty making the Flyers' roster and helping them to a first-place finish in the West Division of the NHL. After a second season with the team, he retired from the game.

William Bops Bowman

IT WAS A BLOW to the head that nobody saw, but there was enough circumstantial evidence to indict NHL tough guy Tiger Williams of the Vancouver Canucks.

It happened in the third game of a 1980 playoff series between the Buffalo Sabres, then coached by Scotty Bowman, and the Vancouver Canucks. At the time Bowman was en route to becoming the NHL's winningest mentor, and Williams was carving a path to the title "hockey's all-time bad man." Eventually he finished with a record 3,966 penalty minutes.

Williams was at his nastiest in game three of the series after his Canucks fell behind two games to none. At one stage of the game played in Vancouver he chopped Sabre forward Bobby Mongrain with his stick, prompting screams from Bowman and the Buffalo players on the bench.

The gritty Mongrain shook off the blow and carried the puck into the Vancouver zone, where he was smashed into the boards by a Vancouver defenseman. Mongrain was injured on the play and lay motionless on the ice.

Wherever Tiger Williams went, trouble was sure to follow. (John Maiola)

All eyes were on the diminutive Sabre. They must have been, because apparently nobody witnessed what happened next over at the Buffalo bench. Suddenly coach Bowman went sprawling backward and was knocked cold. He wound up flat on his back at the feet of his astonished players.

When he was revived, the groggy Bowman complained that Williams had hammered him over the head with his hockey stick while all eyes were on Mongrain. "It was a real two-hander," Bowman beefed. "He whacked me and nobody saw it."

After the game, when questioned about Bowman's accusation, Williams gave reporters an innocent look and said he didn't remember any incident involving Bowman during the game. Later he told me that Bowman had a bad habit of leaning out over the boards during the play. "When a coach does that, Brian," he said, "sometimes accidents will happen."

What Williams didn't know — nor do most people — is that Bowman has a plate in his head, the aftermath of a serious hockey injury suffered during his junior playing days. A stick creasing his head could have killed him.

Prior to game four in the series, Brian O'Neill, executive vice president of the NHL, announced that Williams would have to serve a one-game suspension. O'Neill claimed he had seen enough videotape evidence to reach that verdict. Williams didn't play, the Sabres won the series, and the Canucks' season was over. To this day Williams hasn't confessed to the crime. "Gee, I don't remember hitting Bowman," he says with just the hint of a grin.

Tiger Gets His Favorite Number

WHEN TIGER WILLIAMS was traded from Toronto to Vancouver in 1980, he discovered that his favorite jersey number — 22 — was being worn by the Canucks' Bob Manno. In the dressing room Tiger wasn't shy about speaking up. "Hey, Bob," he said, "I'll give you 10 grand if you'll let me have your number."

Manno looked at Tiger and said, "Nah, I don't think so."

Two weeks later Manno was dispatched to the minor leagues, never to return. When he turned in his jersey with the big 22 on the back, Tiger was there to collect it.

"And it didn't cost me a penny," Tiger said.

Brother Flattens Brother

WHEN TIGER WILLIAMS, former NHL tough guy, was growing up in Weyburn, Saskatchewan, he developed a dislike for referees. His brother Len, who made a few bucks as an official, was no exception.

At the dinner table one day Tiger said to his brother, "Listen, Len, I'm playing a game tonight and I hear you're going to be the referee. I'm warning you right now. If you give me a penalty tonight, I'm going to pop you one."

But Len, like Tiger, wasn't easily intimidated. Sure enough, the game that night was barely under way when Len caught Tiger breaking a rule. He blew his whistle and waved him to the box. En route Tiger flattened his brother, just as he had promised.

When Weldy Lost His Temper

BACK IN 1898 WELDY YOUNG was a hot-tempered player with the Ottawa hockey club. During a playoff game that year, Weldy was having an off night and the fans started to jeer his play. Young ignored the razzing for a while, but when one loudmouth in the crowd got under his skin, he decided it was time to do something. Spotting the critic, Weldy leaped over the boards and went after him. The fans in the area scattered, for Young's mean streak was renowned, and it looked as if the fan he had targeted was in for a beating. But the fan had several friends in the crowd, and Young soon discovered he had bitten off more than he could chew. The spectators ganged up on him and pummeled him into submission. Somehow, bruised and bloody, the Ottawa tough guy was able to stagger back onto the ice and resume play.

Weldy Young wasn't a well-liked player, even by his own teammates. When the team manager decided to make room for Young on the Ottawa roster one season, the club president resigned and two players, Chauncey Kirby and goaltender Fred Chittick, said they would play no more.

When Espo First Met Mr. Hockey

PHIL ESPOSITO HAS A VIVID MEMORY of the night he played against Gordie Howe for the first time.

"I'll never forget it," he told me recently. "It was my first game in the NHL. Well, my second one actually, because I sat on the bench throughout my first game, which was against Montreal at the Forum. I almost got to play in that game. With two minutes to play we [Chicago] were losin' 7–2. Coach Billy Reay looks down the bench and yells, 'Esposito, get out there!'

"Well, I was disappointed I hadn't taken a single shift, so I shouted, 'Okay, Coach, do you want me to win it or tie it?'

"He yelled back, 'Sit down, smartass.'

"Two nights later we're in Detroit, and who do I find myself standin' next to when I get on the ice but Gordie Howe. Geez, he was my boyhood hero. I'm lookin' at Gordie and I'm sayin' to myself, Damn, that's the great Gordie Howe. What am I doin' out here?

"Just before we're ready to face off, Bobby Hull yells at me, 'Watch that old son of a bitch!' With that Gordie blinks once or twice and gets a little grin on his face, and that's when the puck is dropped. I'm still lookin' at him, thinkin' this is unbelievable, when bam! he gives me an elbow in the mouth.

"I stagger back and say, 'Why, you old fart, you!' Then I spear him a good one and we both get penalties.

"In those days, in the penalty box, the players sat close together with a cop or an usher or somebody in between them. So I'm sittin' there holdin' a towel to my split lip and I'm real upset with big Howe. Without thinking, I lean across the guy between us and say to Gordie, 'To think you *used* to be my bleepin' idol.'

"Howe snarls back, 'What did you say, rookie?'"

"Quickly I say, 'Nothin', Mr. Howe, not a word.'"

"To this day, I'll never forget that look."

Hunter Serves Long, Costly Suspension

IT HAPPENED DURING THE FINAL GAME of the Islanders–Capitals playoff series in 1993 in the Patrick Division semifinals. Pierre Turgeon, the Isles' leading scorer, raised his arms to celebrate a goal, and that was the last thing he remembered. He was blindsided by a frustrated Dale Hunter of the Caps and suffered a separated shoulder and a concussion.

NHL commissioner Gary Bettman stepped in and nailed Hunter with a 21-game suspension, the second longest punishment for an on-ice incident in league history. The Capitals were also fined $150,000.

"I picked 21 games because it happened to be the maximum number of playoff games the Islanders could be without Turgeon," Bettman said.

Hunter claimed he didn't know a goal had been scored when he hit Turgeon and that he was merely finishing his check. But video evidence showed him slamming into the Islander player four or five seconds after the scoring play.

The suspension, which prohibited Hunter from taking part in Washington's training camp prior to the 1993–94 season and kept him out of the first 21 regular season games, cost the player approximately $150,000 in lost salary.

The NHL's Longest Suspension

MOST NEWSPAPERS and *The Hockey News* called Dale Hunter's 21-game suspension in 1993 "the longest in league history for an on-ice incident." Somehow they overlooked the lifetime suspension doled out to Billy Couture (often called Coutu) during the 1927 playoffs.

Couture, one of the meanest, toughest defensemen ever to terrorize the NHL, was a member of the Boston Bruins when he was banned forever by NHL president Frank Calder. During a brawl involving several players on the Bruins and the Ottawa Senators, Couture smashed referee Gerry Laflamme in the face. Calder banned him for life, a suspension that was lifted five years later — too late for Couture to return to the NHL.

Rehashing an Old Feud

OLD HOCKEY PLAYERS, like elephants, never forget. In 1963 at a B'nai B'rith banquet in Boston several members of the Hockey Hall of Fame were invited as honored guests. Prior to the dinner, the old-timers gathered in a hotel suite, as was the custom at such gatherings, to reminisce and rehash stories from their athletic youth.

Two of the former greats, Aurel Joliat and Punch Broadbent, recalled a fistfight they had been in 40 years earlier during a game between the Montreal Canadiens and the Ottawa Senators. Joliat's version of the fight differed somewhat from Broadbent's. Harsh words were exchanged, voices were raised, insults exchanged, and punches filled the air. There they were, two men in their sixties, rolling around on the floor, swearing, grunting, and flailing away at each other.

In order to restore order and keep the peace, the two out-of-breath combatants were led to their rooms and locked in until they cooled off.

Randy's One-man Riot

ON MARCH 11, 1979, at the Philadelphia Spectrum, Randy Holt of the Los Angeles Kings declared a one-man war against the Flyers' Frank Bathe. Holt racked up nine penalties totaling an NHL-record 67 minutes. He collected one minor, three majors, two 10-minute misconducts, and three game misconducts — all in the first period. Bathe, the Flyer who scrapped with Holt several times in the opening period, finished the game with 55 penalty minutes, the second highest single-game total ever. While Holt still holds the single-game record for penalty minutes, he failed to hold on to his nine-penalty record. On March 31, 1991, Chris Nilan, then with the Boston Bruins, took 10 penalties in a game against Hartford.

The Night Clancy Goaded Shore

IN THE THIRTIES King Clancy of the Leafs and Eddie Shore of the Bruins were tops among NHL defensemen. Both were fierce competitors, and almost every time they met there were fireworks.

During one playoff series, a two-game, total-goals-to-count affair, the Bruins shut out the Leafs 3–0 on home ice and were heavily favored to advance when the teams met in game two at Maple Leaf Gardens. Many years ago, when I helped King chronicle his memoirs for the book *Clancy,* he recalled the bizarre ending to that story.

"We played terrible hockey in that first game in Boston, and I was ready to try anything to help us win that second match. I made up my mind to needle Shore if the opportunity came up, 'cause he had such a short fuse. I even told my mates when we left the dressing room that night, 'I got Shore in my hip pocket.'

"Well, Boston picked up where they left off and scored the first goal to take a four-goal lead in the series. Then Shore took a penalty, and while he was cooling off, I scored one and Conacher added another, cutting the margin in half. Then Red Horner scored a big goal for us, and Shore was livid, claiming Horner was in the crease on the play. That's when I skated over to Shore and said, 'That was a raw decision, Eddie. Of course, Horner was in the crease. The referee robbed you on that one.'

"Well, Shore blew his stack. He grabbed the puck and whipped it at referee Odie Cleghorn, hitting him in the back. Cleghorn spun around and gave Shore a 10-minute misconduct, and that was the turning point. We scored three quick goals while he was off and rolled to an 8–3 victory. Won the round eight goals to six. Shore never did forgive me for goading him into that penalty that night."

The 80-second Game

WHEN JOHN BROPHY PLAYED for the Long Island Ducks in the old Eastern Hockey League, he teamed up on defense with Don Perry. Both men were tough and mean, the most feared combination on the circuit. They were so intimidating that one game they played in lasted a mere 80 seconds. The New Haven Blades were the opponents, and when Brophy and Perry clobbered a couple of Blades on the very first shift, that was enough. The Blades left the ice, put on their street clothes, and went home. Al Baron, owner of the Ducks, rushed to the visitors' dressing room and offered each player $100 to go back on the ice. To a man they replied, "No thanks, Al, not with those two crazies out there."

Paiement Pays for Polonich Pasting

DENIS POLONICH WAS a scrappy forward for Detroit. Wilf Paiement was a top scorer with the Colorado Rockies. Unfortunately they collided one night in a game during the 1978–79 season, and tempers flared. The sticks came up, and Paiement, wielding his like a baseball bat, struck Polonich in the face, resulting in severe facial injuries. Polonich sued, and in the landmark case that followed, Polonich won a civil action against Paiement. Under the terms of the settlement he agreed to accept over $1 million to be paid over the next two decades.

Little Camille Chases a Fan

THE 1959–60 SEASON was a pathetic one for the New York Rangers. They were submerged in last place and their playoff hopes were nil.

But they earned no sympathy from some lunatic fans in Detroit one night. After they struggled to earn a single point in a 2–2 tie with the Red Wings, they were coming off the ice when they were pelted with an unusual amount of debris. Programs, popcorn boxes, wads of gum, shoe rubbers — they dodged it all. As they entered the corridor leading to their dressing room, little Camille Henry slipped on a program and fell, dropping his hockey stick.

A fan named Eric Steiner, a 37-year-old salesman, was standing nearby. He swooped in and grabbed the stick. Henry reached out to pull it back when Steiner smacked him acrross the face with the blade of the stick, opening up a wound under one eye that later required several stitches.

When Steiner saw the blood and the furious look on Henry's face, he took off and dashed out the nearest exit. Henry, the smallest player in the NHL, leaped up and ran after him. Out of the arena and down the street they raced, sparks flying from Henry's skates. Within a block he tackled the man and held him down until police arrived.

Arrested and charged with assault, Steiner's excuse was that he simply lost his head. Henry got his stick back and retraced his steps to the arena. Along the way fans leaving the game gaped at the sight of a New York Ranger, blood streaming from his face, clutching a stick under his arm, and clomping along in full hockey gear, including his skates.

Hockey More Violent at Turn of Century

THE QUESTION OFTEN COMES UP: Was hockey more violent in the good old days? Picking a month and a season at random, I came up with January 1907 and perused the sports pages for episodes of hockey violence that month — and there were plenty. For example:

- January 2: Referee Magnus Flett has advised the Manitoba Hockey League to expel Dey of Portage la Prairie for his foul play in the game with Brandon. He put Leader and Armstrong out of the game by using his stick on their heads.
- January 4: It is claimed that McIvor of the Goderich club, on New Year's Eve, when neither he nor his check was playing the puck, skated down on Cole (a deaf mute on the Clinton team), striking him from behind with his stick, knocking him down, and fracturing his jaw in three places. The referee at once ruled McIvor off for 10 minutes. McIvor was later arrested, charged with

assault, and suspended for the rest of the season.

- January 7: In the Calumet–Soo game on Saturday night there was a sensational incident when goaltender Jones of the Soo laid out Bert Morrison by hitting him over the head. In the Houghton–Pittsburgh game Campbell of Pittsburgh assaulted referee Melville and was given the extreme International League penalty — three minutes.

- January 9: The *Soo Express* says: "Marty Walsh, one of the cleverest men in hockey, had to be removed to the hospital, suffering from a compound fracture of the ankle. The attack upon Walsh was brutal, two of the heaviest men of the Calumet team jumping onto the boy, and it is said that he was choked and slugged while prone on the ice. Little Walsh was unconscious and suffered intense pain."

- January 9: The first game in the Saskatchewan League was very rough. A Regina spectator fell out of the gallery onto the ice and was unconscious for some time. Later a Regina spectator jumped over the fence and struck Coldwell, the Moose Jaw umpire. A free-for-all ensued, ending in several spectators going to jail.

- January 13: This report followed a donnybrook between Ottawa and the Wanderers in Montreal. "In the match, Baldy Spittal was said to have tried to split Blatchford's head open by bringing down his hockey

Fights have always been a part of hockey, as this dust-up between the Maple Leafs and the Blackhawks back in the days of the old six-team league can attest. (Hockey Hall of Fame)

stick on it with all the force he could muster. Blatchford was carried off with his blood spilling on the ice. Alf Smith was reported to have skated up to Hod Stuart and, hitting him across the temple with his stick, laid him out like a corpse. Meanwhile, Harry Smith was cracking Ernie Johnston across the face with his stick, breaking his nose and spilling more blood." Follow-up coverage in the papers expressed the writers' outrage: "They should get six months in jail is the opinion as to the game's brutalities. And old players say it was the worst exhibition of butchery they ever saw."

• January 16: From a report on the game

between Newmarket and Toronto St. Georges: "Doyle and Kennedy 'rough housed' at every opportunity. Doyle on one occasion let fly his stick at an opponent who was skating away from him. Kennedy bumped into everybody and twice threw his stick at a St. Georges player when a score appeared to be imminent."

- January 27: There was a follow-up story to the January 12 donnybrook between Montreal and Ottawa: "The three Ottawa players, Spittal, Alf Smith and Harry Smith, for whom warrants were recently issued for assault on Wanderer players, appeared in the police court on Saturday and were admitted to bail, to appear on Wednesday next for a hearing." On the following Wednesday Alf Smith and Baldy Spittal were fined $20 apiece and were bound over to keep the peace for 12 months. Nose breaker Harry Smith was found not guilty.
- January 29: A report read: "F. C. Chittick, referee of the final Wanderers–Kenora match in Montreal, will in all probability take legal action against Tom Hodge of Montreal, an ex-member of the Wanderers Executive, for an assault which Mr. Chittick says was committed after the match. It is said that the referee was walking to one of the dressing rooms when Mr. Hodge struck him from behind, being angered at Mr. Chittick's handling of the game, in which Wanderers were defeated, with the consequent loss of the Stanley Cup. Hodge will be remembered as referee at Ottawa when

the Toronto Marlboros went there after the Stanley Cup. He saw nothing wrong so far as Ottawa's tactics were concerned, and they whaled, slashed, cross-checked and fouled the Marlboros to their heart's content."

Was hockey as violent then as it is today? Indeed it was — even more so. If we had chronicled episodes of hockey violence for another six weeks — into March 1907 — we would have come across a fatality on ice. A Cornwall star, Owen McCourt, was killed in a game against the Ottawa Vics. Struck over the head by an opponent's stick, McCourt was rushed to hospital where he died. Charlie Masson of Ottawa was charged with manslaughter and put on trial. He was acquitted on April 10 when teammates testified it was another player's stick that had struck McCourt that night.

Another First for Dino

ON AUGUST 24, 1988, winger Dino Ciccarelli, then with the Minnesota North Stars, became the first NHL player to receive a jail term for attacking a rival player on the ice. Judge Sydney Harris of Toronto sentenced Ciccarelli to 24 hours in jail and fined him $1,000 for clouting Toronto defenseman Luke Richardson twice with his stick (over the head) and punching him in the mouth during a game in January. Released after a two-hour stint behind bars, Ciccarelli called the verdict "utterly ridiculous." Asked to describe his stay in the slammer, he said, "The first thing I saw was a big fat cop eating a jelly doughnut. Then I stood around signing autographs for the other poor guys in there."

When Francis Fought the Fans

EMILE FRANCIS was coaching the New York Rangers at Madison Square Garden one night, and his club was leading Detroit 2–1 late in the game. Then the Red Wings' Norm Ullman split the Ranger defence, went in on goal and scored to tie the game.

But the New York goal judge was slow to react and didn't flash the red light for several seconds. When it did light up so did Francis.

He left the Ranger bench and dashed to where the goal judge sat. He berated the astonished official and demanded to know why he'd been so slow to signal a goal. Was it because the puck didn't go in the net? Should the goal have been disallowed? He demanded an explanation.

That was when a fan intervened and told Francis to butt out. "Leave the poor guy alone," the fan bellowed. Then he came out of his seat and lunged at Francis. The Ranger coach, already seething with frustration, belted the man.

Two more fans jumped up, grabbed the diminutive coach and began beating him. One roundhouse punch caught Francis squarely in the face, cutting him for six stitches. In the scuffle, the coach's suit was ripped.

The Ranger players then came to their leader's aid. Several Rangers scooted down the ice and climbed over the protective glass at the end of the arena. Skates flashing and fists swinging, they jumped into the fray and rescued their coach. Their sudden attack sent dozens of fans scurrying for the exits.

Two days later Francis was told the fans he'd struggled with were suing him for a million dollars.

It took five years for the case to come to trial, and just as the jury was filing out to reach their verdict, one juror whispered "Good luck" to Francis.

"Mistrial," declared the judge when he heard the remark. Two more years went by, and this time the claimants were awarded $80,000 in damages by a new jury.

"The incredible thing is," says Francis, "when the verdict was finally in, the three jokers who punched me and sued me then came over and wanted my autograph."

5

ON-ICE ODDITIES

The Original Two-Goalie System

IT'S QUITE COMMON FOR NHL teams to change goaltenders during a game, but at least once in Stanley Cup competition a team got away with employing two goaltenders at the same time. At the turn of the century, a wily coach of a team from Kenora (then known as Rat Portage) unveiled a unique strategy against a powerful Ottawa club in a Stanley Cup match. He benched one of his forwards and inserted a second goalie in his team's net. There was no rule against it at the time, and the coach thought two goalies would make scoring almost impossible.

He was wrong. The goalies stumbled into each other and left enough openings for the Ottawa boys to score. The strategy was quickly abandoned.

A rule was soon adopted preventing a repetition of the ploy.

Pro Football in a Hockey Rink

THE CHAMPIONSHIP of a professional football league was once decided in a hockey rink. On December 18, 1932, a raging blizzard swept over the city of Chicago, site of the football game that would end the U.S. pro season.

As temperatures dropped and snow piled up on the gridiron, officials decided to play the game in the Chicago Stadium, hockey home of the Chicago Blackhawks. Seats were moved back, several inches of dirt were spread over the floor of the arena, and 11,000 fans turned out to witness the unique sports event between the Chicago Bears and the Portsmouth Spartans.

Because the "field" was a mere 80 yards long, every time a team crossed midfield it was penalized 20 yards. The star of the Portsmouth team didn't play because of a job commitment. He left the team to become basketball coach at Colorado College. And the only touchdown was scored on a pass from Bronko Nagurski to Red Grange — two of the greatest players ever.

The Goalie Wore Boxing Gloves

AUTHOR GEORGE TATOMYR'S BOOK *Beyond the Uke Line* profiles each of 55 hockey players of Ukrainian descent who played in the NHL. One of the most famous was Bronco Horvath, who centered Johnny Bucyk and Vic Stasiuk on the potent Uke Line for the Boston Bruins over 30 years ago. Others who excelled in the NHL were goalies Terry Sawchuk, Johnny Bower, and Turk Broda, and forwards Mike Bossy, Dale Hawerchuk, Bernie Federko, Stan Smyl, Dennis Maruk, Tom Lysiak, Bill Mosienko, and yes, even Eddie "Clear the Track" Shack. Over the years Ukrainians have accounted for close to 8,000 NHL goals.

Tatomyr's research indicates that hockey's start in the Ukraine had shaky beginnings. In the 1930s a team called the Lions competed in a Polish league. The Ukrainian goalie protected his head with a primitive face mask made out of a World War I army helmet. Sturdy metal bars attached to the helmet deflected pucks aimed at his face.

Hockey, like most sports, disappeared from the Ukraine during the war, but it surfaced again in the late forties. This time the players really had to improvise when it came to equipment. For example, the goalie on one team wore boxing gloves. Pieces of quilting protected shins and shoulders and were held in place by long underwear worn over top. During one postwar season, the Lions had only six gloves between them, and players were obliged to take turns wearing them.

They became accustomed to derisive laughter wherever they appeared. In their debut against a German team at Garmisch, their opponents laughed heartily at their ridiculous appearance. But the ill-equipped visitors laughed last by trouncing their hosts 18–4.

The Player Who Couldn't Score

MANY YEARS AGO when the New York Americans were in the NHL, they had a low-scoring winger on the roster named Eddie Convey. Convey was a buddy of King Clancy, then a star defenceman with the Toronto Maple Leafs.

When Clancy heard that Convey might be sent to the minors if he didn't start producing more goals, he decided to give his old pal some help.

When the Americans played in Toronto one night, Clancy enlisted teammate Charlie Conacher to help him propel their mutual friend Convey into the hockey spotlight. "If you follow the plan I've come up with," Clancy told the obliging Conacher, "Eddie Convey will score at least one goal against us tonight."

Clancy's plan depended on the Leafs gaining a two- or three-goal lead over the Americans. After that Convey would be allowed to sail into the Toronto zone unmolested. "You'll wave at him as he goes by," he told Conacher. "And I'll stumble and fall when I try to check him. I'll leave a big opening, and Eddie will have a perfect chance to go in alone and score."

Sure enough, the Leafs were ahead by three or four goals when Convey zipped around Conacher and flew past the stumbling Clancy. Leaf goalie Lorne Chabot was in on the plan, too. He gave Convey at least half the net for a target. But Convey's shot missed the inviting target and sailed high over the cage.

"Let's give him another chance," suggested Clancy. A few minutes later, Convey again grabbed the rubber and started up the ice. He breezed past Conacher and deked his way past Clancy. Chabot hugged the post, giving Convey even more open net. But did he score? No! This time his rising shot caught Chabot under the chin — right in the Adam's apple.

Chabot fell to the ice, choking and gasping. When Conacher and Clancy arrived on the scene, the goalie glared at them and croaked, "That's enough charity for tonight, fellows. That guy doesn't deserve to score."

Conacher looked at Clancy. "Well, King?"

Clancy growled, "Chabot is right. Next time

Convey comes down here, cut his legs out from under him."

Clancy Held a Hot Hand

I often chuckle when I think of an anecdote the late King Clancy once told me about an incident early in his career as a substitute defenceman with the NHL's Ottawa Senators.

"I didn't get much ice time when I first joined the Senators," he said. "Most players were sixty-minute men in those days, so the three Ottawa subs — Morley Bruce, Frank Boucher and I — were used sparingly.

"On bitterly cold nights, the three of us stayed in the dressing room during games. It was a lot warmer in there than on the Ottawa bench. If the coach needed one of us, he simply buzzed the room by pressing a button near the bench. One buzz was for me, two for Bruce and three for Boucher.

"What did we do in there? To tell the truth, we loosened our skates and played cards to pass the time.

"But one night the coach surprised us. He buzzed twice for Bruce, who had his skates off and wasn't ready to play, so Boucher scrambled out in his place. But he was back moments later, saying, 'Coach wants you, Clancy.' Geez, I quickly tied up my laces and hurried out. But there'd been such a delay before I got into the game that everyone was screamin' — the coaches, the players, the fans and the referee.

"It couldn't have happened at a worse time. Wouldn't you know I was holding four aces in my mitts when the buzzer interrupted our card game that night. When I got back to the dressing room I asked my teammates, 'Hey, what happened to the cards I was playing?'"

"Frank Boucher said innocently, 'Why, we put your cards back in the deck. We didn't know when you'd be coming back.'"

"'King, they probably weren't very good cards, anyway,' said Morley. 'Let's deal you some more.'

"I know it's a terrible thing to suspect your teammates of doing anything underhanded, but I can't help but think those two fellows took a little peek at the cards I left on the dressing room table that night.

"And if we did nothing else in that game, we helped to make a little hockey history," Clancy added in conclusion. "Within hours, the league slapped a new rule in the book. From then on, all substitutes were ordered to stay on the bench for the duration of the game, no matter how cold they might get just sitting there."

Oh, Brother

IN AT LEAST ONE NHL GAME, played in Chicago on December 1, 1940, there were four sets of brothers on the ice. Lynn and Muzz Patrick and Neil and Mac Colville played for the Rangers; Max and Doug Bentley and Bill and Bob Carse were in uniform for the Black Hawks.

Ab Hoffman Fooled Everybody

THOUSANDS OF GIRLS PLAY organized hockey, and thousands of women register with hockey associations every year. In 1990 a team of Canadian women won the world's title in Ottawa, defeating the United States in a thrilling championship game. The next showcase for women's hockey could be the Olympic Games — as a demonstration sport initially.

Even though girls and women have been playing hockey for a hundred years, it has traditionally been a game where men and boys come first.

Back in 1955, eight-year-old Abigail Hoffman of Toronto took a good look at organized hockey and decided that girls weren't getting a fair chance to participate in this fast-moving game. Abby had played a lot of hockey with her brothers down at the corner rink, and she figured she was just as clever on skates as most of the boys in her age bracket. So she signed up as a player in the Toronto Hockey League as Ab Hoffman, defence.

And what a player Ab turned out to be! At the end of the season, the league officials named Ab to the all-star team. However, a routine check of Ab's birth certificate revealed an oddity. "He" was said to be a female. "No one noticed it earlier," said Earl Graham, the league chairman. "It knocked the wind out of us when we discovered Ab was a girl. Her birth certificate was mixed in with about 400 others, and nobody even thought about checking gender."

Suddenly, Abby's secret was out. And just as suddenly, she became a celebrity. Her story was in all the papers. She was interviewed on radio and television. She received invitations to see NHL games at the Montreal Forum and Maple Leaf Gardens.

Nobody tried to bar her from hockey. She kept on playing with her team — the Tee Pees — and was a popular member of the club. "She sure fooled us all, but we want her to stay with us," said teammate Russ Turnbull. "She's really good."

After two seasons in boys' hockey, Abby joined a girls' team. But she found it less exciting. So she quit the game and went on to excel in other sports, first swimming, then track and field. In time she became a world-class runner and competed in two Olympics. In 1972, she captured a bronze medal in the women's 800 at the Olympic Games in Munich, West Germany.

But she'll always be remembered as the girl hockey player who fooled everybody.

Mike Walton: Eccentric on Ice

WHEN MIKE WALTON retired from pro hockey a few years ago to enter the real estate business, he left behind a legacy of bizarre behavior in hockey.

Early in his career with the Toronto Maple Leafs, Walton showed up at Maple Leaf Gardens one night wearing a Beatles wig — his way of protesting coach Punch Imlach's ban on long hair and sideburns.

Broadcaster Harry Neale, who coached Walton when both were with Minnesota in the WHA, recalls the time Mike skated off the ice after a game with Houston. Instead of turning into the Minnesota dressing room to shower and change, Walton clomped across the cement floor toward the parking lot, jumped in his car and disappeared into the night. An hour later, according to one witness, Walton was spotted at his favorite bar, nursing a beer and still wearing his hockey uniform.

On a road trip, Neale had scheduled a practice session for his team in a suburban arena outside Winnipeg. Right next to the arena — as part of a sports complex — was a swimming pool. When the Minnesota players passed the pool en route to their dressing room, they saw a familiar figure waving at them through the large panes of glass. There was Mike Walton, perched on the high board and dressed in his full hockey uniform. His swan dive into the pool earned him a round of applause and a perfect 10 from his astonished mates, but with all that gear on, he almost drowned trying to get back to the surface.

Interviewed on television one night, Mike startled the host of the show by appearing naked, covered only in gobs of shaving cream.

Midway through a game in Minnesota, Neale couldn't believe his eyes. He looked down at his bench to see Walton engaged in a fistfight with Gord Gallant, one of his teammates. Neale had never before seen two teammates throwing punches at each other in the middle of a game. When the referee came over to investigate, Neale told the official, "Look, you can't give them penalties. They're both on the same side."

When Walton's play improved after the altercation with Gallant, Neale told his players, "Look, if you want to wake Mike up, take a poke at him."

The Ice Was Littered with Loot

EARLY IN THE CENTURY, many top hockey stars were lured to Northern Ontario by mining moguls who'd struck it rich in the area. Towns like Haileybury and Cobalt paid fabulous salaries — Art Ross once received $1000 to play two games in the Timiskaming Mines League. A game played in the Cobalt Arena ranks as one of the wildest on record.

In a previous game in Haileybury, Cobalt's bad man, Harry Smith, who had been imported from Ottawa at great expense, cut down so many Haileybury opponents that the police rushed to the arena and carted Smith off to jail. But Smith wasn't behind bars for long, and he got a hero's welcome when he showed up back in Cobalt for the return match.

Staggering sums were wagered on the outcome. One man bet $45,000 on Cobalt to win. Wealthy mining tycoon Noah Timmins figured Haileybury was the better team and wagered $50,000 on his hunch. His bet was quickly covered.

Timmins was counting heavily on the goaltending of stout Billy Nicholson, at 300 pounds, the world's largest netminder. When Nicholson took his place in goal, there were very few openings for a puck to go through.

But it didn't take Smith and his Cobalt mates long to find a few chinks in Nicholson's armor. They scored five quick goals against the mammoth goalie. Surprised and delighted to find themselves so far in front, the Cobalt players settled back to play a checking game.

Haileybury kept fighting in the second half, and

with Art Ross showing the way, the visitors struck back for five goals of their own to tie the score before the final buzzer. The teams would rest for a few minutes, then play overtime.

With his $50,000 bet on the line, Noah Timmins invaded the Haileybury dressing room and waved a thousand dollars in the air. "This is for the player who scores the winning goal," he promised. For highly motivated Horace Gaul, the bonus represented a season's pay. When play resumed, Horace grabbed the puck, rushed up the ice, scored the game-winner and collected the cash.

After the contest, delirious Haileybury fans showered the ice with money — unbelievable amounts of money. Players caught the bills and dived after the coins. But goalie Nicholson was the smartest of them all. He dragged a big washtub onto the ice and started filling it with cash. Then he turned the tub over and sat on it — all 300 pounds of him — until the hubbub died down. Nobody was going to dislodge him from his new-found loot.

This Game Was Never Finished

O N MARCH 14, 1933, Coach Tommy Gorman brought his Chicago Black Hawks into the Boston Garden for a battle with the Bruins. The Hawks were leading 2–1 with just two seconds left on the clock when Boston's great defence-man Eddie Shore rushed up the ice, shot and tied the score. Shore's goal forced a ten-minute over-time period. In that era, teams played a full ten minutes of overtime, not sudden death like today.

When the overtime began, the Bruins' Marty Barry promptly scored to put Boston in front 3–2, but the goal was hotly disputed by the Hawks. Referee Bill Stewart, whose grandson Paul is a current NHL official, skated over to the Chicago bench to explain the call to a furious Tommy Gorman.

When he heard Stewart's explanation, Gorman suddenly exploded in rage. He grabbed the official and shook him. He yanked the referee's sweater over his head and began battering him with his fists. The enraged Stewart, struggling to emerge from under his sweater, soon started pushing back. At least two of his punches left their mark on Gorman's ruddy face. It was a dandy fight, the players all agreed later.

Stewart had had enough of Gorman's belligerence. He threw the Chicago coach out of the game, and when Gorman balked at leaving, Stewart called for the cops. "Throw this man out!" he thundered, pointing at Gorman, who was still hurling insults at the referee.

Two of Boston's finest invaded the Chicago bench and began to wrestle with Gorman. The bewildered Hawk players didn't know whether to help their coach or not. But when they saw him being dragged away, they took off in pursuit. The cops called for reserves and threatened the players with jail if they didn't back off. Suddenly the visiting team's bench was empty — no players, no coach.

But that didn't bother Stewart. He pulled out his watch and gave the Chicago players one minute to return. When they failed to appear, he ruled that Gorman and the Hawks had forfeited the match. The Bruins won the abbreviated game by 3–2. It's the only time an NHL game has ended in this manner.

Ironically, it was referee Stewart who, four years later, took over as coach of the Hawks and guided them to the Stanley Cup.

The Player in Green

WOULD YOU BELIEVE ME if I told you that a member of the Toronto Maple Leafs once played in an NHL game while dressed in a green uniform?

It happened on March 17, 1934 — St. Patrick's Day — and the man in green was, of course, that irrepressible Irishman, defenceman King Clancy.

Clancy threw aside his traditional blue and white uniform that night and donned a green jersey with a large white shamrock stitched to the back. It was his night — King Clancy Night at the Gardens — and there's never been a night quite like it.

Before the game, a number of colorful floats were wheeled onto the ice surface. Out of a large potato popped several junior players. Leaf star Harold Cotton emerged from a mammoth top hat. George Hainsworth, the goalie, was hidden in a boot, while Red Horner, the Leaf tough guy, fought his way out of a huge boxing glove.

Then, with the arena lights dimmed, Clancy, the king of hockey, entered the arena riding a float in the shape of a throne. He was wearing royal robes and a silver crown. Clancy's pals, Charlie Conacher and Hap Day, helped him down from his throne, and when he turned to thank them they impishly hurled coal dust in his face.

After receiving a grandfather clock and a silver tea service as mementos of the occasion, Clancy, his face still black and his uniform green, went to work against the visiting Rangers.

But after one period, Ranger coach Lester Patrick had seen enough. He collared King and asked him to please change back to blue and white because his green shirt was too confusing to the Ranger players.

Teams They Never Played for Retired Their Jerseys

I HAVE OFTEN STUMPED fans and friends with the following trivia question: Name the players who had their numbers retired by NHL teams they never played for. The answer is: J. C. Tremblay and Johnny (Pie) McKenzie.

Let me explain how such an oddity happened. In 1972 J. C. Tremblay, a star defenseman for the Montreal Canadiens, jumped to the Quebec Nordiques of the WHA where he played for seven seasons. Just before the Nordiques joined the NHL for the 1979–80 season, Tremblay retired from hockey. A few months later the Nordiques (now in the NHL) retired his jersey number, even though he never played a game for the NHL version of the Nords.

A similar situation happened in Hartford, where Johnny McKenzie, during his WHA days with the New England Whalers, became a favorite with the team owner. Like J. C. Tremblay, Mackenzie retired

*All-Star
defenseman
J. C. Tremblay
checks out the
opposition.*
(Robert B. Shaver)

from the game before the Whalers became a member of the NHL. But the NHL Whalers, even though he never wore one of their jerseys, held a special ceremony for McKenzie and retired his number 19.

Pelted with Pucks

BACK IN 1972, Derek Sanderson was the most highly paid athlete in the world. He jumped from the Boston Bruins and signed a contract, worth a reported $2.65 million over five years, with the Philadelphia Blazers of the WHA.

Blazer fans — more than 5,000 of them clutching free pucks given out before the game — were anxious to see the Blazers perform in their home opener. But Sanderson, who'd been named team captain by coach John McKenzie, was injured in an exhibition game and unable to suit up for the contest.

Disappointed to begin with, the fans grew ugly when the Zamboni resurfacing the ice had a breakdown just before game time. It broke through the surface and was axle-deep in ice and slush. Arena officials deemed the playing surface in the refurbished Convention Center unsuitable for hockey. To make matters worse, hundred of fans arriving late for the game had left their cars parked at all angles in the arena parking lot, creating a massive tangle there.

There was no option — the game had to be postponed.

The team owner, Jim Cooper, asked Sanderson to accompany him on the ice and announce the cancellation to the crowd. When Cooper and Sanderson took the microphone and delivered the bad news, there was a chorus of boos and catcalls. Then the souvenir pucks started raining down — hundreds of them. But just before he ran for his life, Sanderson couldn't resist giving the crowd a parting shot. "Folks, if you think you're mad now, wait'll you try to get your cars out of the parking lot. It's a real mess out there."

Then he took off, dodging a hundred more pucks that came flying out of the stands.

Strange Objects on the Ice

OVER THE YEARS, I've seen some weird objects hit the ice during hockey games, especially during the playoffs.

Some of them were human, like the male streaker who vaulted the boards at Maple Leaf Gardens one night and made a run for the Leaf bench. Another night, in Los Angeles, three curvaceous ladies pranced from goal line to goal line clad only in their birthday suits.

Coins, programs and rotten eggs seem to be the most common items hurled by disgruntled fans. At the Los Angeles Forum one night, a Kings' fan tossed a live chicken, dressed in a purple uniform, over the boards.

A Detroit playoff series simply wouldn't be complete without a squid or an octopus making its annual appearance. Former NHL referee Red Storey says, "There's nothing as ugly or as slimy as one of those things on the ice. I'd always order a linesman or an arena worker to clean up the mess. I never wanted to touch one of them myself."

In 1975 a playoff game in Buffalo between the Sabres and the Flyers was held up by a low-flying bat, another creature players and officials try hard to avoid. Finally, Sabre forward Jim Lorentz whacked it with his stick, drawing a mixture of cheers and jeers from the fans. In the next few days, "Batman" Lorentz was inundated with letters. Most of the writers were sympathetic to the plight of the bat, and some even called Lorentz "heartless" and a "murderer."

In Quebec City several years ago, three little pigs, squealing in fright and dismay, were turned loose on the ice surface.

At the Montreal Forum in an era when it was customary to protect good shoe leather in winter, fans celebrated a big goal by the Rocket, Boom Boom or Big Jean by throwing their toe rubbers on the ice. Former Chicago Black Hawk winger

Dennis Hull likes to tell about the time his father took him aside before a big game at the Forum. Anticipating a fatherly pep talk, Dennis was surprised to hear his father say, "Son, when the Habs score tonight and the rubbers hit the ice, grab me a good pair, will you? Size ten."

One Hot Dog — To Go

RETIRED PRO GEORGE MORRISON recalls an embarrassing moment in his career when he toiled for the St. Louis Blues.

"I was never coach Scotty Bowman's favorite player," said Morrison, "and I was even less popular with him after a caper I pulled during a game at the Los Angeles Forum.

"We were on a long road trip, and I didn't get on the ice for two straight games. During the game in Los Angeles it looked like the same old story — I was told to suit up but not to count on getting much ice time.

"It was late in the game and I'd warmed the bench all evening. Suddenly I realized I was very hungry. Well, next to me at the end of the bench, I saw an usher eyeing my hockey stick. So I whispered to him, 'Pal, get me a hot dog, will you, and I'll give you my stick after the game.' The usher was back in a flash with the hot dog, and I was just sneaking my first bite (I waited until Scotty was looking the other way) when Bowman yelled at me, 'Morrison, get out there and kill that penalty!'

"What to do? As I leaped over the boards, I stuffed the hot dog down the cuff of my hockey glove. I didn't know what else to do with it. And wouldn't you know, seconds later, someone slammed into me in front of our net. Hit me so hard the hot dog popped free of my glove and flew up in the air. Out goalie made a stab at it and tried to knock it to one side while the other players ducked the flying relish and mustard.

"Fortunately, the whistle blew and a linesman moved in to clean up the mess. That's when Scotty Bowman yanked me off the ice. By then, he'd pretty much figured out what had happened and he was furious."

Morrison grinned. "It was a long time before he played me again."

Looking for the Winning Edge

OVER THE YEARS, NHL teams have always looked for the winning edge; the ploy, the maneuver, the little gimmick that might bring success.

Back in 1960, the Detroit Red Wings tried something new — oxygen on their bench. Players gulped oxygen from the tank, hoping it would give them increased stamina and pay off in a goal or two. It didn't help Murray Oliver much. Perhaps that was because he forgot to turn the valve on the tank that released the oxygen.

The Red Wings once kept a container of yogurt in the dressing room. Players were expected to grab a spoonful of it every time they passed by. It, too, was supposed to improve performance.

The Rangers were also noted for off-ice gimmicks. One season coach Lester Patrick ordered his players to drink a glassful of hot water first thing every morning, whether they thought they needed it or not.

A famous restaurant owner in New York came around one time with a so-called magic elixir to sell, made from the secret recipe of Momma Leone. The elixir would put more speed into the feet of the sluggish Rangers, he promised. But after the team suffered a lengthy losing streak, the magic elixir went down the drain, along with the Rangers' playoff hopes.

Another time, a New York hypnotist, Dr. Tracey, was hired to hypnotize the Rangers into believing they were a winning team. The hypnotist knew his stuff. When he talked to the players, eyes soon shut and heads dropped to chests.

One of the Rangers, Tony Leswick, was so deep in a trance that coach Frank Boucher became worried. "They look so listless, so out of it," he complained. "And they've got a big game to play tonight." He ordered Dr. Tracey to snap his players out of their deep sleep.

The hypnotist said, "You're the boss," and in a few moments all the players were wide-awake.

As the players filed out for the warm-up, Tony Leswick winked at Boucher. "You gotta be weak-minded for that hypnosis stuff," he said. "The old doc didn't do anything for me."

The Homeless Hockey Team

COACH TOM WEBSTER knows all about adversity. An inner ear problem threatened to keep him out of the NHL coaching ranks when flying to games aggravated the condition. Because of the pain, loss of balance and dizzy spells, Webster was forced to resign as New York Ranger coach in 1986 after a mere 16 games. Months later, after surgery corrected the problem, he resurfaced in an enviable position as coach of the Los Angeles Kings.

No matter what he accomplishes at the NHL level, Webster will be hard-pressed to surpass an achievement that stands out on his minor-league record. In 1983-84 he took a team destined for the scrap heap and directed it to a championship nobody dreamed it was capable of winning.

Webster was coaching the Tulsa Oilers of the Central League that season. But he had major worries right from the start. The team ran into financial problems early in the year, and by mid-season the owners packed it in. They simply quit — but the players didn't. The players held a meeting and voted to struggle on — without any owners and without a home rink in which to play. League officials, understandably dubious about the future of the franchise, granted them permission to play out the schedule, with all their games to be played on the road.

Leaving wives and sweethearts behind in Tulsa, the Oilers stayed in cheap hotels and often slept on the team bus. They changed their name to the CHL Oilers but they might as well have been called the Homeless Oilers. They were hockey nomads — the only team in history without a home base.

Occasionally, the Oilers were able to practice in Tulsa, on a rink located in a shopping mall. But they skated without sticks or pucks because owners of nearby stores feared broken windows and other damage from flying disks. To stay in shape, the players moved a soccer ball around the ice. Webster borrowed some tennis racquets and kept his goalies jumping by whipping tennis balls at them.

Somehow, Webster's Oilers survived their season of grueling road trips, zero fan support and infrequent pay cheques. Perhaps adversity toughened them because they displayed amazing strength in the playoffs, sweeping Indianapolis aside in the final series to capture the league championship and the Adams Cup.

"I'll never forget our victory parade," says Webster, who was named Coach of the Year. "It was held in the hotel bar. Then we marched outside and paraded around the team bus. The players on the team were very special. They accepted every challenge and overcame every obstacle. I'll always feel very, very close to them."

A Costly Broken Curfew

IN THE CAMPBELL CONFERENCE finals of 1988, the Edmonton Oilers were leading the Detroit Red Wings three games to one. It would take a miraculous comeback for the Red Wings to advance along the playoff trial. One more loss and their season would be over.

Some of the Red Wings obviously gave up all hope of a comeback, for on the eve of game five, seven Red Wings went out partying. They stopped to have a few beers at a popular bar in Edmonton. And wouldn't you know it, they stayed far too late, broke curfew and were caught.

Well now, how much do you figure breaking

curfew can cost a guy? A surprising amount, as it turned out. They were fined, of course — the maximum allowable fine of $500.

But that was just the beginning of their punishment. In the off season some of the curfew breakers were released or traded. That proved costly, because Detroit owner Mike Ilitch is known as one of hockey's most generous owners. When contracts are up for renewal in Detroit, most players leave the bargaining table feeling like lucky lottery winners.

Just ask coach Jacques Demers, who received a $50,000 raise from Ilitch that season, making him the highest-paid coach in hockey at around $300,000 per season. Or ask John Ogrodnick, who, when he scored 50 goals one season, received a $50,000 bonus from the owner, even though he was not compelled contractually to give one.

When the 1988 playoffs were over, and the league forwarded each Red Wing player $16,000 in bonus money, Ilitch generously matched that amount. So the Red Wings received an additional $16,000. All of them, that is, but the seven curfew breakers who stayed late at the bar.

So curfew-breaking proved to be costly for the seven Red Wings. A $500 fine added to the loss of the boss's bonus comes to $16,500. Too bad. That kind of money would have kept them in beer all summer long. Well, most of the summer, anyway.

The Coach Answers the Call

IT HAPPENED IN MONTREAL during the Stanley Cup playoffs of 1928, in a final series between the Montreal Maroons and the New York Rangers.

After losing game one, the Rangers ran into grief in game two. Lorne Chabot, New York's steady goaltender, was felled by a Nels Stewart shot and left the ice with blood streaming from a cut over his eye.

Ranger coach Lester Patrick, with no spare goalie, asked permission to use Alex Connell of Ottawa, who was a spectator at the game. "No way," said the Maroons, aware that Connell had played six consecutive games for Ottawa earlier in the season without allowing a single goal. Patrick was handed an edict — either find a goalie in ten minutes or forfeit the game.

So white-haired Lester Patrick, age 44, who'd played in goal perhaps once in his long playing career, decided to put on the pads himself. He told his players, "You fellows check and check hard. I'll need all the help I can get."

If the Maroons felt that Patrick would be an easy mark when they saw him shuffle awkwardly onto the ice, they were mistaken. Patrick played remarkably well, allowing just one goal on 18 shots as the Rangers won in overtime.

After the game, Patrick was mobbed by his mates. In the dressing room, surrounded by reporters, he played down his remarkable feat. "I stopped only six or seven really hard shots," he said with a grin. "And my teammates saved the old man with their backchecking."

The Rangers, with Chabot back in harness,

went on to win the Stanley Cup, and they were treated like heroes when they returned to New York. Especially Lester Patrick, the coach-turned-goaltender. Mayor Jimmy Walker, who'd recently hailed the return of Charles Lindbergh from France and organized a ticker-tape parade for Babe Ruth after his 60-home run season, embraced Patrick at City Hall while thousands cheered and flashbulbs popped.

Playoff Fiasco in New Jersey

THERE WAS TENSION in the air before game four of the playoff series between New Jersey and Boston in 1988. Game three of the Wales Conference final had ended on a shocking note — with Devils' coach Jim Schoenfeld confronting referee Don Koharski in a hallway at the Brendan Byrne Arena. Schoenfeld was livid and called Koharski a "fat pig" among other things. For his outburst, Schoenfeld was suspended.

Between playoff games, in an unprecedented move, the Devils served the league with a restraining order from a New Jersey court, a directive that allowed Schoenfeld to continue coaching. NHL officials were shocked. They couldn't believe a member club would resort to the courts to plead its case. The repercussions were dramatic, and for a time threatened the completion of the series.

The New Jersey move triggered a wildcat strike by the game officials for game four, led by veteran referee Dave Newell, who demanded safer working conditions in the arena. In effect, the officials, including the backup crew, went on strike.

League officials frantically sought substitute officials and came up with 52-year-old amateur ref Paul McInnis, and two linesmen — 51-year-old Vin Godleski and 50-year-old Jim Sullivan. Only McInnis could find a referee's shirt. The linesmen wore yellow practice jerseys and green pants and skated on borrowed skates. The combined age of the recruits — 153; their NHL experience — 0.

And where was NHL president John Ziegler while all this was going on? He'd disappeared and nobody could find him.

The game was played and New Jersey won. Later, peace was restored when the league agreed to rescind Schoenfeld's suspension until a hearing could be arranged. The NHL's regular officials quickly agreed to return to work.

Boston's Harry Sinden had the final word about the amateur officials. "We took three guys out of the stands," he said, "and the difference between them and our regular guys was marginal."

Dinny "Dollar Bill" Dinsmore

IN 1930 MANAGER DUNC MUNRO of the Montreal Maroons said he was ready to believe in Santa Claus and the tooth fairy after a conversation with chunky defenseman Charlie "Dinny" Dinsmore. Dinsmore, a heavily built little player who had been a popular Maroon until the 1928–29 season, asked manager Munro if he could make a comeback — for the princely sum of a dollar a year.

Munro instantly agreed. How often does a manager get an opportunity to sign a proven big leaguer for the price of a good cigar? Dinsmore, known as "the pest" for his ability to shadow opposing scoring stars, was only 27 years old. He had retired a few months earlier to become a bond salesman, but the lure of the game was strong. So he became the first player in history to sign a contract for a dollar.

Alas, Dinny failed to become the bargain Munro hoped he would be. His skills had faded and he was quickly released.

"I thought I could make a defenseman out of him," Munro said, "but he couldn't handle the position. But hey, it only cost me a buck to find out."

A Bonus in Buffalo

A LITTLE-KNOWN STORY in Buffalo Sabre hockey history concerns a player named Paul McIntosh. He didn't stay around long, but when Floyd Smith was coaching there, McIntosh figured in a most unusual incident. He had played in 39 games for Buffalo one season and his contract called for a $15,000 bonus if he took part in 40 games. Smith had orders from GM Punch Imlach to let McIntosh dress for game number 40, but under no circumstances was he to get any ice time.

With the season just about over, Imlach figured to save his club 15 grand if McIntosh didn't play. But late in the game the Sabre players decided to take matters into their own hands. With two minutes to play, three or four Sabres grabbed McIntosh and, despite his protests, physically threw him onto the ice while the team was changing lines "on the fly." There was nothing Smith or Imlach could do. The few seconds McIntosh played were enough to count as an "official" appearance, and Imlach grudgingly awarded McIntosh his bonus. He even played him in two more games, giving McIntosh a chance to score his first goal of the season. But McIntosh failed to produce.

Let's Get the Puck Out of Here

THE BOSTON BRUINS and the New York Americans played a pair of unique games during the 1931–32 season. On December 8, 1931, in Boston the Americans shot the puck down the ice at every opportunity. Although boring to the fans, it was a great way to take the pressure off while playing a superior team. Since no rules had yet been devised to prevent "icing the puck," the Bruins spent most of the evening chasing the disk back into their own zone. That night it happened 61 times, leaving the Boston players frustrated and their fans furious.

Bruins owner Charles Adams vowed to get even. On January 3, 1932, in a game played on New York ice, Boston "iced the puck" 87 times. The two games rank as perhaps the most boring ever played. Some of the NHL owners felt that Adams should have been fined up to $10,000 for retaliation, but NHL president Frank Calder said no. Under the existing rules his players had every right to do what they did. Then Calder immediately introduced a rule designed to curb icing the puck, one that prevented a recurrence of the farce.

A Hockey Riot in Britain

IN 1937 LONDON, ENGLAND, was the site of the world amateur hockey championships, and British fans were wildly excited about the prospects of a gold medal for their team. The British squad, stacked with Canadians born in Great Britain, had gone through the tournament without surrendering a single goal. Jimmy Foster, a sturdy goalkeeper formerly with the Moncton Hawks, had chalked up seven shutouts in seven games — a remarkable feat — and a victory over Canada in the semifinal game would all but ensure the world title for Britain.

The big game, played at Harringay Arena, attracted over 10,000 fans. They looked on in dismay as Canada's Allan Cup champions, the Kimberley, B.C., Dynamiters, beat Foster for three goals and won 3–0. The angry mob decided at game's end that the referee was to blame, and M. Poplemont of Belgium fled for his life at the final buzzer. He was showered with garbage — tin cans, beer bottles, apples, and oranges — as he made a hasty exit. Several youths chased him, and he was forced to seek sanctuary in a nearby restaurant under police protection.

Back at the arena the mob turned on the Canadian players, and several might have been beaten up but for the intervention of 50 sailors from the Canadian sloop *Frazer*. They surrounded the hockey players and fought off the assaults of the fans, who accused the Dynamiters of dirty tactics.

Frustrated at being unable to pummel the players, the fans then roughed up several attendants and arena employees and smashed countless windows in the building. The riot rocked the arena for close to an hour and was finally stopped by an enterprising band leader. He assembled his musicians, most of whom were changing into street clothes in a dressing room, and led them in a rendition of "God Save the King."

The rampaging throng stood stock-still for a moment, then slowly began removing their hats. A few even sang the anthem. When the last strains died away, everybody was so calm that the arena was cleared in a matter of minutes.

The riot was called the worst in many years in British sport. The Kimberley boys must have been rattled by the experience, because they were hard-pressed to edge Switzerland 2–1 in overtime in their final game. They captured the world crown with eight straight victories, six of them shutouts. England won 5–0 over Germany (a seventh shutout for Jimmy Foster) to take the runner-up position.

Watch Out for the Bandstand!

DURING THE SEASON OF 1885–86, the first college game in Kingston, Ontario, was played between Queen's University and the Royal Military College. The site of the game was in an open-air rink in Kingston harbor, where many games of shinny had been played over the years.

The cadets from the Royal Military College ordered new sticks from Halifax for the big match, sticks made out of small planed-down trees with the curved roots carved into blades. The Queen's players were green with envy when the new sticks arrived, and they insisted on being supplied with a half dozen, as well — otherwise they might not show up for the game.

The most bizarre feature of this historic matchup was a bandstand — right in the middle of the ice. Out of the bandstand rose an electric light standard. Strangely none of the players complained about this hazard, even though the opposing goalies couldn't see what was happening on the far side of the structure.

The play was very close, but in the final few minutes the bandstand turned the tide in favor of Queen's. Their star player, Lennox Irving, swept around the bandstand and looked up to make his shot on goal. Incredibly the RMC net was empty. Off to the side the rival goalie and one of his point men were sitting in a snowbank. The point man was struggling to strap on the goalie's skate, which had slipped from his foot. They had relied on having a few seconds to secure the blade to the boot because the play had moved into the Queen's zone moments earlier.

Now, with Irving racing toward them, the cadets scrambled back onto the ice. But they were too late. Irving's shot found the empty goal. If the cadets thought of registering a protest, it wouldn't have done them much good, for there was no goal judge in this game and no referee. The teams hadn't thought there was any need for outside help. They abided by the rules they had set themselves and everybody agreed that Queen's had won an exciting victory.

Waiting in Wetaskiwin

IN 1948–49 ROY BENTLEY (one of the brothers in the famous Bentley clan from Delisle, Saskatchewan) was coaching the Wetaskiwin Canadians in the northern Alberta Junior Hockey League. Wetaskiwin was little more than a dot on a prairie map, but hockey was a serious business there. Many of the players were imports, and the club had the backing of the NHL's Chicago Blackhawks.

In the league finals Wetaskiwin met the Edmonton Athletic Club "We always had troubles with Edmonton, and that playoff year was no exception," Bentley said. Sure enough, Edmonton won the first two games and the series moved south to Wetaskiwin.

That was when Bentley decided to make full use of home ice advantage and a supportive crowd. Before the start of the first period he kept the Wetaskiwin players in their dressing room an abnormally long time. This ruse allowed the hometown fans a chance to verbally abuse the visitors while they skated in lazy circles around the ice.

Before the second period Bentley's boys stayed in their room even longer, and once again the Edmonton players on the ice were booed and harassed unmercifully. But Bentley's strategy went awry before the third period got under way. The Edmonton players decided to give the Canadians and their fans a taste of their own medicine. Clarence Moher, the Edmonton coach, ordered his players to stay put. They were not to step outside their dressing room until they heard the home team clomping down the corridor toward the ice. And the waiting game was on. The Wetaskiwin players remained behind their dressing room door, while across the hall the Edmonton players waited them out. Players on both teams chewed their gum, sucked on oranges, and waited some more.

The intermission stretched into 10, 15, then 20 minutes. An angry referee and his linesmen banged on both doors and ordered the clubs back onto the ice. The players ignored them.

Occasionally a player would peek through a small hole in the door to see if the other club had budged. "I opened the door a crack and peeked out once," Bentley recalled, "and there was Clarence Moher peeking back at me. Looked like he was determined to sit there all night if necessary."

Finally the referee said, "That's it, boys! There'll be no more hockey tonight." And he called the third period off. The players, no doubt feeling a bit foolish, slowly shed their uniforms and showered while the fans who jammed the arena were left wondering what in blazes had occurred behind the scenes to cause the game to be canceled.

Both coaches were suspended for promoting such ridiculous stalling tactics. Incidentally Edmonton went on to win the series.

He Played for One Club While Coaching Another

THERE WERE SOME mighty strange goings-on in English hockey during the thirties. In 1937 Len Burrage, a defenseman from Winnipeg, made history by playing for one club while coaching another — in the same league.

The British Ice Hockey Association saw nothing unusual in Burrage holding down a defense position with Harringay while toiling as coach of the Manchester Rapids, another member of the 11-team league.

But there was one date on the schedule that troubled the association. On March 2 Harringay was pitted against Manchester. Would Burrage act as player or coach? The fans submitted all kinds of suggestions. One thought he should play a period for each team and then coach in the third period. Another thought his role should be decided by a coin flip. A third thought he should take a neutral position and referee the game. Yet another suggested he stay at home and read a good book.

As it turned out, the association made the decision for Burrage. After a vote was taken, Burrage was ordered to play in the game because he had joined Harringay before accepting the coaching position with Manchester.

That same year another player in the British league had a similar problem. Baron Richard Von Trauttenberg, who played with Streatham, journeyed with his team on a tour of Europe. But when Streatham got to Vienna, Von Trauttenberg deserted his club and joined the opposing team. Seems he had recently been named captain of the Austrian national team and felt honor-bound to play at least one game for his country's representatives.

Ivan Lost His Nose

WHEN IVAN MATULIK left his native Czecho-slovakia to join the Halifax Citadels of the American Hockey League, he thought he was prepared for anything: a new lifestyle, initia-tions, an 80-game schedule, long bus rides, fast food — the works.

One thing he hadn't planned on was losing part of his nose. The accident occurred during the 1991–92 season on a Halifax road trip, and it happened so quickly that Ivan isn't quite sure how it transpired. During the play, players collided. A skate blade arced past Ivan's face and neatly sliced off part of his nose.

Blood flowed as he left the ice to be given immedi-ate attention by the team trainer and doctors. He was told part of his nose was missing. But could it be found? Could it be reattached?

By this time the period was over and the Zamboni was circling the ice. It had already passed over the area of the ice where the accident had occurred. The missing tip of Ivan's nose must be inside the machine, mixed in with a pile of slush and snow.

When the Zamboni dumped its chilly load, the search began. It was like looking for a needle in a haystack. But the searchers were rewarded when one of them held up a pink piece of flesh.

Ivan Matulik and the tip of his nose were rushed to hospital where a surgeon skillfully reattached it. Ivan was told by doctors that operations of this type were often quite successful. It was fortunate, he was told, that the nose tip had been surrounded by ice and snow.

Today Ivan's nose looks and feels perfectly normal. He is thankful he got prompt medical attention and he knows now that a hockey player has to be prepared for anything, even the loss of part of his anatomy.

Bizarre Olympic Victory for Great Britain

IN THE EARLY THIRTIES Bunny Ahearne was becoming a person to be reckoned with in international hockey. And it was Ahearne who was responsible for putting the first blight on Canada's unblemished hockey record at the Olympics in 1936.

Months prior to the Olympic Games the wily entrepreneur compiled a list of all amateur players in Canada who had been born in the British Isles. Most had immigrated to Canada as young children and over the years had mastered most of hockey's skills in Canadian rinks. The best of these amateurs were lured to London by Ahearne, who found a league for them to play in and slipped them as much as $50 a week to cover expenses. One of the most talented was goaltender Jimmy Foster.

Ahearne recruited yet another Canadian, Percy Nicklin, to coach a team in his house league, and when the Winter Olympics of 1936 were staged in Garmisch, Germany, Ahearne assembled a "British" entry composed of the London-based imports with the experienced Nicklin at the helm.

The Canadian representatives that year were from Port Arthur — the Bearcats, a team of little distinction and one that had to be bolstered by five good players from the Montreal area before leaving

Canada. The Bearcats ran into a stone wall when they faced Jimmy Foster and the British entry in what they were led to believe was a semifinal match. Foster played the game of his life and yielded just one goal while his mates managed two. It was the first defeat ever for Canada in Olympic hockey competition. Despite the loss, the Canadian players weren't talking about revenge. Ahead lay the final round of the tournament, and they looked forward to getting another crack at Foster.

Then came an astonishing statement from Ahearne. He insisted that a final-round match was out of the question. It was unnecessary, since Canada had already lost once to his British team. Furious, Canadian officials entered a strong protest, and an emergency meeting was called at which a smiling Ahearne said, "Fine, let's vote on it." To Canada's disgust five nations sided with Ahearne, a man once described by a journalist as "capable of acting unscrupulously to gain his own advantage." Only Germany felt the Canadian team was being cheated of their rightful chance at the title.

Ahearne smirked as Britain was awarded the gold medal, even though the British had played one less game than Canada and had fewer tournament wins. Canada's records was 7–1, Britain's 5–2.

Bizarre? You bet.

For the next four decades Ahearne was a sharp thorn in the hide of Canadian hockey. Jim Coleman, one of Canada's most highly respected hockey writers, in his book *Hockey Is Our Game,* called Ahearne "a Machiavellian strategist" and "a double-dealing, self-serving little rascal from the opening face-off to the final buzzer."

Despite his wily ways and the antipathy he often

showed toward Canadians, Ahearne was honored by the Hockey Hall of Fame in 1977. His induction surprised many, including Jim Coleman, who wrote: "Nothing he did in his old age appeared to qualify him for the honor of enshrinement in the Hockey Hall of Fame, that is, primarily, a Canadian institution."

Leaders in the Futility League

THE 1928–29 CHICAGO BLACKHAWKS were arguably the most inept NHL team ever. That season the Hawks stumbled their way through eight straight games without scoring a single goal. They were shut out 21 times in the 44-game schedule and managed to score only 33 goals for the season. Vic Ripley was their leading scorer with 11 goals and two assists for 13 points.

But were the 1928–29 Hawks any worse than the Washington Capitals, a seventies expansion team? The Caps barely survived 1974–75, their initial NHL season. During an 80-game season, Washington shattered a modern-day record for futility with a mark of eight wins, 67 losses, and five ties. The Caps didn't merely lose games that season; they were humiliated in almost every outing. Twice they lost by 12–1 scores. They lost other games by 11–1 and 10–0. In one 11-game stretch they were shut out five times. By the end of the season they had given up 446 goals while scoring only 181. Along the way they established one NHL record for consecutive losses with 17 and another for consecutive losses on the road —

37. The team went through three coaches — Jim Anderson, who lasted 54 games (4–45–5), Red Sullivan (2–17), and Milt Schmidt (2–5). In the 1992–93 season the Caps did find some relief from their ignominy. The new Ottawa Senators franchise lost 38 consecutive games on the road to break the Caps' record.

One of the Washington forwards was 19-year-old Mike Marson, a black player who wasn't close to being ready for the rough grind of the NHL. Marson was the only player not to wear underwear under his white hockey pants. Under the bright lights, and when Marson started to sweat, it looked as if he wasn't wearing any pants at all. The fans thought it was pretty funny, and after a while the players were given new blue pants and used the white ones only in practice.

Two games stand out in the memory of Tommy Williams, who led the team in scoring and consoled his mates with words like "We've got a good team, fellows. We're just in the wrong league." The Caps finally snapped their 37-game road losing streak with a victory over the California Seals in Oakland in late March 1975. Recently, reflecting on that game with *Washington Times* sportswriter David Elfin, Williams said, "We grabbed an old trash can and painted it with a magic marker. Then, half dressed, we paraded that trash can over our heads and skated around the Oakland Arena. You'd think we'd just won the Stanley Cup.

"And in our final home game of the season," Williams adds, "we beat Pittsburgh 8–4, and Stan Gilbertson, who later lost a leg in an auto accident, scored three goals in three minutes and 26 seconds, a record for an American-born player. An old goat like me [Williams was 34] set a club record in that game with six points. After the game, the fans came out on the ice and we posed for photos with them and signed autographs. It was a nice ending to a very long season."

She Played Like a Man

WOMEN'S HOCKEY IN CANADA goes back a hundred years. When Lord Stanley donated the Stanley Cup in 1893, girls in long skirts were already pushing pucks around the ice at the Rideau Hall rink in Ottawa. One of the best of the lady players was a lass with the intriguing name of Lulu Lemoine.

From 1915 to 1917 Cornwall, Ontario, produced a crack ladies team named the Vics. Whenever the Vics traveled to Ottawa or Montreal for games, huge crowds turned out to watch the action. Fans were particularly fascinated by the sparkling play of a girl named Albertine Lapansee, a high-scoring forward on that Cornwall team. Lapansee scored about 80 percent of her team's goals. She was slight but fast, a beautiful skater, and a remarkable stickhandler and shooter.

By 1918 Lapansee's name disappeared from the Cornwall sports pages, and as a hockey historian and researcher, I wondered why. So I journeyed to Cornwall in the summer of 1992 and met with one of Albertine's relatives, a 72-year-old man named Connie Lapansee.

"Connie," I said, "your famous aunt was the best female hockey player in Canada years ago, but in my research I can find no trace of her after 1917. Whatever happened to Albertine?"

"Brian," he replied, "she had a strange life. Albertine quit playing women's hockey after the 1917 season and moved to New York. There she had a sex change operation and became a man. Of course, she changed her name, too. When she came back home sometime later, well, I should say when *he* came back home, he was known as Albert Smith. He was married by then and he and his bride opened a service station not far from Cornwall."

And that is the bizarre ending to the story of Albertine Lapansee who, for a couple of incredible seasons, was known as the best female hockey player in Canada.

A Strange Penalty Shot Call

LOTS OF NHL PLAYERS get to take a penalty shot in their careers, and two players, Pat Egan and Greg Terrion, even share a record of scoring two penalty shot goals in a season. In the seventies Phil Hoene, a Los Angeles Kings rookie, scored his first NHL goal on a penalty shot, while Chicago goalie Michel Belhumeur once stopped two penalty shots in one game. But only one NHL player has ever scored on two free shots within a matter of seconds.

It happened in the forties when Jackie Hamilton was a budding young star with the Toronto Maple Leafs. Hamilton was pulled down by Boston's Dit Clapper one night, and the referee awarded him a penalty shot. But in those days the league rules called for two types of penalty shots — a major and a minor. For a major penalty shot the referee spotted the puck at center ice and the player taking the shot moved in on the goalie and shot from point-blank range — just as they do today. But for a minor penalty shot the puck was spotted 28 feet out from the goal and the player — without being able to move in on goal — fired it from there.

When Hamilton was preparing for his free shot, the referee became confused. He placed the puck at center ice, not at the 28-foot mark where it belonged. Hamilton promptly grabbed the disk, raced in, and scored.

Then a loud argument erupted. The rival coach banged the boards and pointed out the referee's mistake. He maintained the shot had been taken from the wrong point. Everyone's temper rose except Hamilton's. Finally the referee said, "Jackie, you're going to have to take the shot over again, this time from inside the blue line."

"Fine with me," the obliging Hamilton said. "You're the boss."

Hamilton lined up, blasted a hard shot past the goaltender, and skated away, grinning. Two penalty shots, two pucks in the net. "Yeah," Hamilton said later, laughing, "but I only got credit for one of them."

You're on the Wrong Bench, Picard

WHEN THE ST. LOUIS BLUES joined the NHL as an expansion team in 1967, one of their most popular players was a big defenseman named Noel Picard. But there were nights when Picard didn't appear to be totally focused on the game.

Midway through an important game against Boston Picard finished his shift and headed for the bench. Problem was, he went to the Bruins' bench by mistake. Maybe he was thinking about how to stop Bobby Orr or Phil Esposito. Perhaps, subconsciously, he wanted to get away from the sharp tongue of his coach, Scotty Bowman. He was never able to explain his action.

The Boston trainer, Frosty Forrestal, when he saw Picard approaching, opened the gate to the bench and waved him in. Picard found a spot on the pine, sat down, and play resumed. Only when he looked around did he notice something strange — everyone around him was wearing Boston colors.

What to do? The players and fans were laughing at his predicament, while across the rink Blues coach Scotty Bowman was livid and shaking a fist in his direction. Squirming with embarrassment, Picard decided to act. When the play went into the Bruins' zone, he leaped over the boards, dashed across the ice, and dived in among his teammates. He was praying nobody would notice his three-second sprint to the home team bench.

Alas, out of the corner of his eye, the referee had spotted Picard's leap off the Bruins' bench and blew his whistle just as the red-faced defenseman scrambled over the boards on the far side of the rink.

"Too many men on the ice!" he barked as he penalized the Blues for two minutes, causing Scotty Bowman's blood pressure to soar even higher.

As for Picard, he put his head down like a whipped dog. He knew his gaffe would provide a million laughs for hockey people for decades to come.

King Clancy Serves as a Goal Judge

THE LATE KING CLANCY was hockey's jack-of-all-trades. In his career he was a player, a coach, a referee, and an executive. And on at least two occasions he served as a goal judge during a game — a role he didn't particularly relish. Here is how he described his first stint as the official in charge of the red light.

"When I was with the Leafs in the thirties, I came down to Maple Leaf Gardens one day to watch a junior game between Niagara Falls and the Ottawa Primroses. Midway through the game, there was a problem with the goal judge. Whether the fellow got sick or fell off his stool and hurt himself, I don't recall. But they did ask me to fill in for him. I said, 'Sure, I'll help out. What's so hard about being a goal judge?'

"Remember, in those days, there was no protective cage to sit in. Nothin' like that. The goal judge sat right in with the crowd, more or less. I just got settled in my position when the Ottawa boys scored a goal. At least I thought they scored one because I snapped on the red light.

"I was amazed at what happened next. Some of the fans were jolted right out of their seats when they saw that little red light flash on. They began screaming at me, claiming that the puck didn't go into the net. A bunch of the Niagara Falls fans — a really tough-looking gang — began leaping over the seats, headed in my direction.

"I'll tell you. I cleared out of there in a hurry. The cops were called and it was a long time before I could resume my place. And during the rest of the game, I kept sneaking looks over my shoulder to make sure I wasn't going to get attacked again.

"After that game, I vowed I'd never be a goal judge again, but I was persuaded to take the job on one other occasion. It was another big junior game at the Gardens, and I was handling the job well — that is, until I became the victim of a cruel practical joke.

During the play, the puck was lofted up against the side of the net just in front of me. The puck didn't even come close to going in the net, but suddenly the crowd was in an uproar. Fans were screaming at me and shaking their fists at me and I

Jack-of-all-trades King Clancy — he had a million and one stories.
(Hockey Hall of Fame)

had no idea why they were so outraged. I hadn't flashed the red light. But *somebody* had, because when I looked up it was on.

"The referee skated up to me and asked, 'What's the matter with you, King? Why'd you turn the light on?'

"'I never touched the light,' I told him. 'Maybe there's an electrical problem.' I couldn't believe this was happening to me.

"That's when I glanced over and saw Charlie Conacher standing nearby. He was laughing his head off. Well, I knew right then how the red light got turned on. Charlie had sneaked up behind me, reached around, and flipped the light switch. Right then and there I decided to get out of the goal-judging business. It had too many surprises to suit me."

The Trainer Got into the Game

IT WAS THURSDAY, APRIL 20, 1989, at the Calgary Saddledome. The hometown Flames jumped into a 3–0 lead over the visiting Los Angeles Kings in game two of their best-of-seven playoff series.

Then, in a goal-mouth skirmish, Bernie Nicholls of the Kings punched Flames goaltender Mike Vernon in the head, sending him sprawling to the ice. Referee Bill McCreary signaled a delayed penalty as play moved out of the Calgary zone.

That was when Calgary trainer Jim "Bearcat" Murray, reacting to Vernon's injury, leaped over the boards and onto the ice. He dashed straight for Vernon and began administering to him. Meanwhile the Flames were buzzing around the Kings' goal at the other end of the rink. Moments later they were rewarded when Al MacInnis slammed in a goal.

Some of the Kings protested. "Look, their trainer jumped over the boards while the play was on. Isn't that 'too many men on the ice'?" McCreary, who had never encountered such a situation before, opted for a commonsense decision and allowed the goal to stand.

The NHL's director of officiating, the late John McCauley, said, "I'd never seen anything like it, either. McCreary didn't see Murray come on the ice and he let the play continue. In his judgment he had to count the goal. It was the right call."

Someone who keeps track of such things figured the Flames had an extra man on the ice — Bearcat Murray, the trainer — for about 12 seconds when MacInnis tallied. Murray came in for a lot of postgame kidding from the Flames, but he had the perfect answer. "Boys, all I know is I'm plus one for the playoffs."

Game Delayed — the Coaches Are Missing

DURING THE 1988 Stanley Cup playoffs, in a game between the St. Louis Blues and the Chicago Blackhawks, Chicago coach Bob Murdoch called for a strategy meeting during the first intermission. He and his assistant coaches entered a small room next to the team dressing room. Murdoch was the last man in, so he slammed the door hard behind him. A bit too hard obviously, for when the meeting broke up, none of the coaches could get the door open again. Arena workers arrived on the scene, but they, too, were unable to open the door. Meanwhile the fans were growing restless and many clamored for a resumption of play. Suddenly an unsung hero saved the day. Riding up on a forklift, he wheeled his machine toward the door, crashed into it, and sent it flying. The three coaches stepped over the broken pieces, dusted themselves off, and returned to their coaching duties.

Pilous Pulled His Goalie — with Amazing Results

IN THE LATE FIFTIES the St. Catharines Tee Pees were playing the Toronto Marlboros in a critical playoff game. During the last minute of play, with the Marlies leading 5–4, many fans headed for the exits of the St. Catharines Arena. They wanted to beat the rush to the parking lot.

With 28 seconds left on the clock, there was a face-off in the St. Catharines zone. That was when Tee Pees coach Rudy Pilous decided to take his biggest hockey gamble. He pulled his goalie. Netminder Marv Edwards was furious when Pilous waved him to the bench. "Have you lost your friggin' mind?" he squawked. "The face-off is right next to our net."

"Sit down, kid!" Pilous ordered. "Let's see what happens."

Anticipating an easy empty-net goal, the grinning Marlboros couldn't wait for the puck to be dropped. Meanwhile the fans howled their displeasure, and the Tee Pee players glared at the man who appeared to be handing the game to the Toronto boys.

When the puck was dropped, the Marlies pounced on it, all of them eager to fire the disk into the empty net. But somehow it was a Tee Pee who came up with the rubber. Hugh Barlow raced down the ice with 12 seconds to play and banged in the tying goal.

There was bedlam in the arena. In the parking lot fans leaped out of their vehicles and raced back to reclaim their seats for the overtime.

Pilous made all the right moves in overtime. His team won the game and went on to capture the Memorial Cup. Even today in St. Catharines old-timers love to talk about the day Pilous pulled his goaltender and dared the Marlies to score into the nearby empty net.

PLAYOFF HEROICS
AND CUP CAPERS

Lord Stanley Missed All the Excitement

WHO IS THE ONLY MAN named to the Hockey Hall of Fame who never played, coached, refereed, managed or owned a hockey club? He never broadcast a game or wrote about one in the papers. In fact, he never even witnessed a Stanley Cup championship game.

The answer? Why, Lord Stanley of Preston, of course, the man who as governor general of Canada donated the Stanley Cup to hockey in 1893. Shortly after that, Queen Victoria called him back to England, so he never witnessed any of the great contests for the trophy that bears his name.

Bill Barilko's Final Goal

I never knew Bill Barilko but I wish I had. His Toronto Maple Leaf teammates from the fifties — men like Harry Watson, Sid Smith and Howie Meeker — tell me he had style and charisma. On the ice he was tough and fearless. Away from it his blond good looks and sunny disposition captivated everyone.

In the spring of 1951, Barilko was the most popular defenceman on the Toronto team. Called up from the Hollywood Wolves of the Pacific Coast League four years earlier, the cocky rookie from Timmins, Ontario quickly earned a place on the Leaf roster and would not let it go. He was an instant hit with the fans, who loved his enthusiasm, his belligerence and his daring rushes that inevitably wound up in the opposing team's goal mouth.

He didn't score often — only 26 times in 252 regular season games. But one goal he scored, captured in all its beauty through the lens of ace sports photographer Nat Turofsky, will live forever as one of hockey's shining moments. It was the 1951 Stanley Cup winning goal, and sadly, the final goal of Barilko's brief NHL career.

Montreal and Toronto collided in the Stanley Cup finals that season, a thrilling series that lasted five games, every one of them decided in sudden-death overtime. Never before, never since, have all games in a final series required extra time to decide a winner.

The Leafs, on home ice, took a 1–0 lead in the series when rookie Sid Smith scored after 15 seconds of overtime. In game two, also played in Toronto, Montreal superstar Rocket Richard evened matters with a dramatic overtime goal. Despite the split, Toronto had peppered Hab goalie Gerry McNeil with 75 shots in the two games. As a result, the Leafs displayed plenty of confidence as they boarded the train for Montreal and the next two games.

Overtime in game three ended suddenly when Leaf centre Ted Kennedy ripped a long shot past McNeil, and in game four, big Harry Watson scored the overtime winner, to give the Leafs a commanding 3–1 lead in the series.

Back at Maple Leaf Gardens in game five, McNeil's brilliance was a decisive factor in what seemed sure to be a 2–1 Montreal victory. But then leaf coach Joe Primeau pulled goalie Al Rollins from the net with 93 seconds left in regulation time. The strategy paid off when Tod Sloan tied the score, slipping a rebound under McNeil with just 32 seconds on the clock.

Another win in overtime would bring the Stanley Cup to Toronto. Early in the overtime, the Leafs' Howie Meeker gained possession of the puck behind the Montreal net and shoveled it out to the onrushing Bill Barilko.

The big defenceman, never one to hesitate when boldness was called for, galloped in from the blue line and threw his 185-pound body into a desperate shot at McNeil. His aim was true, the red light flashed, and Barilko's dramatic goal won the Stanley Cup for the Leafs.

But there's a sad footnote to this story. A few weeks later, back home in Timmins, Ontario, Barilko and a friend decided to embark on a fly-in fishing trip to the coast of James Bay. Barilko's mother had a premonition something bad might happen and urged him not to go. But he insisted and early on the morning of departure, when he tiptoed into his mother's bedroom and said softly, "Goodbye, Mom," she pretended she didn't hear and refused to answer. It was a decision she would regret for the rest of her life.

The hockey star and his friend flew their small Fairchild pontoon plane to the Seal River, near the northern extremity of James Bay. They fished for two days, caught several dozen trout, which they stored in the pontoons, and started back. After stopping to re-fuel at Rupert House on the southern end of the bay, Barilko's pilot friend had difficulty getting the plane, weighed down with fish, off the water. Finally he succeeded. The plane cleared the treetops and disappeared in the clouds. What happened to the Fairchild and its two occupants after that remains a mystery. One thing soon became clear — the plane went down somewhere between James Bay and Timmins.

Despite a million-dollar search lasting several weeks and covering thousand of miles of bushland, it wasn't till eleven years later that the wreckage of the plane, with skeletal remains of two men inside, was discovered.

Bill Barilko is gone but not forgotten.

The Alfie Moore Saga

IN THE SPRING OF 1937 he was just another goalie, a minor leaguer named Alfie Moore. His season at Pittsburgh was over, and he was back in Toronto, relaxing in a tavern. He wished he had tickets for the big game at the Gardens that night, the first game of the Stanley Cup finals between Chicago and Toronto.

Suddenly two Black Hawk players, Johnny Gottselig and Paul Thompson, burst into the tavern and grabbed Moore. "Come with us," they ordered. "You're playing goal for the Hawks tonight."

It seems Hawks' regular goalie, Mike Karakas, had broken a toe and could not play. When the Hawks pleaded with Leaf owner Conn Smythe to let them use Davie Kerr, a Ranger goalie, Smythe just laughed and said, "No way. Kerr's too good. No, we'll loan you Alfie Moore, our Pittsburgh goalie — that is, if you can find him."

Moore was found, not quite sober perhaps, but eager to play. "I'll show Smythe he made a mistake keeping me in Pittsburgh," he told his new mates.

After giving up an early goal to the Leafs' Gord Drillon, Moore blanked Toronto the rest of the way. Gottselig, who scored twice in the 3–1 Hawk victory, said he could hardly find his name in the paper the next day. All the praise was for Moore.

Smythe was so upset he refused to let Moore play in game two, which the Hawks lost. But at home in Chicago, with Karakas back in goal, the Hawks won two straight and captured the Stanley Cup.

When the playoff loot was divvied up, the Hawks asked Moore what his services were worth. "Oh, about $150," he said. Bill Tobin, the Hawks' manager, gave Moore twice that amount and later sent him a suitably engraved gold watch.

The legend of Alfie Moore, the goalie they pulled from a tavern, endures to this day.

"Sudden Death" Hill

When Mel Hill, a 140-pound right winger from Glenboro, Manitoba tried out for the New York Rangers in the mid-1930s, he was rejected. Too light, they said. So Hill played amateur hockey for a year, added some weight and was good enough to catch on as a regular with the Boston Bruins in the 1938–39 season.

But the rookie didn't score very often — no goals at all by Christmas, and only ten for the entire regular season. With first-team all-stars Eddie Shore and Dit Clapper on defence, and high-scoring forward Bill Cowley (league MVP and scoring champion), Milt Schmidt, Bobby Bauer, Porky Dumart and Roy Conacher up front, Hill soon became accustomed to playing in the shadow of more talented players. Indeed, he considered himself fortunate to be able to cling to a spot on the Bruin roster.

But in the 1939 playoffs, Hill stood out like a beacon. Boston met New York in the first round, and rookie Hill scored a dramatic winning goal in game one after almost three periods (59 minutes, 25 seconds) of overtime. It was 1.10 a.m. when Hill's shot ended proceedings. In game two, he scored again in overtime to give the Bruins their second straight victory.

The Bruins won game three in regulation time, but the Rangers fought back with three straight victories, forcing a seventh and deciding game at the Boston Garden. The score there was tied 1–1 at the end of regulation time, and the first overtime period was scoreless. So was the second.

Late in the third overtime, Bill Cowley threw a pass from the corner onto Hill's stick and Mel slapped it past Ranger goalie Davie Kerr to win the game and end the series. The red light flashed after 48 minutes of extra time. With three overtime winners, Hill acquired the nickname Sudden Death, a monicker that stuck to him for the rest of his life. When fans sought his autograph, they even asked him to preface his name with "Sudden Death."

Hill's Bruins went on to win the Stanley Cup that spring with a final series' triumph over Toronto. Hill's bonus money, $2000 for the Cup win and a special bonus of $1000 for the three overtime goals, equaled his $3,000 regular-season salary.

Cool Head, Nervous Stomach

DURING WORLD WAR TWO good goalies were scarce, but the Toronto Maple Leafs came up with a stellar stopper in Frank

McCool. There was just one problem with McCool. He had ulcers. When he faced the pressure of play-off hockey, his ulcers flared up and made every game a painful experience.

In the spring of 1945, the Leafs managed to reach the Stanley Cup finals, even though they'd finished 28 points behind first-place Montreal in regular-season play. It was considered a stunning upset when the Leafs eliminated the Habs in six games in the semifinals. Montreal had lost only eight games all season, and the Canadiens' famed Punch Line of Toe Blake, Rocket Richard and Elmer Lach had finished one, two, three in the NHL scoring race.

Playing a large role in the upset was rookie net-minder Frank McCool, whose nervous stomach made playoff competition an agonizing experience. Each pressure-packed game brought him to the brink of collapse.

Now the Leafs prepared to meet a strong Detroit team in the Cup finals. Despite their dramatic win over Montreal, no one figured the Leafs for a sec-ond straight upset — not with a sick and inexperi-enced goaltender carrying their Stanley Cup hopes. There was concern that McCool, unable to cope with the stomach pain that plagued him, might have to be replaced.

But McCool was magnificent in game one and stopped Detroit 1–0. In game two he came up with another shutout, this time 2–0. In game three he blanked the Red Wings again. Three games, three shutouts and a record for stinginess unequaled in postseason play.

Between games, and between periods of each game, McCool soothed his flaming ulcers by drink-ing plenty of milk.

Then, with the Stanley Cup almost within his grasp, he faltered. The Red Wings stopped his shutout streak after 193 minutes (a playoff record), staving off elimination with a 5–3 triumph in game four. They used McCool's own weapon, the shutout, to stop the Leafs in games five and six.

By then the rookie's stomach was on fire and his confidence sagging fast. His chance to win the Stanley Cup appeared to be slipping away.

Game seven quickly heaped more pressure on McCool's shoulders as neither team was able to score. The most important game of the year remained scoreless for over two periods. Midway through the third, with the score tied 1–1, McCool's ulcers almost knocked him right out of the game. He doubled over in the Leaf net, then pleaded with the referee for time out in order to take some stomach medicine.

Today, he would be denied a respite, and a back-up goalie would come off the bench to replace him. But in that era there were no backups. Every goalie was a sixty-minute man. So McCool got the break he requested and left the ice. He spent ten minutes in the dressing room sipping milk to soothe his ulcer pangs.

Soon after he returned, the Leafs' Babe Pratt scored the game-winning goal and Toronto won the Stanley Cup with a 2–1 victory. McCool, with four playoff shutouts, had played the best hockey of his career while suffering almost unbearable pain.

The following season, McCool shared the Leaf goaltending job with returned war veteran Turk Broda. The 1945 playoff hero played in 22 games, failed to collect another shutout and quickly faded from the NHL scene. But "Ulcers" McCool left behind an enviable record — three consecutive shutouts in the Stanley Cup playoffs.

Sawchuk's Dazzling Playoffs

ASK ANY OLD-TIME HOCKEY BROADCASTER to name the greatest goalie he's ever seen and chances are he'll tell you it's Terry Sawchuk. One of Sawchuk's remarkable records — 103 shutouts in a 20-year NHL career — may never be broken.

It was shutout goaltending that made Sawchuk famous back in 1952 when he was a second-year man with the Detroit Red Wings. In 1951, having captured the Calder Trophy as top rookie and having been named to the all-star team, he'd already established himself as one of the best netminders in the game. But nobody expected him to be almost flawless when the Wings met Toronto in the playoffs in 1952.

Sawchuk blanked the Leafs in the first two games 3–1 and 1–0, and allowed only 3 Toronto goals in the next two games (6–2 and 3–1 for Detroit). The Red Wings skated off with a four-game sweep of the semifinals.

The young goalie was just as hot against powerful Montreal when the final series opened at the Montreal Forum. Sawchuk gave up a single goal in game one and another lone score in game two. Both games went to Detroit, 3–1 and 2–1. Back on home ice, Sawchuk was even stingier. He chalked up two straight shutouts with identical 3–0 scores. Reporters agreed it was Sawchuk's brilliance that enabled the Red Wings to become the first team in history to sweep eight straight games en route to the Cup.

In the eight games, Sawchuk recorded four shutouts. He gave up a mere five goals and his goals-against average was an incredible 0.62. No playoff goaltender has come close to matching that performance.

The Winnipeg native went on to other Cup triumphs — two more with Detroit in 1954 and 1955 and one with Toronto in 1967. But the Stanley Cup playoff that pleased him the most was the eight-game sweep in the spring of '52.

Baun Scores the Winner — On a Broken Leg

FORMER LEAF STALWART BOBBY BAUN doesn't play old-timers' hockey with us anymore — his doctor advised against it because of a broken neck the hard-rock defenceman suffered in an NHL game an injury that ended his career. We miss the man who is often asked about his biggest moment in hockey — the time he scored a winning playoff goal while skating on a broken leg.

Baun's memorable moment came in 1964 in Detroit, in the sixth game of the final series between the Leafs and the Red Wings. If the Wings won they would capture the Stanley Cup. With the score tied 3–3, Gordie Howe of the Wings rifled a shot that caught Baun just above the ankle. The Leaf defenceman had to be carried off on a stretcher.

In the dressing room, Baun had local anesthetic

injected in the ankle to kill the pain, and when the game went into overtime, there he was back on the ice.

After one minute and 43 seconds of overtime, Baun took a pass from Bob Pulford and slapped the puck at Red Wings netminder Terry Sawchuk. The disk deflected off Detroit defenceman Bill Gadsby and found the net for the winning goal. In 55 previous playoff games, Baun had scored only twice.

So it was back to Toronto for the seventh and deciding game. Baun disregarded doctors' advice to have his aching leg x-rayed. "Later," he said, "I'll do it later. Look after Kelly, Brewer and Mahovlich first." Leaf centre Red Kelly was nursing sprained knee ligaments, defenceman Carl Brewer had a rib separation, and left-winger Frank Mahovlich had a bruised shoulder.

For the final game, Baun's leg was once again injected with painkiller. He played a regular shift despite severe pain. It wasn't until the Leafs won the game 4–0 and had the Stanley Cup firmly in their grasp that he consented to have his leg x-rayed. The medical technicians confirmed what Baun already suspected. A cast would be needed for the leg he'd broken a couple of nights earlier.

Wacky Happenings in Winnipeg

IN 1902 THE WINNIPEG Victorias hockey team held the Stanley Cup, and the city of Winnipeg was tremendously excited about a forthcoming challenge from the Toronto Wellingtons. There was such a rush for admission to the first game in

the best-of-three series that four men at the front
of the line were almost crushed to death against
the arena doors by the mob behind; when the
gates opened the men were trampled underfoot.
Pulled to safety by arena officials, the unconscious four were passed over the heads of the
onrushing fans until fresh air revived them and
they were able to take their places in line again,
this time at the end of it.

Some fans traveled all the way from central
Saskatchewan to see the games and estimated
they spent two hundred dollars apiece on the jun-
ket — almost a year's salary for many Westerners
in that era.

The series was highlighted by some most unusual occurrences.

Before each game, the Winnipeg players warmed
up on the ice while wearing long gold dressing
gowns over their uniforms. Midway through the
first game a Newfoundland dog jumped on the ice,
halting play and precipitating a merry chase. The
dog's owner finally followed his pet onto the ice
and dragged him off by the ears.

Then the puck, lifted high in the air in an early-
day attempt at icing, became lodged in the rafters
over the ice. The players gathered below and
threw their sticks at the rafters until one of them
knocked the disk free. He received a standing ovation and bowed to the crowd.

When a player was penalized by the referee,
he was told to "sit on the fence." Because there
was no penalty box, the player sat down on the
low boards (in some arenas they were only a
foot high) until the referee waved him back into
the play.

In those early days of hockey, when the puck flew into the crowd, it was traditional for the fan catching it to throw it back on the ice. However, in one of the 1902 games, a Winnipeg fan caught the puck . . . and kept it! He didn't know it, but he was starting a now familiar hockey tradition. He also caused a long delay while officials searched for a second puck. There was another delay when Fred Scanlan of Winnipeg broke a skate. Play was halted until he was fitted with a new one.

It was during this series, won by Winnipeg, that the puck actually split in two during a game. A Toronto player named Chummy Hill trapped half the broken puck with his stick, fired it into the Winnipeg net . . . and the referee ruled it a goal. Winnipeg goalie Brown complained to the referee, stating he thought play should have stopped with the breaking of the puck and he was taken by surprise.

How did Toronto fans, in those days before radio and television, hear about the outcome of the Winnipeg games? In the offices of the Toronto *Globe*, a newspaperman awaited the bulletins wired in from the arena in Winnipeg. When he was given the final score, he rushed to the telephone and called the Toronto Street Railway Company. A man on duty there gave three blasts on the railway whistle, which signaled the Toronto defeat.

It's reported the railway whistle could be heard from one end of Toronto to the other.

Winnipeg Fans Wildly Excited About Cup Series in 1902

THE WINNIPEG VICS CAPTURED the Stanley Cup in 1902, defeating the Toronto Wellingtons. It was after one of these games that newsmen accused the visitors of smoking on the bench while the game was in progress. The Wellingtons had a complaint of their own. The penalties, under western rules, were often far too long. The penalized player had to serve a "game," which was a common word for the time leading up to a goal. In other words, he couldn't return to the ice until a goal was scored. It was finally agreed that the penalty time for a minor infraction would be two minutes.

For the second Cup series against Montreal the teams couldn't agree on a referee. Two men qualified, McFarlane and Quinn. Finally there was a coin toss and McFarlane won. But that gentleman refused the assignment initially. Why? Because Montreal had favored Quinn, which hurt McFarlane's feelings.

Prior to the series the temperature in Winnipeg soared, reaching 62 degrees Fahrenheit. The ice began to melt in the Winnipeg arena and workers mopped the surface with blankets. Even though much of the water was absorbed, the games were played in slush.

According to the *Winnipeg Telegram,* young men "climbed, squeezed, burrowed their way in — free. One fan would pay and once inside he would open a window 30 feet above the ground. His friends used ladders 'borrowed' from the nearby Hudson's Bay Company and snuck in the window. A whole squad of policemen missed the illegal entry. They were too busy watching the game and thinking of the four dollars they were to receive for keeping an eye out for gatecrashers."

Interest in the series was equally high back in Montreal. Over 500 fans jammed the Montreal Amateur Athletic Association gymnasium to get wireless reports, while in the streets of the city an estimated 10,000 watched and waited for the newspapers to put out bulletin boards with updates on the action.

Winnipeg won the first match, played in pools of water, by a 1–0 score. Montreal bounced back with a 5–0 shutout in game two. Big Billy Nicholson, Montreal's 300-pound goalie, handled all shots thrown his way in a masterly fashion.

It was in game three that the visitors earned a nickname that would stay with them forever. The bigger Winnipeg players crashed through time after time, but the Montrealers didn't flinch and hung on tenaciously, protecting a 2–1 lead, which became the winning score. A telegrapher at rinkside flashed the news to Montreal. "The visitors are taking terrible punishment but they are hanging on like little men of iron." From that day on the Montrealers were known as "the little men of iron."

The goaltending of big Billy Nicholson was the difference in the series. He allowed just two goals in the three games.

As a final note, Nicholson's daughter, Helen Nicholson Wolthro, from Cornwall, Ontario, visited my hockey museum at Colborne, Ontario, recently and was surprised to find a photo of her late father on display. Later I visited Mrs. Wolthro at her home in Cornwall, and she placed (on loan) the goal stick used by her father in the 1902 Stanley Cup series. Mrs. Wolthro (née Nicholson), in the 1930s at age 15, was a star player on a Montreal women's team, the leading scorer in her league. She played before as many as 6,000 spectators in one championship series.

Whenever Kate Warbled the Flyers Won

AT THE SPECTRUM IN PHILADELPHIA, somebody decided that the American national anthem was too hard to sing. So, one night before the game they played a recording of Kate Smith singing "God Bless America" instead.

The crowd booed the rendition, and they booed it the next time it was played and every time after that. The Flyers would have switched back to the regular anthem except for one important fact — the team always won whenever Kate sang. They were 8–0 with Kate warbling them to victory. By then, the fans had warmed to the idea of an over-the-hill singer bringing the Flyers good luck.

Then somebody got the bright idea of bringing Kate in "live" to sing "God Bless America" — right at centre ice in the Spectrum.

But Kate turned down the first request for a personal appearance. "Hockey fans don't want to hear an old lady sing," she said. "I'm 66 years old. They'll laugh me out of the building."

It was true that Kate was 30 years past her prime. Nevertheless, the Flyers offered her $5,000 if she'd appear, and promised her first-class treatment, so she finally agreed to go to Philadelphia.

She arrived secretly before a big game against Toronto. The red carpet was rolled out, then the organ. The voice of the announcer boomed out over the PA: "Now ladies and gentlemen, 'God Bless America." Then he paused for effect and added, "With Kate Smith!"

Kate stepped onto the ice and the crowd almost knocked the roof off the Spectrum with the ovation they gave her. And when she belted out the song, everybody in the place had goose bumps. The Flyers won that night and when Kate made a second appearance at the Spectrum (by then her record was something like 37–3–1) prior to the sixth game of the Philadelphia-Boston Stanley Cup series in 1974, she sparkled again. The Flyers won the game 1–0 and the cup, and Kate was credited with playing a big role in the triumph. It was one of the most memorable chapters in Philadelphia hockey history, combining the talents of a remarkable old woman with a bizarre hockey club known as the Broad Street Bullies.

Why Wait for the Opening Whistle?

IT HAPPENED in the spring of 1987, in the Stanley Cup playoffs, and it brought shame to the National Hockey League. It was a playoff "first," and it caused the start of the sixth game of the Montreal-Philadelphia series to be delayed 15 minutes.

What was it? It was an incredible ten-minute brawl between the Flyers and the Habs, and it happened *before the game even started.*

The brawl was sparked by a silly superstition,

nothing more, nothing less. Some of the Montreal Canadiens, for some obscure reason, had developed a habit of shooting a puck into the opposing team's empty net at the end of the pregame warm-up. They did it when most of the players had left the ice. Few people noticed, and few people cared. It was just a silly superstition.

But this night, when Shayne Corson and Claude Lemieux slipped the puck into the Flyer net at the end of the warm-up period, out stormed Flyer tough guy Ed Hospodar. He was incensed that the Habs would invade the Flyer end of the rink — even in the warm-up — and he attacked Lemieux.

That did it. Players from both clubs jumped back on the ice and a major brawl ensued. Forum fans had never seen anything like it. The next day reporters called the brawl "disgusting," "appalling" and "shameful."

The two teams were fined more than $24,000 each, and Hospodar was suspended for the balance of the playoffs as the instigator of the ugly brawl. He explained his attack on Lemieux by saying, "If it was that important to him, then it was important to me. Everyone is looking for a little edge in the playoffs."

It was the low point of the playoffs, and all because of a ridiculous superstition.

The End of a Streak

SHORTLY AFTER the turn of the century, the Ottawa Silver Seven reigned as Stanley Cup champions. By 1906 they had defended the cup through eight consecutive series and won them all. They had lost only three of 20 Stanley Cup games played.

In March 1906, the Silver Seven met the Montreal Wanderers in Montreal in the first game of a two-game, total-point series. The Wanderers stunned Ottawa, thought to be invincible, with a 9–1 trouncing in game one. Did this signal the end of the Ottawa dynasty?

Back on home ice for game two, the Ottawa club began an incredible comeback in the series. After Lester Patrick scored for Montreal to give the Montrealers a nine-goal lead, the Silver Seven went relentlessly on the attack. They poured shot after shot at the Montreal goal, and at halftime the score was Ottawa 3, Montreal 1.

In the second half, the Ottawa attack was even more intense. The Silver Seven scored six consecutive goals to tie the series at ten goals apiece. There was bedlam in the arena. Nobody could recall such a comeback, the visitors were reeling in their skates and victory for the pumped-up Ottawa club seemed assured. It would be a triumph hockey fans would speak of a hundred years hence.

But wait! Montreal's canny Lester Patrick called for time. He took his panicky teammates aside and gave them a little talk. He told them to stop playing defensive hockey, to fight back with some offensive rushes. He reminded them of the disgrace involved in losing after holding a 10–0 lead. The strategy worked. When play resumed, Montreal went straight to the attack. Patrick himself scored two quick goals and the Ottawa firepower was suddenly defused.

Montreal held on to win the series 12 goals to 10,

and Ottawa's long reign as Stanley Cup champions was finally over.

The Ref Went Home

IT WAS EARLY SPRING IN 1899. Eight thousand hockey fans filled the arena in Montreal for a two-game, total-goals Stanley Cup series with Winnipeg.

In game one, Winnipeg was leading by a goal with a minute to play. Then Montreal broke through to score twice in the final sixty seconds to win the game 2–1 and take a one-goal lead in the series.

Game two was equally close and just as thrilling. Late in the contest, with Montreal leading 3–2, Tony Gingras of Winnipeg was slashed across the legs by Bob McDougall of Montreal.

"Two minutes," said referee Jim Findlay, pointing at McDougall as Gingras, writhing in pain, was carried off to the Winnipeg dressing room.

"Not enough," screamed the Winnipeg players. "McDougall should be thrown out of the game for such a vicious slash."

When the referee refused to change his decision, the Winnipeg players berated him, then stomped off to their dressing room to cool off. Referee Findlay followed them into the room. When Gingras showed him the deep cut on his leg, he said, "All right, I admit I made a mistake but I'm not going to change my call now. And since you men don't like my refereeing style and you don't appear to be willing to resume play, I'm all through refereeing this game and I'm going home."

With that he got up and left. Took off his skates

and went home. Officials from both teams were stunned. They chased after him in a sleigh and pleaded with him to come back. After all, this was no ordinary game. The Stanley Cup was at stake. Finally, Findlay agreed to return to the rink and complete his duties.

But by the time he returned it was too late. An hour or more had passed and most of the 8,000 fans had gone home. The Winnipeg players, some of whom still lingered in their dressing room, ignored Findlay's ultimatum — return to the ice within 15 minutes or forfeit the game. Some of the Winnipeg boys, it's said, had already dressed and started off on a pub crawl of old Montreal.

When the deadline expired, Findlay had little choice. He awarded the unfinished Stanley Cup series to Montreal.

The Strangest Cup Challenge

OF THE MANY CHALLENGES in Stanley Cup history, the 1904–5 season provided the most unusual. That was the season the famous Ottawa Silver Seven were challenged by a team from Dawson City in the Yukon, men who'd joined the Klondike gold rush a few years earlier.

The Dawson City Nuggets left the Yukon on December 19, 1904, and didn't arrive in Ottawa until mid-January 1905. Three of the players, including 17-year-old Albert Forrest, the youngest goalie ever to play in a Stanley Cup series, had started out on their bicycles. But the bikes broke down in the snow, and the three players were forced to walk 40 and 50 miles a day until they reached Whitehorse, where they were reunited with their teammates.

From Whitehorse, the Nuggets took the train to Skagway in Alaska, where they were stranded for two or three days. They travelled by steamship to Seattle, Washington, by train to Vancouver and then by another train across Canada to Ottawa. They were 23 days on the road, with no chance to practice.

When they finally reached Ottawa, without having skated in more than three weeks, they requested a postponement of the series. "Give us a day or two to get our skating legs back," they pleaded. "We haven't been on skates for almost a month."

"Sorry, boys," was the Ottawa reply. "We play tomorrow night."

The Dawson City players, stiff and sore from their long journey, lost the first game 9–2. In game two, Ottawa star One-Eyed Frank McGee went on a scoring spree that left the visitors reeling. McGee scored a record 14 goals in Ottawa's 23–2 thrashing of the Klondikers.

Despite the humiliating defeat, Albert Forrest, Dawson City's beleaguered teenage goaltender, was highly praised by Ottawa reporters covering the game. "Young Forrest was sensational," one of them wrote. "If it hadn't been for him, the score would have been double what it was."

Ice Hockey or Water Polo?

ARTIFICIAL ICE MADE its first appearance in Canada in 1911 when Lester and Frank Patrick had it installed in arenas in Vancouver and Victoria. Before its use became common, many Stanley Cup playoff games were decided on ice that was soft as butter.

In 1905, for example, when Rat Portage, now called Kenora, challenged Ottawa for the Stanley Cup, the Thistles zipped around the slow-footed Capital City boys to capture the first game of the series 9–3. The Rat Portage players wore new tube skates invented by a man named McCullough, and many credited the thin-bladed skates for their superior speed.

After game one, Ottawa fans resigned themselves to the loss of the Stanley Cup. Another win for the speedy Thistles in the best-of-three series and the trophy would go west.

But somebody in Ottawa — the canny (some say devious) perpetrator was never identified — came up with an ingenious plan to rob the visitors of what appeared to be certain victory.

When the Thistles showed up for game two and glanced out on the ice, their mouths dropped open in amazement. Someone had flooded the ice surface with two inches of water an hour earlier — even though it was well above freezing and there was no chance the water would freeze.

The Ottawa strategy worked. The thin-bladed tube skates worn by the Thistles cut deep into the soft ice while the layer of water on top nullified their superior passing and stickhandling skills. Ottawa, a more physical team, appeared to be quite at home in the water and slush, and tied the series with a 4–2 victory.

The screams of outrage from the visitors over the flooding of the ice forced the arena manager to produce a somewhat better ice surface for the deciding game. This greatly disappointed the Ottawa fans, who had enjoyed the swimming pool atmosphere of game two. Ottawa's Frank McGee scored the winning goal in a 5–4 triumph, and the westerners returned to Rat Portage, furious but empty-handed.

Their howls of protest echoed from one end of Ontario to the other. "Some sneak in Ottawa flooded the ice deliberately and it cost us the cup," they told one and all. Ah, but who could prove it?

Unpredictable Ice Conditions

IN MANY EARLY-DAY Stanley Cup matches spring weather made for atrocious ice conditions. Sometimes there would be bits of grass and mud showing, and pools of water on the ice were quite common. In one playoff game the puck fell through a hole in the ice and couldn't be recovered. In Toronto one spring there was so little ice covering the floor that players were said to be "running back and forth on the board floor." After another playoff game, a reporter wrote: "Thanks to the good work of the lifesavers, all the players were saved from drowning."

Occasionally too much ice would be a problem. In Edmonton in 1909 the ice was measured and found to be 18 inches thick. A man in Calgary who had invented a machine that shaved ice was hired. He came to Edmonton and used his amazing machine to shave several inches of surface ice away, creating ideal conditions for a forthcoming playoff game.

Too Many Rings, Not Enough Fingers

TWO MEN SHARE the record of being on the most Stanley Cup winning teams. Henri Richard of Montreal played on 11 championship clubs. Toe Blake, also of Montreal, is the only other man to garner 11 Stanley Cup rings. He played on three championship teams and was the winning coach of eight other Cup-winning clubs.

The Cup Was Never Won

IN 1919, WHEN THE NATIONAL HOCKEY LEAGUE was only two years old, the Montreal Canadiens defeated Ottawa in a playoff series, then journeyed west to meet the Seattle Metropolitans, the champions of the Pacific Coast League, in a best-of-five series for the Stanley Cup.

In these days, "western rules" and "eastern rules" were in force in alternate playoff games, the major difference being that western teams used a seventh skater or "rover."

Under western rules, Seattle won the first game when the Canadiens had trouble making good use of their extra man. Under eastern rules, Montreal took the second game 4–2, with superstar Newsy

Lalonde scoring all four goals. Seattle captured game three, and game four ended in a scoreless tie, despite 100 minutes of overtime.

Montreal evened the series by taking game five, but many of the players felt sick during the contest. Cully Wilson of Seattle fell to the ice complaining of dizziness and fatigue, and Montreal's Bad Joe Hall, also very ill, could not continue playing. He was rushed to hospital with a temperature of 105°F.

The so-called black flu epidemic was sweeping the continent in 1919, killing thousands of people, and several players on both teams were afflicted. At least five of the Canadiens found it impossible to skate and were confined to bed on the eve of the deciding game. Montreal manager George Kennedy, himself a flu victim, asked permission to use several players from Victoria as substitutes for his ailing stars, one of whom was Lalonde, who had already scored six goals against the Metropolitans. But Seattle refused to go along with the request. As a result, officials had no choice but to cancel the remaining game. It's the only time in NHL history a Stanley Cup series went undecided.

When the Canadiens staggered onto their train for the return trip to Montreal, they left Joe Hall, their popular teammate, behind. On April 5, he died of his illness in a Seattle hospital.

One Strike and You're Out

IN THE SPRING OF 1925, the Hamilton Tigers enjoyed the best record of any team in the NHL. As league champions, they drew a bye in the first round of the Stanley Cup playoffs and sat back to await the winners of the Toronto St. Pats–Montreal Canadiens series.

However, all was not happy in the Hamilton camp. Red Green, a star player, claimed that he and his teammates had played in six more regular season games than they had contracted for. He had a point, because the NHL had increased the schedule from 24 to 30 games, and many players hadn't been compensated accordingly. The sum the Hamilton boys had in mind did not seem excessive — only $200 per player.

When management said no, the entire team voted to go on strike. They vowed there'd be no playoff games involving Hamilton if their demands weren't met. NHL President Frank Calder angrily claimed the players' demands were outrageous, and slapped a suspension on the rebellious Tigers. "Your season is finished," he told them. Then he announced that Ottawa, as fourth-place finishers, would replace them.

That decision infuriated the other two playoff teams, Montreal and Toronto. "Why should Ottawa get the playoff bye?" they complained. "They finished behind us." Calder also drew criticism in the press, and ultimately announced that Ottawa would not participate in the playoffs after all, and that the winner of the Toronto-Montreal series would be the NHL's representative in the Stanley Cup finals.

The players' strike marked the end of NHL hockey in Hamilton. After the season, the franchise was sold to New York interests for $75,000, and the team was renamed the Americans. The striking Hamilton players were ordered to pay their fines and apologize to the league before being permitted to join the Americans for the following season.

A Tantrum Cost Him the Cup

IN THE SPRING OF 1942, the Detroit Red Wings were sure they were about to win the Stanley Cup, and so was everybody else. After a so-so regular season — a fifth place finish in a seven-team NHL and a record of 19–25–4 — the Wings were on fire in the playoffs. They polished off the Montreal Canadiens two games to one in one series and ousted Boston 2–0 in another.

In the final series against the Toronto Maple Leafs, the line of Don Grosso, Eddie Wares and Sid Abel was unstoppable. The Red Wings, with Grosso scoring twice, took game one 3–2. Grosso scored two more goals in game two and the Wings won it 4–2. They took a 3–0 lead in games over the Leafs with a 4–3 win in game three. One more victory and the Cup would be theirs.

But the Leafs fought back in game four after benching Gordie Drillon and Bucko McDonald and replacing them with Hank Goldup and rookie Gaye Stewart. Toronto was leading by a goal when a series of incidents set in motion a tidal wave that eventually submerged the Red Wings.

When referee Mel Harwood gave Detroit's Eddie Wares a penalty, for some reason the player picked up a hot water bottle from the bench and handed it to the ref. Moments later, a second Red Wing penalty was called on Don Grosso. He dropped his stick and gloves in front of the referee and showered him with verbal abuse.

Toronto went on to win the game, but right after the match, Detroit coach Jack Adams was so incensed, he vaulted the boards and began pummeling referee Harwood with his fists. League President Frank Calder, who was at the game, subsequently suspended Adams until further notice, and he fined the two players, Wares and Grosso.

Without Adams to coach them, the Red Wings seemed to lose their confidence and most of their desire. The Leafs, paced by the Metz brothers, Syl Apps and Bob Goldham, rebounded to win three straight games and capture the Stanley Cup. No other team has ever accomplished such an amazing comeback in the Stanley Cup finals.

The Chicago Cup Caper

AFTER WINNING a record five straight Stanley Cups in the late 1950s, the marvelous Montreal Canadien streak came to an end in Chicago in the spring of 1961.

The final series between the Hawks and the Habs was an emotional one; Rocket Richard called it the dirtiest he'd ever witnessed. After game three, won by Chicago in the third overtime frame, Montreal coach Toe Blake's temper sizzled. He was so furious over an injury to Bernie Geoffrion and the officiating of Dalt McArthur that he chased after the referee and took a wild swing at him, a rash act that resulted in a $2000 fine.

Midway through game six, played in Chicago, Black Hawk goalie Glenn Hall was blanking the famous Montreal snipers for the second straight time. It was obvious to everyone that the Hawks were going to snatch the Cup away from the Habs.

In the crowd, shocked and angry, was a rabid Montreal fan. Ken Kilander couldn't stand the thought of a Chicago victory. But he was powerless to do anything about it. Or was he?

Impulsively, Kilander leaped from his seat and raced to the lobby of the Chicago Stadium where the Stanley Cup was on display, locked inside a glass showcase. He smashed open the showcase and scooped up the trophy, then ran out of the stadium into the night, with ushers and police in hot pursuit. The thief didn't get very far before he was apprehended and arrested.

In court the next morning he tried to explain his actions. "Your honor, I was simply taking the Cup back to Montreal where it belongs," he said.

"It doesn't belong there anymore," snapped the judge. "But you do. And you'd better get back there before I lock you up and throw away the key."

Graybeards Win the Cup

PRO HOCKEY in the 1990s is a young man's game. Most players are burned out — or nearly so — by age thirty. And yet not so many years ago, the Toronto Maple Leafs won the Stanley Cup with a whole team of graybeards; it was said they used rocking chairs in the dressing room and swigged Geritol from the water bottles.

When these geriatrics won their third and final Stanley Cup in 1967, the average age of the 20 players involved was a nice round 32 years. Three of them — Johnny Bower, Red Kelly and Allan Stanley — were in their forties, and eight more in their thirties.

Perhaps the most amazing player on the club was Bower. Determined to finish his career with Cleveland of the American League after kicking around the minors for 13 seasons (including a brief stint with the New York Rangers), Bower had been reluctant to join the Leafs. "I've had my day," he told Leaf management. "I probably can't help your club anyway." In time, he was persuaded to give the NHL one last fling.

Nobody knew for certain how old Bower was when he joined the Leafs in 1958 — he was at least 33 — and nobody seemed to care. For the next 12 years he supplied the Leafs with spectacular goaltending and led them to four Stanley Cups. But none was sweeter than the 1967 Cup victory over Montreal, when skeptics said the Leafs were far too old to be champions.

Old-timers they may have been, but most of the stars on that team — men like Bower, Stanley, Horton, Sawchuk, Moore, Armstrong, Keon, Mahovlich and Kelly — are now enshrined in the Hockey Hall of Fame.

Adventures of the Stanley Cup

SOME OF THE STORIES about the Stanley Cup and the men who've hungered after it border on the incredible.

You've heard, of course, about the Ottawa player at the turn of the century who drop-kicked the Stanley Cup into the Rideau Canal on a dare. The Cup was small then, just a football-size silver bowl, and fortunately the canal was frozen over.

Then there's the story of the Cup being left in a photographer's studio after he took a team picture, and when it went unclaimed, his wife used it as a flowerpot.

One spring, when the Cup could not be found, Harry Smith of Ottawa vaguely recalled tossing it into a closet in his home a few months earlier. Sure enough, a quick search of the closet produced the coveted silverware.

Then there's a tale from the twenties of a Stanley Cup celebration involving the Montreal Canadiens. The victorious Montrealers were en route to the home of team owner Leo Dandurand where a big victory party awaited them. In the back seat of their sedan, the Cup rested on the laps of the players.

Suddenly a flat tire halted the journey. While the tire was being changed, the Cup was deposited on the street corner. Repairs finished, the players jumped back into the car and sped off to the party.

With the victory celebration well under way, someone said, "Hey, where's the Cup we fought so hard to win?" Someone else remembered the flat tire and how the Cup had been placed on the curb.

Several players dashed for their cars and raced back through the streets until they came to the corner where the Cup had been placed. And there it was, waiting to be claimed.

Secrets of the Cup

THE STANLEY CUP is a handsome piece of silverware weighing about 37 pounds, and only the names of legitimate hockey champions are engraved on its shiny surface.

But such has not always been the case. For the Cup held high each spring by the proud captain of a celebrating team is not the original Stanley Cup. The original Cup — a small silver bowl about the size of a football — was passed from team to team for the first seven decades of its existence — ever since Lord Stanley of Preston, Canada's governor general, donated the trophy in 1893.

In the mid-sixties, NHL officials decided the original silver bowl was getting old and brittle, so League President Clarence Campbell quietly ordered a new one. Carl Pederson, an experienced Montreal silversmith, produced an exact duplicate of the original bowl and, when his facsimile was complete, he secretly substituted his creation for Lord Stanley's original gift. It was years before anyone outside the NHL was aware the switch had been made.

It has often been reported that only one woman's name has ever graced the Stanley Cup — Marguerite Norris, a former president of the Detroit Red Wings. Not so. Early in the century, Lily Murphy, a member of the Ottawa Social Club, scratched her name on the Stanley Cup — the first woman to do so.

And surely the youngest person to have his name inscribed on the Cup was Master Thomas Stanley Westwick, son of the famous player Rat

Westwick, who starred for Ottawa shortly after the turn of the century. Young Westwick was just one year old at the time of the inscription.

Would you believe that at least two politicians have elbowed their way into the Cup-inscribing business as well? Of course you would. In Westwick's era, Dennis Murphy, a member of Parliament, and Sam Rosenthal, an Ottawa alderman, proudly scratched their names on the Stanley Cup during a victory celebration.

Lafleur Kidnaps the Cup

DID YOU KNOW THAT GUY LAFLEUR, one of hockey's greatest scorers, once kidnapped the Stanley Cup? It happened during a victory celebration after the Montreal Canadiens won the trophy in the spring of 1979.

The Canadiens were hockey's most successful team in the seventies and had just swept to their fourth consecutive Stanley Cup triumph, humiliating the New York Rangers in the final series four games to one.

After the traditional Stanley Cup parade through the streets of Montreal, and a further celebration in Henri Richard's tavern, Lafleur impulsively slipped the Stanley Cup into the trunk of his car. He then drove off to the home of his parents in Thurso, Quebec.

There he placed the gleaming trophy on the front lawn where friends and neighbors could see it and have their photos taken next to it. Word spread quickly, and it wasn't long before hockey fans from miles around, many of them clutching cameras, were hurrying to the Lafleur household. It's a day they still talk about in Thurso.

When the crowds began to thin out, Guy looked out the window to see his son Martin, garden hose in hand, filling the Stanley Cup with water. "That's enough," said Guy, rushing out to retrieve hockey's most important symbol. "The Cup is going back to Montreal right now, before something happens to it." And back it went.

While the residents of Thurso were enjoying Guy's little prank, the hockey men responsible for the Cup's safety, who had spent several anxious hours trying to track it down, were less amused. Guy was told never to repeat his stunt . . . or else.

The Cup Winners Promised to Double the Score

IN THE SPRING OF 1908 the Montreal Wanderers were the hottest team in hockey. Over the previous three seasons they had won 27 league games and lost only three. In the 1907 season they had established a record that has never been matched, going undefeated and *averaging* over 10 goals per game. In one game they routed the Montreal Vics 16–3, and in two outings against the Shamrocks they won by 18–5 and 16–5. Ernie Russell, their top scorer, compiled the staggering record of 42 goals in the nine games he played — an average of over four goals per game.

They were just as formidable in the annual chase for the Stanley Cup in those years, winning the trophy in three straight seasons. In 1908 they walloped Ottawa 9–3 and 13–1 in one Stanley Cup series.

They immediately accepted a challenge from the Winnipeg Maple Leafs and crushed the westerners by scores of 11–5 and 9–3.

That triumph seemed like a fitting end to a hugely successful season. But just as the Wanderers were preparing to put their skates away, they were handed a third Stanley Cup challenge — this time from the Toronto Maple Leafs, champions of the Trolley League, the first outright professional league in Canada. The Trolley League was so named because teams traveled by electric trolley between games in Ontario hockey hotbeds like Toronto, Brantford, Guelph, and Berlin (later renamed Kitchener).

But the arrogant Wanderers treated the Maple Leaf challenge as a joke. "Toronto doesn't have a chance against us," a Wanderer spokesman told reporters. "If the Cup trustees order us to play a two-game series against Toronto, it would be a travesty. We'd more than double the score against them. And who would show up for a boring second game? So let's make it a one-game affair and get the season over with." The Cup trustees agreed, and the Toronto boys were given only one chance against the mighty Wanderers.

The game was played in Montreal on March 14, 1908, and the Wanderer fans who turned out bet huge sums that their heroes would double the score on the Maple Leafs, even though the visitors had young Newsy Lalonde in their lineup. Lalonde had been the leading scorer in the Trolley League with 29 goals in nine games.

The Stanley Cup game seesawed back and forth and was tied four times. Montrealers exhorted the champions to pick up the pace, for they were in grave danger of losing their wagers. Some of the fans, during a halt in play, motioned three or four Wanderer players, including goaltender Riley Hern, over to the side boards. "You promised to double the score on these chaps," they shouted. "If you pull up your socks and do it, there'll be some bonus money for you to divide up after the game."

While the players were listening to these entice-ments, one of the strangest goals in Stanley Cup history was scored. The referee, ignoring the dis-traction at rinkside, dropped the puck at center ice, and Lalonde fired it quickly toward the Wanderer net. His aim was true and the disk sailed past the opposing players, who scrambled back too late to prevent the goal. However, Lalonde's empty-net goal so fired up the champions that they stormed back with two goals of their own and won the game by a 6–4 score.

The Wanderers retained the Stanley Cup, but their supporters lost a bundle when the score wasn't doubled. The Toronto boys, on the other hand, had been in on the wagering and returned with a pot of $2,500 to divide among themselves — a small fortune in that era.

The Team That Never Should Have Won the Cup

TAKE THE CHICAGO BLACKHAWKS — please! That was what Chicago fans were saying in 1938 when the Hawks stumbled their way to a mere 14 wins in a 48-game schedule. The Hawks scored only 97 goals all season, less than two per game, the puniest goal production of the eight NHL clubs.

"No wonder they're a lousy team," some fans grumbled. "The club is coached by a former baseball umpire and a referee. What does he know about running a hockey team?"

They were referring to 43-year-old Bill Stewart, who indeed spent his summers umpiring big league ball games and his previous winter as chief of NHL referees. But Hawks owner Major Frederic McLaughlin took a fancy to Stewart's fiery umpiring style and figured he could inject some of that same spirit into his hockey team. So he awarded Stewart a two-year coaching contract.

Even though Chicago squeaked into the playoffs in 1938, they were given virtually no chance of advancing to the finals. One Hawk defenseman, Roger Jenkins, even bet goalie Mike Karakas a wheelbarrow ride through Chicago that the Hawks wouldn't win the Stanley Cup.

Predictably the Hawks lost the first game of their two-out-of-three first-round series with the Montreal Canadiens. Then Karakas caught fire and the Hawks won two straight games, eliminating the surprised Habs.

In their next series versus the New York Americans, the Hawks again fell behind, losing game one. But once more they fought back to win two in a row, leaving the Amerks shaking their heads in disbelief. Suddenly the team that was scorned and humiliated all season found itself in the Stanley Cup finals, facing the powerful Toronto Maple Leafs and their ace goaltender Turk Broda.

Prior to game one the Hawks were plunged into dire straits when goalie Mike Karakas couldn't fit his skate on over a broken toe suffered in the previous series against New York. When Toronto owner Conn Smythe turned down Stewart's request to use a capable substitute, a frantic last-minute search was conducted for little-known netminder Alfie Moore, a Leaf castoff who was found nursing a few beers in a Toronto tavern.

"Don't worry, Bill," Moore said when he was led into the Chicago dressing room. "I haven't been on skates for a couple of weeks, but I'll make those bastards eat the puck."

He did. He made 26 saves, most of them brilliant. One save was a real laugher. The puck hit him in the seat of the pants, and he spun around to see if it was in the net. The Hawks went on to win the game 3–1, and Moore thumbed his nose at the Leaf bench as he left the ice.

Smythe, mad as hell at Moore, banned him from any further competition, and the Hawks, for game two, were forced to employ Paul Goodman, a 28-year-old minor leaguer with no NHL experience. The Leafs not only beat Goodman (who hadn't been on skates in three weeks) by a 5–1 score, but they laid out several Hawks during the contest with crushing checks and flailing fists.

Coach Stewart told the press that he had to visit the hospital before game three to look in on a half-dozen of his boys. "They were laid out with cuts and bruises, and my star center, Doc Romnes, had a broken nose," he complained.

Romnes was wearing a Purdue University football helmet to protect his nose when he took to the ice at the Chicago Stadium before 18,496 fans two nights later. It was the largest crowd in NHL history. Luckily coach Stewart had Karakas back by then.

The injured goalie was able to squeeze his broken toe into his skate boot and went on to play an outstanding game. Doc Romnes scored the winner late in the third period, and Chicago took a 2–1 lead in the series.

Karakas and Turk Broda provided most of the thrills in game four, stopping shot after shot. Late in the second period, with the score tied 1–1, the Hawks' Carl Voss stole the puck and beat Broda to give Chicago a 2–1 lead. Then came one of the most incredible goals in playoff history. Jack Shill of the Hawks, hoping to kill some time on the clock, lofted a shot toward Broda — from 150 feet away. Broda moved out and dropped to his knees to trap the puck, but it skipped past him and into the open net. Chicago led 3–1.

The Leafs pulled out all the stops in the third period, but the strategy backfired when Mush March broke away to make it 4–1. With time running out Stewart instructed Johnny Gottselig, a marvelous stickhandler, to "rag the puck," and that was just what he did, stickhandling around and through the Toronto players as if they were pylons.

When it was over, the team that didn't have a chance threw their coach up onto their shoulders, almost dropping him in the process, and Karakas reminded Jenkins to show up for the wheelbarrow ride. In the weeks that followed, Bill Stewart, the umpire who won the Stanley Cup, was the toast of Chicago. But the backslapping he happily endured soon stopped. The team owner, Major McLaughlin, fired him the following season.

Smitty Made *The Guinness Book of Records*

IN THE HOCKEY RECORD BOOKS Toronto-born Normie Smith is listed as the winning goalie in the opening game of the semifinal round of the 1936 NHL playoffs. He starred in the longest game of hockey ever played.

On March 24, 1936, the Detroit Red Wings faced off against the Montreal Maroons at the Montreal Forum. Who could have known the teams were about to set an endurance record that would last for over a half century and maybe forever?

There was no scoring through sixty minutes of regulation time, and the teams moved into overtime. Period after period of overtime play was played, taking the game into the wee hours of the morning. Finally, in the sixth overtime period, after 116 minutes and 30 seconds of extra time, Detroit's Mud Bruneteau, a two-goal scorer during the regular season, slipped the puck past Lorne Chabot in the Montreal goal. The winner came at 2:25 a.m.

"The *Guinness* people did some research into that game and figured I'd set a world record with 92 saves in hockey's longest shutout," Smith said from his retirement home in Florida in 1987. "I remember the ice was very soft that night and my pads were soaking wet from the water on the ice. My underwear was soaked right through. We were all totally exhausted at the end.

"Between periods the coach gave us a little brandy to drink — just a sip or two — to give us energy and keep us going. A lot of the fans left when the game passed midnight. They had to get up early in the morning."

What is often overlooked is that Smith shut out the Maroons again two nights later, and it wasn't until game three of the series, when Montreal's Gus Marker finally scored on Smith at 12:02 of the first period, that the Detroit netminder's remarkable shutout streak — 248 minutes and 32 seconds — was ended. It remains an NHL playoff record.

While Smith's regular season play was just average (81–83–35), he sparkled under the pressure of playoff competition. In nine games he chalked up three shutouts and registered a 1.23 goals-against average.

The Cinderella Leafs Oust the Gentlemanly Rangers

IN 1958 GEORGE "PUNCH" IMLACH took over as general manager and coach of the Toronto Maple Leafs. The Leafs were mired in last place in the six-team NHL, but in the next few weeks, with Imlach cracking the whip, they caught fire. On the last night of the season the Leafs scored a come-from-behind victory over Detroit in a game the Leafs had to win to make the playoffs. Their last-night triumph, combined with a Ranger loss, put Toronto in the playoffs by a single point. The dramatic finish was front-page news across Canada, and the Leafs became hockey's latest Cinderella team.

Left in the lurch were the disappointed Rangers, coached by Phil Watson. Sometime later Watson revealed an interesting postscript to the story of that playoff race.

With the 1957–58 season winding down, Watson's Rangers were beaten one night by Boston. After the contest, Watson checked the rules and discovered that Boston had used an ineligible player in the game — a goaltender. The goalie was listed as an "emergency replacement" for the Bruins. But the regular Bruins goaltender had returned to health and there was no emergency. Watson decided to protest the game.

His boss in New York, General John Reed Kilpatrick, wouldn't hear of it. "There'll be no protest, Phil," he said. "We don't operate like that. We're gentlemen in this league."

Watson wanted to scream. Gentlemen? In hockey?

"I was certain my protest would have been upheld," he told reporters. "And the Rangers would have been awarded two more points. We would have finished one point ahead of Toronto and been in the playoffs. But it never happened because, well, I guess it's because we're gentlemen."

The First Expansion Team to Win the Cup

HOCKEY BROADCASTERS FORTUNATE enough to be in the booth when a Stanley Cup final series is decided never forget the moment. One that shines in my memory is the 1974 championship won by the Philadelphia Flyers, the first so-called expansion team to capture the Cup.

I was with NBC then, working with Tim Ryan and Ted Lindsay, and our playoff coverage was seen throughout North America. The Flyers had two major obstacles to overcome before capturing the

Cup. The first was the New York Rangers, with a lineup boasting talented old pros like Ed Giacomin, Brad Park, Rod Gilbert, Jean Ratelle, and Vic Hadfield. The series produced seven tension-packed, bruising games, and in game four in New York, Flyer defenseman Barry Ashbee's career came to a sudden end when he was struck in the eye by a Dale Rolfe shot. When Ashbee went down, I was holding a wireless microphone at rinkside. As the gate in front of me opened, I impulsively followed the medical people onto the ice and got a report on the injury from linesman Matt Pavelich. It was a television "first," and later it brought a reprimand from NHL president Clarence Campbell: "Mr. McFarlane, don't go on the ice!"

After ousting New York, the Flyers faced the even more formidable Boston Bruins. There was Orr, Esposito, Hodge, Cashman, Bucyk — one of the highest scoring machines ever assembled. Boston won the opener on home ice 3–2 with Orr the hero, scoring the winning goal in the final half minute of play. The second game has often been called the most decisive in Flyer history. Moose Dupont tied the score with 52 seconds on the clock, and Bobby Clarke popped in the winner after 12:01 of overtime. Clarke leaped into the air like a high jumper when the red light flashed.

The Flyers won two more at the Spectrum, then lost in Boston 5–1. For game six there was a surprise. Kate Smith, the Flyers' good-luck charm, made a personal appearance at the Spectrum, and when she sang "God Bless America" before the opening whistle, the roof almost came off. While Bernie Parent performed like a wizard in the Flyers' goal, Rick MacLeish slammed in the only goal of the game and the Flyers were champions at last. I remember the incredible ovation, the fans leaping and skidding over the ice, the bedlam in the dressing room where I did postgame interviews. Off to one side, wearing dark glasses, stood Barry Ashbee, tears of happiness running down his cheeks. Three years later Ashbee, at age 37 and groomed to be the next Flyers' coach, would die of leukemia.

The following day there was a hastily organized mammoth parade to celebrate the Flyers' victory and the turnout was incredible. It was the largest victory parade in Stanley Cup history. An estimated two million Philadelphians honored their beloved team with an unprecedented outpouring of affection and gratitude.

Boston's 45-year Jinx

IN 1943 THE BOSTON BRUINS lost a playoff hockey series to the Montreal Canadiens. From that wartime year to the spring of 1988 the Bruins met the Habs 18 times in postseason play — and lost every time. In 1988 the long string of losses came to an end when the Bruins pushed Montreal aside four games to one in a division semifinal series.

Who Pulled the Plug?

THE EDMONTON OILERS and the Boston Bruins were locked in a 3–3 tie at the Boston Garden. It was May 24, 1988, the fourth game of the Stanley Cup finals, and 14,500 frantic fans screamed their support for the hometown Bruins. Suddenly the screaming stopped and so did everything else. With 3:23 left to play in the second period, an overload on a 4,000-volt switch knocked out the lights in the run-down old building, leaving players, referees, and fans in the dark. After a long delay, an auxiliary generator was put into use, providing some light, but not enough to play by. Officials evacuated the building, and NHL president John Ziegler declared the game would be replayed in its entirety two nights later in Edmonton. With the unexpected home ice advantage, the Oilers breezed to a 6–3 victory and their fourth Stanley Cup win in the past five years.

7

BEHIND THE
SCENES

A Million for Mahovlich

IT WAS OCTOBER, 1962. Harold Ballard, who, along with Stafford Smythe and John Bassett, had recently bought the Toronto Maple Leafs from Conn Smythe, was having a drink or two with Chicago Black Hawks owner Jim Norris at the Royal York Hotel in Toronto.

Although the Hawks had won the Stanley Cup the preceding year, with Bobby Hull leading the way, Norris had his eye on another great left-winger. The man he had in mind was the Leafs' young star Frank Mahovlich. What a pair! The Big M and the Golden Jet. Norris knew the Leafs were having difficulty signing Mahovlich. Maybe he could be pried loose with a bundle of cash.

His hunch was accurate. Several drinks later a deal was made. The Leafs agreed to sell Mahovlich to Chicago for a record price — one million dollars.

Ballard and Norris shook hands on the deal, and Norris handed Ballard a one-thousand-dollar bill as a deposit.

Next morning came and there were sober second thoughts — not in the Chicago camp but in Toronto. Former Leaf owner Conn Smythe told his son Stafford the deal was ridiculous — it was bad for hockey. Many others agreed, including thousands of Leaf fans once the news leaked out.

Meanwhile, Chicago general manager Tommy Ivan wasted no time attempting to finalize arrangements. He hurried to the Gardens to deliver a cheque to the Leafs in the amount of one million dollars.

At an emergency meeting of Leaf executives a lot of emotional voices were raised. Then Stafford Smythe emerged and sheepishly announced,

"Frank Mahovlich is not for sale. Not at any price. The money is going back."

When asked to comment, Jim Norris said angrily, "Toronto welched on the deal."

Keep Your Eye on Bobby's Slapshot

IN THE SIXTIES Bobby Hull of the Chicago Blackhawks was hockey's biggest gunner. With a powerful slapshot that was timed at over 100 miles per hour, Bobby terrorized opposing goaltenders. In 1965–66 he scored a record-breaking 54 goals and added 43 assists to win his third Art Ross Trophy as NHL scoring champion. A year later, in the Stanley Cup playoffs against Toronto, Leaf executive Harold Ballard proclaimed, "If we can stop Hull and his bleeping slapshot, we can win this series."

Ballard never figured he would play a personal role in stopping one of Hull's slapshots, but that was what happened midway through the series. During the warm-up before a game at Maple Leaf Gardens, Hull unleashed a slapshot that soared much higher than he intended. It flew over the protective glass and smashed into the face of Ballard, who was occupying his private box at the Gardens' north end. The bones in Ballard's nose were crunched in four places, his glasses were shattered, and blood flowed freely all over his expensive suit.

Pal Hal was rushed to the Gardens' medical clinic where team doctors treated his injury. By then both of his eyes were swollen almost shut, and the skin around them was beginning to change color. Just then, through the open door, he saw Hull and the

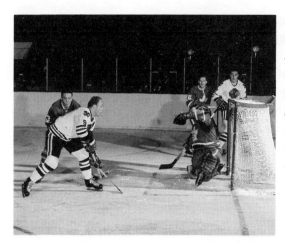

In the sixties the Golden Jet was hockey's biggest gunner.
(Graphic Artists/ Hockey Hall of Fame)

Blackhawks leave their dressing room and begin to make their way toward the ice.

Ballard bolted from the table, grabbed Hull's arm as he passed by, and pulled him into the clinic. "Get a photographer in here quick!" he ordered one of his staff. "I want to get a picture of Bobby and me together. It'll make the front page of every paper tomorrow."

Hull was willing to oblige, but Billy Reay, his coach, who suddenly appeared at the door, had other ideas. "Get the hell out on the ice, Bobby," Reay barked. "This is no time for picture taking."

It took Bobby a few seconds to figure out why his coach reacted the way he did. Then he remembered. Years earlier Reay had been fired by Ballard and the Leafs. Obviously he had a long memory and was in no mood to do Ballard any favors.

The Curse of Muldoon

THE CHICAGO BLACK HAWKS joined the NHL in 1926, and under rookie coach Pete Muldoon, the Hawks finished third in their division. Most hockey men thought that Muldoon had done a commendable job with the talent available.

But the eccentric owner of the franchise, Major Frederic McLaughlin, disagreed. He's reported to have accosted Muldoon and told him the team should easily have finished on top of their division.

"Not in my opinion," snapped Muldoon.

"Well, your opinion doesn't matter much anymore," McLaughlin answered, "because you're fired. I'll get somebody else to coach my hockey team."

And he did, hiring Barney Stanley.

That might have been the end of the story, with Muldoon fading into hockey obscurity, But Jim Coleman, a Toronto sports columnist and prankster of some renown, decided the story of Muldoon's dismissal needed embellishment, a humorous twist — if only for the chuckle or two it might provide his readers.

Coleman was a drinking man in those days, and soon after the cork was pulled from the bottle his creative juices were flowing. At the typewriter he concocted an angry exchange between Muldoon and the Chicago owner.

"You fire me," Coleman had Muldoon threaten McLaughlin, "and I'll put an Irish curse on your team that will last forever. The Hawks will never finish first in the NHL."

Coleman's readers, aware of his fertile imagination, chuckled when his story saw print. Coleman himself thought his column, like Muldoon, would be forgotten in a matter of days. And in a way, it was.

But a decade went by, then a second and a third. In all that time the Hawks never finished atop the NHL standings. Somebody, somewhere, vaguely remembered why. They'd been cursed by a former coach, Pete Muldoon. And the curse was working.

A story appeared about the famous Muldoon curse as if it were fact, and as the Hawks continued to be denied a first-place finish year after year, other wrote about Muldoon's strange hex over the Hawks.

Finally, after 40 years, with Bobby Hull and Stan Mikita leading the way, the Black Hawks surged to a first-place NHL finish in 1966–67. Finishing last was never a problem. In the 40 years since Muldoon's heave-ho, they had managed to do that on 14 occasions.

The All-American Team

IN JANUARY 1937, Major Frederic McLaughlin, wealthy owner of the Chicago Black Hawks, made a startling announcement. He said he was very unhappy with his team's start (only one win in 12 starts by mid-December), and he was going to get rid of the Canadian players on his club and build a powerful team with American-born players.

"I'll rename my team the Chicago Yankees," he declared. "By this time next season there'll be only American-born players on the Chicago roster."

He already had four bona fide major-leaguers on his team, all of American birth. They were goalie Mike Karakas, defenceman Alex Levinsky and forwards Doc Romnes and Louis Trudel. All but Karakas, however, had learned their hockey in Canada.

Late in the season, with five games left to play and his Black Hawks destined for a last-place finish in their division, McLaughlin signed five more American-born minor-leaguers to NHL contracts, giving him a total of nine, or half the team's roster. The newcomers were Ernie Klingbeil and Paul Schaeffer on defence, center Milt Brink and wingers Bun LaPrairie and Al Suomi.

In their first game, the two rookie defencemen were on the ice for all six Boston goals as the Bruins trounced the revamped Black Hawks 6–2. Manager Art Ross of the Bruins was happy to get the two points, but he protested bitterly to the league that McLaughlin's use of the American-born "amateurs" was farcical. "Not one of them had a single shot on goal," he griped.

McLaughlin stubbornly kept the new players in the lineup despite widespread criticism. His team won only one of the five remaining games, and the rookies looked particularly inept in a 9–4 loss to the New York Americans and a 6–1 loss to Boston.

Perhaps it was the outcome of those two games that convinced McLaughlin to abandon his dream. His Black Hawks never did become the Yankees of the NHL. But today, more than fifty years later, McLaughlin would have no difficulty finding enough American-born talent to ice a winning combination.

When You Hear the Whistle, Pass the Puck!

IN 1926, WHEN THE CHICAGO BLACKHAWKS joined the National Hockey League, Major Frederic McLaughlin, the eccentric team owner, hired Pete Muldoon as the first of many Chicago coaches. Muldoon will be remembered for his Don Cherry-like shirt collars and little else, and when he was fired months later, it was said he placed a curse on the Blackhawks, a hex that kept them from a first-place finish in the NHL until 1967. Actually there was no curse. The story was concocted by an inventive sportswriter Jim Coleman after wrestling with a rum bottle most of the night.

Of the dozen or so coaches who followed Muldoon, a man named Godfrey Matheson brought the strangest theories to hockey. Matheson's main claim to fame was the fact that he had guided a team of Winnipeg kids to a midget league championship. When McLaughlin heard about this monumental accomplishment, he hired Matheson on the spot.

Matheson soon introduced some ultramodern coaching ideas that left his players, the fans, and ultimately the team owner in a state of bewilderment, if not shock. His most notable innovation was the whistle system of coaching. From behind the bench Matheson would signal plays by blowing a whistle. One blast was a signal for the puck carrier to pass the puck, two blasts called for a shot on goal, three toots on the whistle meant the Hawks were to tighten up defensively, and so on. Matheson's system may rank as the goofiest coaching strategy ever conceived. The players found it impossible to count or keep track of the whistles. Some shot when they should have passed, others passed when they should have shot, and a few ignored the whistle-tooter altogether. One can only imagine how the referees reacted to all those piercing whistles from the bench.

Before Matheson could come up with any more bright ideas to revolutionize coaching, owner McLaughlin sent him packing. But it wasn't long before he made another oddball coaching choice. He hired Bill Stewart, a baseball umpire and hockey referee, to guide the Hawks. And this time he got lucky, for Stewart took the Blackhawks all the way to the Stanley Cup in 1938.

Coaches Do the Silliest Things

ROGER NEILSON, when he coached the Buffalo Sabres, once threw sticks and a water bottle onto the ice because he didn't care much for the officiating in a game one night.

Tom Webster, coach of the L.A. Kings, hurled a hockey stick, javelin-style, at a referee during an NHL game, hitting the official on the foot.

Billy Reay, when he coached Buffalo in the American Hockey League, once got into a fistfight with the team's announcer.

Murph Chamberlain, another Buffalo coach, once threw a bucket of pucks onto the ice while a game was in progress.

Jacques Demers and Mike Keenan are two NHL coaches who have been accused of tossing pennies onto the ice to create a time-out during games.

Toe Blake of the Montreal Canadiens once

stormed across the ice and punched a referee. He was subsequently fined $2,000.

A coach of a junior team in western Canada once stripped to the waist during a game. Nobody knows why.

Toronto's Punch Imlach once put his skates on at the Leaf bench, opened the gate, and was about to skate out and argue a point with the referee when he had second thoughts and retreated.

Emile Francis of the Rangers once scooted around the rink to tell a goal judge off. Fans intervened, Francis found himself in the middle of a battle, and his players had to climb over the high glass, leap into the throng, and rescue him.

Jack Adams of Detroit, with his team leading Toronto 3–1 in games, jumped onto the ice at the end of game four of the 1941 Stanley Cup finals and started punching referee Mel Harwood. It marked a turning point in the series. Adams was suspended indefinitely, his team sagged, and Toronto won three in a row and captured the Stanley Cup in what has been called "hockey's greatest comeback."

The Innovative Roger Neilson

THEY CALLED ROGER NEILSON Captain Video when he first coached in the NHL because he was clever enough to introduce videotape to professional hockey. He was always on top of things, introducing new methods, looking for an edge.

When he coached junior hockey in Peterborough, Ontario, Neilson astonished the fans by replacing his goalie on penalty shots with a lanky defence-man named Ron Stackhouse. When the penalty shooter moved in, Stackhouse moved out and checked him — before he could get a shot away. It always seemed to work and finally the league revised its rules and banned the Neilson ploy.

When he pulled his goalie from the net late in a game, the goalie was instructed to break his goal stick and leave it in the crease. If an opposing player took a shot on goal, there was a good chance the puck would hit the broken stick and not go in the net. Again, the league was forced to revise its rules.

Neilson even looked to his dog, Jacques, for help on the ice. In practice sessions, Jacques would stand on the ice in front of the net. Behind the net, a defenceman would try to draw Jacques out of position by moving from side to side. When Jacques refused to go for the moves, Roger would day, "See, fellows, if old Jacques won't be fooled by fancy fakes, you shouldn't be either."

Neilson was equally inventive when he coached baseball teams in Peterborough. One day he sub-stituted a peeled apple for a game ball in the mid-dle of an important game. With the bases loaded and two men out, Roger went to the mound to talk to his battery. Unobtrusively, he slipped the apple into the pitcher's glove. Then he secretly gave the ball to his catcher.

When the opposing runner took a lead off third, the pitcher threw a wild pitch over third base. Peterborough fans groaned for it looked like a failed pickoff play. Smirking, the runner on third trotted home, only to be tagged out by the catch-er, who'd been hiding the game ball in his glove.

No wonder Neilson's reputation as a canny coach preceded him to the NHL.

Foster Hewitt's First Broadcast

FOSTER HEWITT, the dean of hockey play-by-play broadcasters, died of Alzheimer's disease in 1985. During the sixties, I shared space in the famous gondola at Maple Leaf Gardens with this broadcasting legend, and from time to time he would reminisce about some of the most memorable moments in his brilliant career.

One date he would never forget was March 22, 1923. On the morning of that day Basil Lake, the radio editor of the *Toronto Star,* gave Foster a unique assignment — to broadcast a hockey game that night between the Kitchener Seniors and Toronto Parkdale from Mutual Street Arena. Foster, then an 18-year-old cub reporter, accepted the assignment with a great deal of reluctance. He had been on the job since dawn that day and he was weary, there was a storm sweeping through Toronto and, most important, he had no idea how to broadcast a fast game like hockey.

But Lake insisted he do the job. Hadn't Foster expressed an interest in getting involved with this new medium of radio? Hadn't he dabbled in boxing and other sports? Then give it a try.

That night, fortified with a five-cent hot dog for nourishment, Foster helped set up the space required at rinkside. His booth was an airtight, glass-enclosed box — about the size of a broom closet.

Fortunately he remembered to purchase a program listing the players' names and numbers, and when the puck was dropped, he began talking. Early in the broadcast he even introduced a phrase that would become internationally famous — "He shoots . . . he scores!" He told me once: "I didn't plan to use it. It just came out. And in time it seemed to catch the fancy of a lot of listeners."

The air in his booth soon became warm and stuffy. He began to perspire, and the glass surrounding his tiny cubicle misted over. He was so uncomfortable that he couldn't wait for the final whistle. But the game ended in a 3–3 tie and overtime was ordered. Foster talked on through three 10-minute overtime periods before the action finally came to a halt. Had he been given a say in the matter he would have vowed then and there never to enter a broadcasting booth again under any circumstances.

However, the response from listeners to his first broadcast was astonishing, so overwhelming that more play-by-play broadcasts were scheduled and Foster was ordered to do them — whether he liked it or not.

Before his second game he wisely had some holes for ventilation drilled through the glass enclosing his booth. "I really didn't mind becoming Toronto's first play-by-play man," he told me. "I just didn't want to be the first to suffocate on the job."

Foster Wasn't the First

ASK A MILLION HOCKEY FANS who broadcast the first hockey game and they will tell you it was Foster Hewitt. On March 22,

1923, Hewitt handled the play-by-play of a senior game from Mutual Street Arena in Toronto between the Parkdale team and Kitchener.

But was he shinny's first commentator? Not according to the *Regina Leader-Post.* Reporter Ron Campbell, writing in that newspaper in 1972, reveals that Pete Parker, a hockey fan turned broadcaster, called the play-by-play of the Western Canada Hockey League playoffs between Edmonton and Regina on CKCK radio on the night of March 14, 1923 — nine days before Foster's historic broadcast in Toronto.

A special closed-in cubicle was built to house Parker and his equipment. The front of his booth was covered with a huge sheet of celluloid, which Parker lifted with one hand when he thought crowd noises would enhance his delivery.

Parker, in relating the story of the first hockey broadcast to the *Leader-Post,* recalled that "the players didn't wear numbers on their sweaters, but that represented no problem because I was familiar with all of the boys and knew them all by sight."

Dick Irvin, Senior, who went on to a great coaching career in the NHL with Toronto, Montreal, and Chicago, played for Regina in that game. Duke Keats was the star forward for Edmonton. Keats set up the winning goal by Art Gagne in a 1–0 Edmonton victory. Two nights later, back in Edmonton, Keats scored the series-winning goal in overtime.

Parker's broadcast of the first playoff game brought dozens of letters from listeners throughout southern Saskatchewan and from many U.S. centers, as well. The next season he was hired to broadcast all of the home games of the Regina Caps on CKCK.

Parker's friends and fellow broadcasters always

resented the fact that Foster Hewitt received the credit for being the game's first play-by-play man.

The First Play-by-Play Announcer

IN MY PREVIOUS VOLUME, *More It Happened in Hockey,* I dispel the myth that Foster Hewitt was the world's first play-by-play hockey announcer. Credit is given to Pete Parker of Regina, who preceded Hewitt into a rinkside booth by several days. On March 14, 1923, Parker handled the first complete broadcast of a professional game heard on radio station CKCK in Regina. Eight days later, on March 22, 1923, Hewitt called the play of a senior amateur game from the Mutual Street Arena in Toronto over the *Toronto Star*'s radio station CFCA.

Parker was obviously miffed that Hewitt always maintained that he was the first. In a letter to me dated March 4, 1972, Parker stated: "On at least two TV panel shows on which he has appeared, Hewitt has calmly stated that his game on March 22, 1923, was the first ever to be broadcast via radio. In Foster's book, *Hockey Night in Canada,* published in 1953, Foster moves the date back a year, declaring, 'In 1921 I broadcast my first hockey game . . .' This is a ridiculous statement for the simple reason that the *Toronto Star*'s radio station, CFCA, didn't start operating until late in 1922."

Parker was quick to add a third name to the mix, that of Norman Albert of Toronto. In his view Albert may warrant the title "World's First Hockey Announcer." According to *Toronto Star* files, Albert broadcast a portion of a game between Midland and North Toronto from the Mutual Street Arena — six weeks before Parker made his debut and seven weeks prior to Hewitt's first broadcast. In a second letter to me in 1972, Parker writes: "I sent a letter to Norman Albert in Toronto and a few days later I received a reply from his wife. She said her husband was too ill to write. She mentioned that Norman had often told her he had broadcast a hockey game before Foster Hewitt but had never done anything about it. Norman worked in the editorial department at the *Toronto Star* at the same time as Foster and was 'drafted' to do the game on February 8, 1923. Unfortunately, Foster has chosen to let the public continue to think that the achievement belongs to him, instead of to Norman Albert. Apparently his conscience never bothered him."

Others may argue that Foster Hewitt wasn't the first play-by-play announcer, but who can deny that he became the most famous? Almost single-handedly he made Saturday night hockey an institution across Canada.

Hockey's First Telecast

MORE THAN HALF A CENTURY AGO, in the winter of 1940, a game played in New York's Madison Square Garden made history. When the Rangers hosted the Canadiens that night, hockey fans at home could catch the action for the very first time, on a miraculous new invention called television.

Not many fans, mind you, because television was in its infancy in 1940. There were only about

300 sets in all of New York City. Their screens were a mere seven inches wide. Incredibly, there was only one camera to follow the play. The announcer's name was Skip Waltz, although he preferred to use the name Bill Allen.

A dozen years later, during the 1952–53 season, the first hockey games were televised in Canada. The Montreal Canadiens presented their first televised game from the Forum on October 11, 1952, and the Leafs' TV debut took place three weeks later, on November 1.

Incredibly, the first producer of the Montreal hockey telecasts was the 24-year-old sports editor of an Ottawa newspaper. Gerald Renaud applied for the job and landed it, even though he had never seen television and had no idea how to produce a game on TV. He hastily read some library books on the subject, asked other CBC production people how things worked and eventually did a praiseworhty job.

But televised hockey was not welcomed with open arms by certain league owners and executives. Many of them feared the medium would dramatically hurt ticket sales. Leaf owner Conn Smythe, for example, charged a mere $100 per game for TV rights to Leaf games during *Hockey Night in Canada*'s initial season. He wanted to make certain televised hockey would be in his team's best interests before locking himself into a long-term contract. At the same time, NHL President Clarence Campbell took a jaundiced view of television, calling it "the greatest menace in the entertainment world."

Smythe's Folly

BACK IN 1927, a man named Conn Smythe bought a Toronto hockey team for $160,000. The team was called St. Patricks and the players wore green uniforms. They played in the old Arena Gardens in Toronto, which had a seating capacity for only 8,000 fans.

Smythe made many changes. He changed the team colors to blue and white, renamed the team the Maple Leafs, obtained some classy players, and soon he was turning fans away at the door.

That was when he decided to build a mammoth new arena for his team. But Smythe's timing was questionable. By then — the early thirties — the Great Depression was causing tough times, and people said the task was impossible. Some called the arena dream "Smythe's Folly."

But the skeptics didn't know Smythe. He and his assistant, Frank Selke, solved most of the problems. For example, the construction workers had to dig through 26 feet of quicksand before they could lay the footings for the building to be called Maple Leaf Gardens. Selke talked the workers into accepting shares in the company in lieu of cash. And just six months after construction began, the 12,000-seat arena was ready for the opening of the 1931–32 season.

On November 12, 1931, the new home of the Toronto Maple Leafs opened on schedule and fans filled the place. They saw the visiting Chicago Black Hawks beat the Leafs in the initial game, but the setback was temporary. Smythe fired coach Art Duncan and brought in Dick Irvin to assemble a winning combination. Irvin did a masterful job, and in the spring of 1932, the Leafs captured the Stanley Cup.

Smythe's vision was rewarded with a world championship and full houses for all home games. In fact, people came from all across Canada just to see the new home of the Leafs. "Smythe's folly" no longer was heard when fans talked of the modern ice palace.

Late in life, when Smythe was asked to name his best year in hockey, he said, "That's easy. It was the year we built the Gardens and then went on to win the Stanley Cup."

A Race to the Wire for Clancy

IN 1930 THE OTTAWA SENATORS of the NHL found themselves in serious financial trouble. The Senators needed an infusion of cash, and the team's directors decided to sell their most colorful player, King Clancy, for the staggering sum of $35,000. Was any player worth that kind of money? That was the question other NHL operators had to ask themselves.

The Montreal Maroons expressed interest and so did the Toronto Maple Leafs. Leaf manager Conn Smythe wanted Clancy badly, but his team's directors refused to pay more than $25,000 for the little Irishman — even if he was regarded as one of the best players in the game. If Smythe wanted him badly enough, he'd have to find the extra $10,000 somewhere else.

Somewhere else turned out to be the racetrack. One of Smythe's horses, Rare Jewel, was entered in a big race. The filly was a nag, a real loser that

Smythe had purchased for a mere $250. In a previous race, she'd finished dead last. Her trainer tried everything, including a flask of brandy, to stimulate her interest in racing. Even the jockey aboard Rare Jewel told his wife to put ten dollars on the nose of the favorite and to forget about Rare Jewel.

In the big race, Rare Jewel went off at 106 to one. But somehow she staggered home in front, paying $214 for a two-dollar wager.

Conn Smythe was the only one at the track that day who bet heavily on Rare Jewel. He walked away with close to $11,000. Smythe took $10,000 of the money and added it to the $25,000 agreed upon the Leaf directors and purchased Clancy. Later he said, "I paid a fortune for a heart, the gamest heart in pro hockey. Clancy also brought character, courage and devotion to the Toronto Maple Leafs." Smythe even sent Ottawa two fringe players as part of the deal — Art Smith and Eric Pettinger.

"With Clancy the Leafs have a chance for the Stanley Cup," said Smythe. And shortly after Clancy arrived, they won it.

The Ref's Last Game

THE OLD REDHEAD, Red Storey, once scored three touchdowns for the Toronto Argos in a Grey Cup game. He starred in lacrosse and hockey, too. But it was in the NHL, as a referee, that he became most famous, especially after a playoff game between Montreal and Chicago on April 4, 1959.

It was game six of an emotional semifinal series, and the score was tied 3–3 when Ed

Litzenberger of the Hawks was tripped up by Marcel Bonin of Montreal. When Storey failed to call a penalty on Bonin the crowd screamed. They howled even louder when the Hawks' Golden Jet, Bobby Hull, went sprawling after a collision with Junior Langlois. Again, no penalty.

The partisan Chicago fans screamed at Storey. When play stopped, one irate Chicago supporter leaped onto the ice and chased after the referee, dousing him with beer. Storey grabbed the interloper while Doug Harvey, Montreal's all-star defenceman, rushed over and belted the fan a couple of times. Then another Chicago fan jumped over the boards and leaped on Storey's back. Storey flipped this fellow in the air and Harvey caressed him with his hockey stick on his way down.

The game was delayed for 35 minutes until order could be restored. After the Canadiens went on to win the game and eliminate the Black Hawks with a 5–4 victory, the shaken Storey said, "Now I know what it's like to have people coming at me, ready to tear me apart. There were 20,000 people screaming for my blood. They hated my guts. How can so many people hate so much?"

A couple of days later, Storey was in Boston, preparing to work another game, when he heard that NHL president Clarence Campbell had been highly critical of his work in the Chicago playoff game. Campbell told an Ottawa sports editor that Storey "froze" on the two penalty calls that so infuriated the Chicago fans.

That was it for Storey. Even though Campbell said his remarks to the reporter had been off the record, Storey's pride was deeply hurt. He turned in his resignation immediately and never went back to the game he loved.

After hockey, he turned to sports broadcasting and the banquet circuit, where he's always been in demand with his fascinating tales of days gone by.

Rebellious George Hayes

IN 1965, NHL LINESMAN George Hayes was fired by League President Clarence Campbell after a 19-year career in hockey. He had officiated in more than 1500 games, plus 149 playoff and 11 all-star games.

Sounds like Hall of Fame material, wouldn't you say?

But Hayes, who died in 1987 at age 67, always scoffed at the idea of a Hall of Fame berth. He maintained some of the capers he'd pulled upset too many people.

Once, for example, he threatened to throw the referee-in-chief off a moving train. Then there was the time he got in a fight in a restaurant, was hit over the head with a ketchup bottle and couldn't see for two weeks.

When the NHL instituted an insurance program for officials, Hayes was the only one who refused to contribute. The following season, he was irate when he discovered he'd signed a contract that contained an insurance clause. So he named his dog, Pete, as beneficiary.

Hayes's downfall came after he refused to take an eye test as ordered by Clarence Campbell. He told Campbell his eyes were perfect, that he tested them by reading the labels on the bottles in his favorite Montreal bar. That was when Campbell fired him for "gross insubordination." Hayes says, "Here they were worried about my eyes when their top referee at the time, Bill Chadwick, had only one eye."

But there were other transgressions. The NHL had a rule that game officials must travel first class on the trains and sleep in a berth. Hayes preferred to travel in the day coaches. He didn't mind sleeping sitting up, and he also saved the money he would have spent on first-class accommodation.

His dismissal by Campbell was the culmination of a long-standing feud between the burly linesman and the league president. Hayes said, "Campbell didn't speak to me for years except to give me

Hall of Fame linesman George Hayes (center) tries to break up a brawl between the Canadiens and the Bruins. (Hockey Hall of Fame)

hell. I never respected him much, either."

Nobody ever criticized Hayes for what he did on the ice. He was regarded as one of the finest linesmen ever to skate in the NHL. Hayes predicted his career would never be recognized by the league. He'd been too much of a rebel, he'd told too many people what he thought of them.

But big George was wrong. Less than a year after he passed away, the Hall of Fame selection committee voted him in. A little late, perhaps, but a popular choice. And how we'd have loved to hear his acceptance speech.

Not Your Normal Pregame Meal

THE LATE GEORGE HAYES, one of hockey's most colorful and eccentric linesmen, liked to save a little money on road trips by packing his own lunches. One day he packed some canned meat and fresh bread in his bag, added a "bottle or two" to wash things down, and jumped onto the train for Detroit.

En route, spurning the costly dining car, he opened the canned meat, spread the contents onto the bread, added thick chunks of onion on top, and sat back to enjoy his meal. It was only when he went to throw the empty can into the trash that he noticed a photo of a dog on the label.

"I admit I had a snort or two beforehand," he told his pal, referee Red Storey, when they met before the game in Detroit. "But I can't believe I made sandwiches out of dog food. Whatever you do, Red, don't breathe a word of this to anybody."

Laughing so hard he could barely answer, Red said, "Sure, George, sure. I promise. Your secret's safe with me."

They went on to Detroit, and Red was still chuckling over the dog food story. He was bursting to share it with somebody. As soon as the warm-up was over and the anthem was played, he skated over to Gordie Howe and Bill Gadsby and told them about Hayes eating the dog food sandwiches.

The two Red Wings knew what to do. Gadsby skated up close to Hayes and started howling like a dog. Howe came along and added a few "Woof, woofs," then attempted to pat Hayes on the head. After that Howe and Gadsby couldn't stop laughing.

But Hayes didn't think it was funny. Fuming, he skated up to Storey and said, "You son of a bitch. You told those guys, didn't you? And you promised you wouldn't."

Storey didn't answer. He was too busy getting set to drop the puck for the opening face-off.

Colleen Howe Steps In

FOR YEARS THE NHL refused to draft amateur players until they reached the age of 20. In the early seventies, that didn't seem right to Colleen Howe, wife of Gordie and mother of two talented teenagers, Mark and Marty.

"It's an asinine rule," she declared before the draft in 1973. "Say you had a son who played the piano. You put a lot of time and money into coaching him and sending him to top conservatories. Then, at 19, when he's ready for Carnegie

Hall, they tell you he can't play there because he's not old enough. That's ridiculous."

Her words triggered a reaction from Bill Dineen, then coach of the Houston Aeros of the WHA and a good friend of the Howes. Everyone assumed the WHA, like the NHL, had a rule against signing players under the age of twenty. But no such rule existed and Dineen knew it.

Dineen created a huge stir at the WHA draft meetings in 1973 when he drafted Mark Howe from the Toronto Marlboros. Officials from other clubs shouted, "It's illegal. The kid's a teenager. He can't do that." Others scoffed at Dineen's selection and said, "Dineen just wasted a top draft choice. He's violated the agreement that exists between the pro hockey clubs and the Canadian Amateur Hockey Association."

Dineen replied, "Since Mark Howe is American-born, he's not governed by that edict."

To show how confident he was that the courts would back his decision, which they ultimately did, Dineen drafted Mark's brother, Marty, who was almost as good a prospect, in the 12th round.

The next day Gordie Howe received a phone call from NHL President Clarence Campbell. Campbell urged him not to let his boys sign with Houston, for it would be a devastating blow to the NHL. But Gordie said he couldn't deny his sons an opportunity to play professional hockey. The boys had worked toward that goal all their lives.

A few days later, Gordie had a suggestion for Dineen. If he was going to sign two Howes for Houston, why not sign three? "Great idea," said Dineen. So Howe, at age 45 and after two years in retirement, fulfilled a lifelong dream of his own, by playing on the same hockey team as his sons.

Downfall of an Agent

IN THE MID-SEVENTIES Dick Sorkin of Long Island was one of the most successful player agents in hockey. This former sportswriter with *Newsday* corralled many of the game's top stars, players like Bob Nystrom of the Islanders, Tom Lysiak of Atlanta and Lanny McDonald of the Leafs.

When McDonald turned pro, Sorkin negotiated a million-and-a-half-dollar deal with the Toronto Maple Leafs. He negotiated a similar contract for Lysiak, and in both cases the money was spread over five years. Needless to say, Sorkin's clients were happy with the services he provided. They predicted big things for him in the agency field.

Sorkin was one of the first agents to haunt the junior hockey playoffs and sign up young kids long before they were ready for the pros. He was a charming guy, and many young players were flattered when he showed an interest in them.

The players he signed had total confidence in him. In most cases, they allowed him to look after all their finances, a decision most of them would later regret. With each signed contract, and when the money started pouring in from the pro clubs, Sorkin maintained what was later called a "nickel and dime" accounting system. The players' confidence in his business procedures would have been badly shaken had they ever seen it.

In order to make more money for his clients — and for himself — Sorkin took the players' funds, and without consulting them, invested thousands of dollars in the stock market. When the market collapsed in the seventies, his losses were staggering — about half a million dollars. He began to panic — someday the players would ask for an accounting — and he sought an easy way to get the money back. In a matter of weeks he lost another $200,000 desperately gambling on sports events.

Finally, Lysiak, Nystrom and others became suspicious. They called for an investigation and Sorkin's reckless handling of their financial affairs was finally revealed. Most — if not all — of their money was gone. The agent was charged with fraud, found guilty and sentenced to three years in jail.

Sorkin served part of his sentence and when he got out he flourished again, but not in hockey. In his third career, he became a successful painting contractor in New York.

Rolling in Dough

HE WAS A DOOR-TO-DOOR SALESMAN in the 1950s, selling pots and pans and struggling to make ends meet. But he had a dream — a dream of making pizzas and someday owning hundreds of pizza parlors across the land.

He saved enough money to open one tiny pizza store in 1959. Two years later, he opened another. Today, Mike Ilitch can point with pride to more than 3000 Little Caesar pizza store franchises across North America.

He was always a sports nut — he'd been an outstanding ball player in his youth — and with millions rolling in each year from pizza sales, he fulfilled another dream — that of owning a big-league franchise. He purchased the Detroit Red Wings from Bruce Norris in 1982 — a once-great NHL franchise that had fallen on hard times. Since then he's spent many millions trying to turn the Red Wings into Stanley Cup winners.

In the eighties, he spent a million alone on fading stars like Darryl Sittler, Tiger Williams and Ivan Boldirev. Warren Young, Harold Snepsts and Mike McEwen cost him another bundle of cash.

But his desire for college free agents cost him the most. A cool million for RPI's Adam Oates (later traded to St. Louis) and even more for Ray Staszak from Illinois-Chicago. When Staszak signed for five years at $1.4 million he became the most highly paid rookie in NHL history. It turned out to be a dreadful waste of money, because Staszak faded faster than a tan in Toledo.

Other Red Wings were well rewarded. John Ogrodnick was handed a $50,000 bonus when he scored his 50th goal one year, and Brad Park received a huge contract plus two pizza outlets for signing on with the Wings. Coach Jacques Demers became hockey's most highly paid mentor in Detroit.

Mike Ilitch is a generous owner. But he's learning a fact of hockey — big spenders seldom win Stanley Cups.

The Strange Entry
Draft of 1974

TODAY THE ANNUAL NHL entry draft is a showcase event, with future stars parading to the teams drafting them and proudly donning team jerseys while flashbulbs pop and a nationwide TV audience looks on. Let a Mario Lemieux or an Eric Lindros show the least reluctance to embrace the drafting club and instant headlines are created.

So it is hard to believe that the annual draft of teenage talent was once conducted in secret, with all the choices being made over the telephone. In 1974 the hush-hush draft was held behind closed doors because of increasing competition for young players by the World Hockey Association.

Some oddities of that draft:

- While it was touted as a secret draft, there were some major leaks. Reporters seemed to know all about the selections — and announced them to the public — almost before they were made.
- Washington, an expansion team, made 20-year-old defenseman Greg Joly the number one choice after Pat Price, the player the Capitals really wanted, skipped to the WHA.
- The Montreal Canadiens, thanks to some shrewd wheeling and dealing by Sam Pollock, owned no less than five draft choices in the first round. After Greg Joly (Washington), Wilf Paiement (Kansas City), Rick Hampton (California), and Clark Gillies (Is-

landers) were selected, the Canadiens took Cam Connor (5th). They also acquired Doug Risebrough (7th), Rick Chartraw (10th), Mario Tremblay (12th), and Gord McTavish (17th).

- The telephone draft was found to be incredibly slow, spanning three days.
- The Buffalo Sabres contributed the most amusing twist. General manager Punch Imlach selected a little-known Japanese star, Taro Tsujimoto, in the 12th round. Tsujimoto was described as a five-foot-eight, 180-pound center from the Tokyo Katanas. It marked the first time an Asian player had been drafted, *The Hockey News* reported. Weeks went by before Imlach confessed it was all a joke. He had plucked Tsujimoto's name from the Buffalo telephone book. No such hockey player existed. "I just wanted to add a little fun to those dreary proceedings," Imlach said.

Grab a Stick, Governor!

THERE WAS A MAJOR SURPRISE when the World Hockey Association held its first player draft in 1972. The Minnesota Fighting Saints, even though they had no hope of landing him, drafted Minnesota Governor Wendell Anderson. Actually the choice wasn't as ridiculous as it appears. Anderson was a key player in the 1956 U.S. Olympic hockey team, silver medalists at the Games held in Cortina, Italy.

A Behind-the-Scenes Battle for the Canada Cup

CANADA HAS AN IMPRESSIVE RECORD in Canada Cup play, dating back to 1976. Team Canada has won four of five championships with the only blot on the record an 8–1 pummeling administered by the Soviets in the 1981 championship game. That was the year the Soviets learned that winning the sparkling trophy is one thing — keeping it is another.

When the teams left the Montreal Forum that September night, the Soviets packed the Canada Cup into a hockey bag and were hurrying for their bus when they were intercepted by tournament chairman Alan Eagleson.

"What's in the bag?" Eagleson asked Soviet official Valentin Sytch.

When Sytch replied, "None of your business," or

Alan Eagleson, Canadian hockey's international impresario.

some similar retort in the Russian language, Eagleson made a grab for the bag.

"You buggers, you've got the Cup in there. Now hand it over!"

While Eagleson clutched one end of the bag, Sytch latched onto the other end. The two men pushed and pulled, arguing all the while, and finally Eagleson's strength won out. He threw open the bag and collared the Cup.

"It's the Canada Cup," he shouted as he hustled the trophy away, leaving the Soviet delegation gnashing their teeth. "That means it stays in Canada."

And it always has.

A Sponsorship Scandal in Germany

IN 1986–87 THE ISERLOHN TEAM in the West German Federal League was in financial difficulties. Two players with NHL experience, Slava Duris (Toronto) and Jaroslav Pouzar (Edmonton), discovered that collecting paychecks from the team owner, Hans Weissenbach, was tougher than stopping a three-on-one.

"There were arguments over money all the time," Duris said. "And pretty soon he wasn't paying us anything at all. So Pouzar and I said, 'That's it. We won't be back for the next game.' And we stayed away. It wasn't long before the owner came around and gave us a few bills — just enough to keep us from bolting — but we could tell the situation was grave and the team might fold at any moment."

The City of Iserlohn wanted to save the franchise. Civic officials offered to bankroll the team, but Weissenbach said no. He would find a new sponsor for his club, one with plenty of ready cash. And he did.

An important source of income for European clubs is the sale of advertising space on team uniforms. The smooth-talking Weissenbach sold space on two sets of uniforms. One set was used in the pregame warm-up and a second set was used during the game itself. After the warm-up before their next game, when the Iserlohn players reached the dressing room, they were handed game jerseys with the words "Green Book" written across the front.

Green Book! Duris and Pouzar knew what that meant. Surely they weren't going to be a skating advertisement for the infamous book written by Moammar Khaddafy, advocate of terrorism.

During the game, the players found themselves getting more attention than they had ever received before. Still photographers and television cameras followed their movements on the ice and, within hours, the scandalous advertising on their jerseys created a furor throughout the league. The West German Hockey Association, when it discovered that Weissenbach was paying off his considerable debts with a wad of bills acquired from Khaddafy, held an emergency meeting and voted to turf Iserlohn out of the circuit.

The players couldn't wait to ditch those god-awful jerseys and get out of town. Duris signed on with Landshut and Pouzar was acquired by Rosenheim. In both places, they reported, the uniforms were much more attractive. And the paychecks much more frequent.

The Missing Choppers

A MINOR MYSTERY was part of the 1981 All-Star game played in Los Angeles. But it was quickly solved before anyone even thought of calling Columbo, the famous Hollywood detective.

While the teams were being introduced, overzealous maintenance employees entered the team dressing room with brooms, vacuums, and dustpans. Their orders were clear: keep the rooms spotless. Dutifully they swept up every scrap of paper and tape — and every paper cup. What they failed to notice in one of those paper cups were Bill Barber's false teeth.

During the first intermission, when the Philadelphia Flyer star reached his place in the dressing room, to his horror he noticed the cup — and his teeth — were missing. At first he thought it was a practical joke. Hadn't Guy Lapointe of Montreal once gathered up his teammates' dentures from similar paper cups and mailed them back to the Montreal Forum — while the Habs were on an extended road trip? And hadn't Toronto's George Armstrong once switched teammate Johnny Bower's teeth with a similar-looking set, claiming later that he had picked up the substitute dentures from an undertaker?

But this was no joke. Barber's teeth had simply vanished.

A frantic search was quickly organized. All maintenance workers were assembled and ordered to find the missing dentures — or else. Searchers spent the second period sorting through a ton of garbage and looking into a thousand paper cups.

Still no choppers. The search went on through the final period, and just when everyone was beginning to despair, a young hero-to-be, pawing through the contents of a garbage can he had overturned, flipped over a paper cup, looked inside, and smiled. Smiling back at him were Barber's dentures.

The discovery came in the nick of time. Barber was runner-up to Mike Liut as MVP of the game, and he came in for plenty of attention in the postgame press conference. The smile he gave all the cameramen was one of happiness — and relief.

Clarence Campbell Goes to Jail

IN MARCH 1980 Clarence Campbell, former president of the National Hockey League, spent five hours in a Montreal jail cell. It was part of his sentence after he was convicted of wrongdoing in the Dorval Sky Shops scandal. Campbell was also fined $25,000.

The 74-year-old hockey Hall of Famer's stay in jail was "a symbolic sentence," according to Mr. Justice Melvin Rothman of the Quebec Superior Court. It was lenient because of the judge's consideration for Campbell's failing health.

The previous month Campbell and businessman Gordon Brown were found guilty of conspiring to give Senator Louis Giguere $95,000 in exchange for an extension on the lease of the duty-free Sky Shops at Dorval Airport. The sentence placed a shameful blemish on the reputation of the man who had preached integrity in hockey throughout his long career as NHL president.

The Youngest Referee

AGES OF EARLY-DAY hockey referees were seldom recorded, but since many arbiters were players recruited from other teams, their youth was taken for granted. Frank Patrick would certainly rank among the youngest of the players chosen to handle important matches. On nights when he wasn't starring for his own club in Montreal, this 18-year-old was often the referee in games played elsewhere. By age 20 he was selected to referee two important Stanley Cup series.

The Missing Officials

ON JANUARY 15, 1983, a blizzard swept through New England and prevented NHL referee Ron Fournier and linesman Dan Marouelli from getting to their next assignment — a game in Hartford between the Whalers and the New York Islanders. So linesman Ron Foyt, who did make it to the game on time, consulted the NHL rule book and found a solution to the problem. If he took over as referee, he was permitted to recruit a player from each club to serve as linesmen in the game. He had no trouble finding volunteers. Gary Howatt of the Islanders and Mickey Vulcan of the Whalers were both nursing minor injuries. But both could skate. And both were happy to assist Foyt because "it was a once-in-a-lifetime" opportunity.

So the game was played and the first period went by without a hitch. During the intermission, Fournier and Marouelli finally arrived and replaced the two players who had helped create an NHL "first." The two volunteers, Howatt and Vulcan, are the only two modern-day players ever to act as game officials in the NHL.

When Goal Judges Were Stripped of Their Power

IN HOCKEY'S CRADLE DAYS the goal judges — often men selected at random and pulled from the stands just before game time — were compelled to make the final decision when a goal was scored. If they erred, or were thought to have erred, the fans howled their displeasure. The referee, if he felt so inclined, had the authority to send one or both judges back to their seats and call on a couple of volunteers to replace them. It was a bizarre system by today's standards, but perfectly acceptable to turn-of-the-century hockey fans.

Later the power of awarding a goal was stripped from the goal judges and awarded to the referee, and it is easy to single out the reason for the change. Goal judges were most often residents of the community in which the game was played. Therefore it was assumed that their decisions, more often than not, favored the home team. Referees, on the other hand, were often "outsiders," imported from another community some distance away and therefore (it was fervently hoped) they were unlikely to hold any bias toward one team or the other. It was also thought that the referee might have a better vantage point to see whether or not a goal was actually scored.

One game, played in Morrisburg, Ontario, shortly after the turn of the century, may have precipitated the change. While hosting archrival Cornwall, one of the Morrisburg players skated down the ice and apparently scored. The goal judge, a Morrisburg native, waved his little flag, signaling a goal. The Cornwall players protested, claiming the puck didn't enter the net. When their complaints were shrugged off, the players and their fans drew up an affidavit bearing the names of 200 spectators who swore the goal hadn't been scored. One of their number, a Cornwall lawyer, presented the affidavit to league officials. It was an impressive-looking document.

When the Morrisburg fans got wind of this initiative, they were quick to respond. They, too, scurried around seeking witnesses, and overnight they collected the names of 200 witnesses who swore they saw the puck enter the net.

The Cornwall supporters never did get the original ruling overturned, but the pressure they exerted did force a change in league policy. Shortly afterward league officials declared that the referee would have the final say whenever a goal was scored.

Now It Can Be Told

THE BOSTON BRUINS WERE one of the first NHL clubs to sign a Swedish player. They had high hopes for Sven (Tumba) Johanson, a four-time Olympian who joined the Bruins at training camp over 30 years ago. Johanson's stay in the

NHL was a brief one, however, mainly because of a practical joke he concocted.

"I don't think the Bruins accepted me," he said on his return to Sweden, "and I think it was because of a practical joke I played on them one day. I saw that they all joked around with each other in the dressing room, and I wanted to be a part of it. So I asked myself what I could do to become accepted by them. Well, I noticed that they all put their false teeth in little cups before a game or practice. So I thought I'd have some fun. When they went onto the ice, I sneaked back in the room and switched all the teeth around. When they came back in, they found that none of their teeth fitted.

"Did they laugh at my little prank? No, were they ever mad. And they knew it was me who'd done it because I was laughing like crazy. From then on it was very cool between us, and a few days later the manager took me aside and told me he was sending me back to Sweden."

How the Leafs Lost Two Future Stars

IN 1932 THE TORONTO MAPLE LEAFS captured the Stanley Cup, and for the next few years owner Conn Smythe relied on the nucleus of that team. But soon younger, fresher players were needed.

In western Canada Leaf scout Beattie Ramsay phoned Smythe and told him he was sending three bright prospects to the 1938 Leaf training camp. He was certain Smythe would be impressed with at least two of the three men he was sending. Their names were Doug Bentley and Elmer Lach. The third player was Harvey Barnes.

At training camp the shy young westerners were all but ignored by the other Leafs. No one knew much about them, except that Beattie Ramsay had recommended them. The boys were awed by the big city and intimidated by the reputations of the men who dressed next to them for the training camp scrimmages. Many of the Leafs — stars like Conacher, Primeau, Jackson, and Horner — had been their boyhood idols. In the workouts the westerners felt awkward and self-conscious. They found it difficult to fit in with the famous NHL players.

Into the dressing room one day strode Leaf owner Conn Smythe. After kibitzing with his regulars, he noticed the trio of rookies huddled in a corner.

"I thought Beattie Ramsay was sending me some men," he snorted. "Looks like he sent me three little peanuts instead."

Some of the Leafs laughed, others felt badly about Smythe's putdown.

"Don't worry about it, kids," one of them said. "Mr. Smythe is always popping off. None of us will get swollen heads so long as he's around."

But Smythe's words had left the boys from the West dazed and humiliated.

The next morning they didn't show up for practice. When coach Dick Irvin called their hotel, he was told they had left the city.

"They said they were going back home, Mr. Irvin. They took last night's train for Regina."

It was true. Lach, Bentley, and Barnes all vowed they would play hockey as far away from Toronto as possible. And they did — for a year or two.

Then Bentley got a break with the Chicago Blackhawks and soon became a star, scoring 33 goals and 73 points in the 1942–43 season. He told the Hawks he had a brother Max who was "even better than me" and brought him to training camp. Soon the Bentleys and Bill Mosienko formed the Pony Line, one of the highest scoring lines in hockey.

Elmer Lach, meanwhile, had distanced himself from the Leafs by playing with the Moose Jaw Millers. It wasn't long before his stylish play caught the eye of Paul Haynes, a Montreal scout. In 1940 Lach headed east for another training camp, and this time he had no trouble catching on with the famous Montreal Canadiens. Coach Dick Irvin, who had left Toronto to become the mentor of the Habs, was delighted to see Lach again, one of Smythe's "little peanuts." And thankful for Conn Smythe's acid tongue and the words that had driven young Lach away from Toronto.

In time Lach, too, helped form a famous line, the renowned Punch Line of Lach, Toe Blake, and Maurice Richard. With Lach in the the lineup for the next 13 years, the Habs rolled to four consecutive first-place finishes and captured three Stanley Cups.

It would be nice to report that Harvey Barnes, the third "little peanut," found big league stardom, too. Alas, it was not to be. But two out of three isn't bad.

Hockey's Iron Man Might Have Been a Leaf

BACK IN 1975 the Montreal Canadiens had a problem. They were searching for a solid defensive forward, preferably a centerman who could win face-offs.

Scotty Bowman, the Habs' coach, was engaged in casual conversation with Roger Neilson one day. Neilson, then coaching the junior Peterborough Petes, happened to mention that one of his players, Doug Jarvis, was the best face-off man in hockey.

"Of course you mean in junior hockey," Bowman said.

"No, I mean in all of hockey," Neilson replied.

With this information stuck firmly in his mind, Bowman went to Sam Pollock, general manager of the Canadiens, and asked, "How can we acquire Jarvis? Roger Neilson tells me he's the best face-off man in hockey."

Pollock admitted Jarvis might be a problem to acquire because he had been drafted earlier that year by the Toronto Maple Leafs. So, one of the first things Pollock did was to make sure Leaf owner Harold Ballard was aware that Jarvis was a devout Christian. He asked Ballard, "How is that religious kid you drafted doing?" Ballard's antipathy toward "religious" players had been firmly established when he dumped Laurie Boschman, another good centerman and born-again Christian.

Then, in trade talks with Leaf general manager Jim Gregory, Pollock mentioned a player named Greg Hubick, a Montreal farmhand. "He needs a chance to play, and we've no room for him. Maybe he could help your Leafs," he told Gregory.

Gregory said he could use Hubick, but asked, "Who can I give up in return?"

"Why not make out a list of five players in your farm system and I'll pick one in return for Hubick," Pollock suggested.

Gregory's list included a couple of players he thought Pollock would find too attractive to pass up. He must have been surprised when Pollock selected the fifth name on the list — Doug Jarvis.

At the Montreal training camp there was only one spot open on the Hab roster — and rookie Jarvis grabbed it. He excelled at winning face-offs and his defensive play was superb. He played in every game and his team won the Stanley Cup. They won it again in 1977, 1978, and 1979. Jarvis barely missed a shift in four straight seasons and collected four Stanley Cup rings.

He played 80 games in each of seven seasons for Montreal before he was traded to Washington as part of a blockbuster deal — Jarvis, Rod Langway, Brian Engblom, and Craig Laughlin for Ryan Walter and Rick Green. In Washington he played three more 80-game seasons before moving on to Hartford in another deal. His attendance record at Whaler games was also perfect. On December 26, 1986, he surpassed Gary Unger's consecutive-game record of 914. Jarvis went on to establish the current NHL ironman mark of 962 games, which dates back to April 5, 1987.

He came close to missing a game only once, when he was knocked out during a game in Detroit. Team doctors kept him in hospital overnight, then gave him the green light to play that evening.

And his fondest memory?

"Game number one. Just stepping on the ice at

the Montreal Forum that night was the fulfillment of a lifelong dream."

That'll Be 30 Bucks, Mr. Day

WHEN HAP DAY, a star player for the Toronto Maple Leafs in the late 1920s, signed his contract with Conn Smythe one year, he noticed an unusual clause in the pact. It stated: "The hockey club shall furnish the player with a complete hockey uniform with the player placing a $30 deposit with the club, said deposit to be returned to the player at the end of the season upon the return of the uniform."

Cherry Calls Time-out to Sign Autographs

EVER HEAR OF AN NHL COACH calling a time-out in a game to sign autographs? Don Cherry did it on the night he coached the woeful Colorado Rockies to an upset victory over his former team, the Boston Bruins. It was December 2, 1979, and Cherry was itching for a win when he brought his Rockies into the Boston Garden for the first time since he was dismissed as the Bruins' coach in the off-season. Not only was he still miffed at Boston general manager Harry Sinden for firing him, he had just heard that two Boston players, Gilles Gilbert and John Wensink, had bad-mouthed him to the press.

"I can understand Gilbert criticizin' me," Cherry

snorted to the reporters. "Did he tell you how I tried to start him five times last season and he came up with five different excuses why he couldn't play? And every time we'd go into Montreal he'd give me some excuse why he couldn't play there. It got to be a joke.

"And for Wensink to say I played favorites really disappoints me. He should get down on his knees every night and thank the Lord that I did play favorites, or he'd have been battin' his brains out in the International League."

But the Boston fans were quick to show Cherry he was missed and still loved, rising to give him a standing ovation when he took his place behind the visiting team's bench. As usual the Rockies got off to a sluggish start and fell behind 2–0. Then someone said, "Come on, guys, let's dig in and win this for Grapes." And they did, squeezing out a 5–3 victory, with the last shot hitting the empty Boston net. The most talked-about moment in the game came in the third period when Cherry called a time-out. His players gathered at the bench, but he discussed no strategy, offered no words of encouragement. To their amazement, and to the delight of everyone in the building, he turned his back on them and started signing autographs.

"It was just somethin' that happened," he told me later. "I didn't plan it. I wasn't tryin' to twist the knife in or nothin'. I was just tryin' to give my defensemen a rest. Then people started askin' me for my autograph, so I signed some things. You can bet my bosses in Colorado weren't too happy about that."

One of Cherry's supporters that night was D. Leo Monahan, a longtime Boston hockey writer. The following day he wrote: "Grapes couldn't have written a better script. The man may showboat a bit but he's a gem among his drab, colorless, cliché-speaking brethren. Hail, Don Cherry, hail."

An Embarrassing Moment for Grapes

DON CHERRY WOULD PROBABLY like to forget the following incident. During a playoff series between the the Los Angeles Kings and the Edmonton Oilers, Don found himself in the Los Angeles airport waiting for a flight. Across the airport waiting room he spotted a familiar figure, that of Brant Heywood, the

Dressed up to the nines: Don Cherry posing as a Maple Leaf.
(Graphic Artists/ Hockey Hall of Fame)

Hockey Night in Canada isolation director. Heywood was bending over to tie an errant shoelace. Approaching his friend from behind, Cherry gave Heywood a friendly pat on the bum. But the man who straightened up, the man who turned and gave Cherry a withering look, didn't look like Heywood one bit. "Do you meet many men this way?" he asked Cherry before he hurried away.

Look, Up in the Sky, It's a Referee!

HALF A CENTURY AGO, when Frank Carlin managed the Montreal Royals hockey club, life on the road was full of surprises. "We went into Boston once," Carlin told me, "and there didn't appear to be a referee for the game. There were two linesmen, but no ref. When I mentioned his absence to the linesmen, they just laughed and said, 'He's up there.' Then they pointed skyward. Sure enough, high over the ice, sitting in a gondola, was the referee. Somebody figured he'd have a better overall view of things if he was high over the ice in a kind of basket. I swear it was the only time I'd ever seen such a thing. So we played in the only game in which the referee was perched forty or fifty feet above the action. If he called a lousy penalty, the players below had nobody to argue with except for the linesmen. And all they said was, 'Don't tell us about it. He's the guy who made the call.' And they'd point skyward again."

Wrong Man, Wrong Time, Wrong Place

REMEMBER NED HARKNESS? He was the coach and later general manager of the Detroit Red Wings for a couple of seasons in the seventies. He had made his reputation in U.S. college hockey and become the first man to jump from campus rinks to coach in the pros, only to fall flat on his tush in Motor City.

Was it Ned's rah-rah approach, treating the pros like college kids, that killed his chances for success in Detroit? Or was Fred Shero right when he said, "Harkness had many things going for him, but hockey players and club owners are afraid of outsiders. They're afraid of shocks."

There was no question that Harkness jolted the Wings right from day one. At training camp he introduced new methods, such as a novel forechecking system and some interesting conditioning drills. His chalk talks annoyed the veterans, who complained about being treated like "collegians." Gordie Howe, Alex Delvecchio, and Frank Mahovlich all got their digs in.

Harkness fought back, pointing the finger at general manager Sid Abel. He complained about the complacency within the organization. He griped about the lack of scouting reports and was annoyed when Abel told him, "Don't worry, Ned. Things will work out."

Eventually Abel, irritated by the criticism, delivered an ultimatum to team owner Bruce Norris. "Either Harkness goes or I go."

"We're going to miss you, Sid," Norris replied.

"I'm sticking with Harkness."

But the veteran players sided with Abel. Like them, he was old school. The Red Wings drew up a petition. If Harkness wasn't fired, they would refuse to play. Gordie Howe was chosen to hand Bruce Norris the edict. When he saw it, Norris was shocked.

Still he backed Harkness and asked him to be both coach and general manager. But Harkness was ready to throw in the towel as coach. He knew it was hopeless. The Wings were never going to play Harkness-style hockey. He resigned and accepted Abel's old job as the Wings' general manager.

The poisonous stories spread about Harkness by the players and passed along to the press were translated into animosity by the fans. His car windows were broken and his home was splattered with eggs. One fan attacked him physically, while others sent him death threats. Before long, bags of hate mail streamed into the Red Wings' offices.

By February 1974 the situation had become intolerable. When Harkness resigned from the organization, he made no explanation, only saying, "I guess I was the wrong man, with the wrong team, at the wrong time."

I knew Ned Harkness long before he reached the NHL. Our St. Lawrence University hockey teams often played against his Rensselaer Polytechnic Institute (RPI) squads in the fifties. Harkness was the greatest college hockey coach I had ever seen. We knew him as the Miracle Man at RPI for his ability to take teams with little depth right to the heights. In 1954 his RPI team had two lines, a pair of defensemen, and a goalie. He guided it past powerful Michigan and Minnesota to win the NCAA title at Colorado Springs. His record at RPI was 187–90–7, despite the fact that he never had the luxury of coaching talent-laden teams.

In the 1960s he moved on to Cornell and molded a hockey powerhouse. His record there was truly astonishing — 163–27–2. And that was in his first three years on the job before he was able to stock his teams with players he had recruited personally. From 1967 to 1970 Cornell captured two national titles, four straight ECAC crowns, and five straight Ivy League championships. One of his stars was goalie Ken Dryden, who played in only three losing games during his college career. During one stretch in 1970, Cornell went a record 29 games without a loss.

After the disaster in Detroit, Harkness embarked on a program to bring top college hockey to Union College in Schenectady, New York. He began with no arena and no team, and when he was able to ice a team of freshmen and sophomores, he quickly ran up a record of 48–6–2 against varsity competition. He resigned in 1978, stating, "I'm a hockey coach, not a politician," a remark aimed at college administrators who were said to be harassing him.

Buying a Time-out . . . with Cash

DURING THE 1986 STANLEY CUP PLAYOFFS, St. Louis coach Jacques Demers tried to buy a little time for his team. And he was brought up to believe that whenever you buy something, you are expected to pay for it. So whenever he needed a little extra time to give his players a breather, he tossed some pennies onto the ice. When warned by the referee not to do it again, Demers said, "It's true. I got caught. But I'm not the first coach to get a few extra seconds that way. I've seen tape tossed out there, a player's mouth guard dropped over the boards, lots of things."

When a reporter asked him how he would have felt if a security man had tossed him out of the rink for throwing objects onto the ice, he replied, "I never thought of that. I would have been very embarrassed."

Breaking Up Is Not Hard to Do

HOCKEY BROADCASTERS HAVE their moments. I know. I have been one. One day I asked Toronto Maple Leaf announcer Joe Bowen and his then partner Bill Watters if there was one incident they could recall that really cracked them up.

Bowen says, "Oh, yeah, the Leafs are playing in Edmonton one night and the club had just signed, at great expense, that noted plumber from Czechoslovakia, Miroslav Ihnacak. Lasted half a season. Anyway, the kid had just arrived and it was his second or third game and he wants to make an impression. So he takes a run at Mark Messier who's in along the boards with his big elbow stuck out like this [demonstrates]. Now here comes this rookie from across the rink and rams his nose right into Messier's elbow. What a smack when he hit! Well, down he goes and Billy and I start to laugh. It was hilarious. Poor Ihnacak is lying there quivering, and there's blood all over the place and we're hysterical. Then Billy says, 'I think the poor guy's got CCM tattoed on his bugle.'

"Well, that did it. Now we're really laughing. Here they're scraping poor Ihnacak off the ice and we're busting our guts in the booth. Then the game is under way, and I still can't control the laughter, so I went to a commercial — right in the middle of the play. I'd never done that before, but I had to. Luckily no goals were scored while we were away. And the game was on radio, not TV, so nobody said anything or noticed anything except maybe they thought a couple of damn hyenas were calling the play."

Bill Watters adds, "We were under control when we came back from the commercial, and everything was rolling along just fine . . . until we saw Ihnacak jump back onto the ice . . ."

"That's when we lost it again," Bowen interjects. "We both thought of Ihnacak taking dead aim on Messier's elbow, running right at it from 50 feet, and going down like a sack of wheat, so we started cackling and howling again. I can't believe we got through the rest of that period."

A Message for the King

WHEN KING CLANCY RETIRED as a hockey player, he turned to refereeing. One day he told me about a game he worked in New York.

"It was during World War II and some soldiers were on hand for the opening ceremonies. It was very dramatic the way they dimmed the lights as everybody stood for *The Star-Spangled Banner.* Then the soldiers raised their rifles and prepared to fire a volley. It was a solemn moment and a hush fell over the crowd. Then, way up in the top balcony, some leather-lunged fan bellowed out, 'When you get through with all that — shoot Clancy!'"

Ballard Fires Neilson, or Does He?

ON MARCH 1, 1979, the struggling Maple Leafs met the Montreal Canadiens at the Forum. It was a big game for Toronto coach Roger Neilson. Prior to the match, his boss, 75-year-old Harold Ballard, told reporters, "Neilson will be gone . . . fired if the Leafs don't win."

Late in the game, with Toronto trailing 2–1, Ballard told Dick Beddoes, then a member of our telecast crew, that Neilson indeed was toast. The dismissal of Neilson, a very popular guy, made headlines everywhere. I ran into the coach in a Toronto restaurant the next day and commiserated with him. He, in turn, said he was confused because he hadn't heard anything yet from Ballard. The Leaf players, meanwhile, led by Tiger Williams and Darryl Sittler, huddled with Ballard and pleaded with him to bring Roger back. There was even a rumor that they might refuse to take the ice for their next home game if Roger wasn't behind the bench.

By Saturday Ballard had either reconsidered or he couldn't find a competent replacement for Neilson. He talked to John McLellan about taking over, but McLellan said he wanted no part of the assignment. So Ballard called Neilson in and rehired him. But the Leaf boss, always the showman, kept the move a secret. Ballard even suggested that Neilson wear a paper bag over his head when he took his place behind the Leaf bench that night. It would be quite a sensation, especially since the game was on *Hockey Night in Canada.*

Neilson wisely decided against the paper bag suggestion, and when he did make his appearance, the ovation he received was tremendous. Alas, his return was short-lived. A few weeks later Ballard decided not to renew his contract.

"They Asked Me to Coach"

IN ALL THE CONFUSION SURROUNDING the firing and rehiring of Toronto coach Roger Neilson in March 1979, I wound up with a great deal of egg on my face.

Prior to Neilson's surprising return — without a bag over his head — for the Saturday night game at Maple Leaf Gardens following his "dismissal" in Montreal, I tried frantically to learn the identity of the man Ballard had selected to replace him as Leaf coach. As the color commentator on the telecast, it was important that I say something about the new coach at the beginning of the program.

Minutes before game time, seeking the latest developments, I dashed into the Leaf front office where I encountered head scout Gerry McNamara. "Help me out, Gerry," I pleaded. "We're going coast-to-coast in a few minutes and I've got to know who's coaching tonight."

"You've come to the right place," he said. "They've asked me to coach tonight."

"That's all I need to know. Thanks, Gerry."

I raced to the gondola and moments later announced to a huge television audience that Gerry McNamara would be the new Leaf coach. At precisely that moment Roger Neilson emerged from the Leaf dressing room and strolled to the Leaf bench while the crowd roared its approval.

I was dumbfounded. Where was McNamara? Why had he lied to me about taking over as coach? Was he deliberately trying to make me look like a buffoon?

On Monday morning I walked into McNamara's office and confronted him. "Gerry, why did you lie to me on Saturday night?" I asked him, my collar still warm.

"But I didn't lie to you," he replied calmly. "I told you on Saturday that they had asked me to coach. I didn't say I would be coach. There's a difference, you know."

Perhaps there was a difference . . . a small one. But there was no doubt he had led me to believe he would be Neilson's replacement. Hence the egg all over my face.

"Wipe That Tan Off, Miller!"

BOSTON COACH DON CHERRY was preparing his Bruins for a playoff series with Montreal one year. After a morning workout in Boston, the team reassembled later that day for the bus ride to the airport and the flight to Montreal. The weather had turned exceptionally balmy in

Boston, and forward Bobby Miller had taken advantage of the soaring temperature to lie out in the sun for a couple of hours. The result — a beautiful tan. When Miller boarded the bus, Cherry had a fit.

"Look at you, Miller," he snorted. "You're all brown, for God's sake. You've got a tan. The rest of us is white and you've got a tan."

As Miller scurried down the aisle of the bus, Cherry gave him a parting shot. "I'm tellin' you right now, Miller. Get rid of it!"

Those Crybabies

ON FEBRUARY 28, 1902, team executives of the the Montreal Victorias held a meeting after which they lodged a protest with the league over the result of a game played two days earlier. The Vics maintained that the puck used in the match wasn't a regulation one. It was slightly smaller than the regulation disk. Furthermore, it wasn't a new puck. Therefore, they maintained, the score shouldn't count and their defeat should be erased from the records.

The Vics' protest was not only thrown out but the team was ridiculed and universally accused of being a "bunch of poor sports and crybabies." One Toronto sports editor wrote: "The Montreal Vics must expect their protest to be considered by a committee from some institution for the feeble-minded if they have any idea it will prevail." Another editor wrote: "They're grown up but still babies. They claim that the puck was not regulation size but they agreed to play with it. Only when they lost did they decide to protest."

Dopey Deals

IN JANUARY 1983 the Seattle Breakers of the Western Hockey League traded the rights to forward Tom Martin to Victoria — for a team bus. "It was no big deal at the time," Martin said. "I heard it was a good-looking bus."

On June 18, 1987, New York Ranger GM Phil Esposito announced he had traded a number one draft choice and $100,000 to the Quebec Nordiques for the Nords' coach Michel Bergeron. During Bergeron's second season on the job, Esposito fired him.

Colorful, Controversial Conn Smythe

ON MARCH 15, 1932, during the first period of a Toronto–Boston game played in Boston, Leaf goalie Lorne Chabot tripped the Bruins' Cooney Weiland. Chabot was sent to the penalty box for two minutes, and three Leafs — Red Horner, Alex Levinsky, and King Clancy — took turns defending the goal. There was only one goalie per team in those days. All three failed their netminding test as the Bruins rattled in three goals. The penalty to Chabot infuriated Leaf manager Conn Smythe, and when referee Bill Stewart skated past the visitors' bench, Smythe reached out, grabbed him by the sweater, and refused to let go. Finally Charles Adams, the Bruins' president, with several policemen in tow, persuaded Smythe to release the referee and allow the game to continue.

When Toronto star Ace Bailey suffered a fractured skull after being upended by Boston's Eddie

Shore at the Boston Garden in December 1933, Smythe was one of the first men on the scene. While rink attendants carried the stricken Bailey off on a stretcher, hundreds of fans left their seats and filled the corridors of the Boston Garden. When one Bruin fan refused to get out of Smythe's way, he punched the man and was promptly arrested and charged with assault. The charge was later withdrawn when the judge ruled that Smythe had acted under great stress.

During the 1936–37 season, Smythe accused Montreal officials of a sneaky trick. He claimed that an attempt had been made to slow down his fast players by blunting the blades of their skates. "Someone sneaked into our dressing room and

The Stanley Cup is presented to the Maple Leafs' Conn Smythe (center) in 1942. At extreme left is coach Hap Day with star player Syl Apps. (Turofsky)

spread sand on the floor," was his accusation. General manager Tommy Gorman of the Maroons dismissed Smythe's charge as nonsense. "If there's sand on the floor, Smythe must have brought it from Toronto — from one of those sandpits he owns."

When the Toronto Maple Leafs invaded the Boston Garden for a game in January 1937, Smythe appeared on the Toronto bench wearing a cutaway evening jacket, striped trousers, spats, and a top hat. His attire, he told reporters, was designed to add some much-needed class to Boston hockey circles. The attendant publicity he received in the Boston papers pleased Smythe and infuriated his archrival, Boston GM Art Ross.

During the same season, when his Toronto club lost a game in New York, Smythe leaped over the boards and began a heated argument with the referee and the goal judge. When big Art Coulter of the Rangers skated in between Smythe and the officials, the diminutive Smythe threw a wild punch that caught Coulter right in the mouth.

At a Montreal–Toronto match in Maple Leaf Gardens, Smythe leaped into the penalty box to blister the ears of the Canadiens' player-coach Sylvio Mantha, who was serving a minor penalty. When referee Mike Rodden skated over to order Smythe out of the box, the Leaf owner grabbed Rodden by the sweater and wouldn't let go. During the struggle, Smythe took an usher's hat and slapped it on the struggling referee's head. Leaf coach Dick Irvin joined the fracas and belted Mantha. Then NHL president Frank Calder rushed to the scene, along with Ernest Savard, governor of the Canadiens. Fans gaped at the astonishing sight. There was the

NHL president and two of his governors, plus a coach and a player-coach, all pushing, shoving, and shouting in the penalty box.

One year Smythe accused the Toronto sportswriters of not telling the truth. As a result, he made the newspapers pay to have their reporters attend Leaf games. "Newspapermen are crooks!" he declared. "They are glad to take my money, glad to put my ads in their papers, glad to take my free seats to the games. And then they don't write the truth! From now on let them pay to get into Leaf games."

On the eve of a Toronto–Boston game in Boston, Smythe bought advertising space in all the Boston papers. Addressed to the Bruin fans, it read: "If you're tired of what you've been looking at lately, the sleep-producing hockey as played by the Boston hockey club, come out tonight and see a decent team play the game the way it should be played."

The Bruins' Art Ross was furious with Smythe and demanded the NHL censure him. The league governors met in time and decided to censure both Smythe and Ross for their constant bickering.

LEGENDS AND LORE

One of Hockey's Oldest Records

ON MARCH 12, 1912, defenceman Frank Patrick of Vancouver scored a phenomenal six goals from his defence position in a game against New Westminster. This record has never been matched.

A Moving Tribute to Orr

THAT JANUARY NIGHT IN 1979 was a night to remember at the Boston Garden. The Bruins were entertaining a team of touring Soviets. But the visiting team wasn't the reason this game was a hotter ticket than any Stanley Cup final.

The occasion was Bobby Orr Night, with starting time postponed for 30 memorable pregame minutes while friends and fans honored the greatest Bruin of them all.

Play-by-play broadcaster Bob Cole and I sat in our cramped booth above the ice, all but deafened by wave after wave of applause and the din of the cheering. The thunderous ovation went on and on and on . . . and rose to a peak when at centre ice, Bobby Orr, with his wife Peggy by his side, took off his suit jacket and slipped on his famous number-4 jersey.

No Bruin, no player anywhere, ever did the things that Orr did on ice. He scored 264 goals in a ten-year career and twice led the NHL in scoring. One year he collected 135 points . . . this at a time when 100-point seasons were not as common as they are today.

Orr won the Norris Trophy eight straight times, the Hart Trophy as MVP three times, and he was a perennial first-team all-star.

Almost single-handedly he took the Bruins from last place to first in the NHL standings and pushed them to two Stanley Cups. He revolutionized hockey with his rushing, offensive style, and he did all this while playing on a gimpy left knee that required six operations and forced him out of hockey much, much too soon.

In the Boston Garden that night, a banner was raised in Bobby Orr's honor. His name and number were on the banner and the years he served the Bruins so well — 1966–76. Boston management had let him slip away to Chicago for a couple of years — a big mistake — but now he was back, back to stay if not to play.

With their prolonged ovation, Bobby's fans let him know how much they appreciated all he had done for them, and how much they loved him.

Gretzky Goes to L.A.

IN JUNE 1988, when the Edmonton Oilers were celebrating their fourth Stanley Cup victory, team captain Wayne Gretzky said he'd like to be around to celebrate ten more Stanley Cups as an Oiler. Two months later, Gretzky was gone from Edmonton, traded by the Oilers to the Los Angeles Kings in a blockbuster deal that stunned hockey fans everywhere.

Oiler fans were shocked and furious. They needed someone to blame because they felt they'd been robbed of a priceless possession.

Some of them blamed Wayne's wife, American actress Janet Jones. They called her Jezebel and Yoko Ono and said she'd persuaded Wayne to leave for Hollywood. Others blamed the greed of Oiler owner Peter Pocklington.

Pocklington claimed that Bruce McNall, the dynamic new owner of the Kings, had approached him during the summer and asked what it would take to get Wayne. Pocklington said he would never have considered dealing his superstar if Wayne hadn't called him to say he wanted to move on. It's true that Wayne expressed an interest in the Kings, saying, "It would be beneficial for everyone involved to let me play for Los Angeles."

But Eddie Mio and Paul Coffey, Wayne's best friends, said Wayne was devastated at the thought of leaving the Oilers. Coffey said, "There's no bloody way he wanted to leave. I don't care if he married the Queen of England." Mio added, "It was only after the papers were drawn up that Wayne decided he'd had enough of Peter Pocklington. And nobody should blame Janet for this move. She does not deserve to be persecuted . . . not for a minute."

The terms of the deal? Gretzky, along with Marty McSorley, Mike Krushelnyski and minor leaguer John Miner to the Kings, in return for Jimmy Carson, Martin Gelinas, the Kings' first-round draft choice in 1988, three first-round choices in '89, and '91 and '93, the rights to minor-leaguer Craig Redmond, plus 15 million dollars.

No matter who's to blame or who won the deal, there's never been a trade like it. Not in hockey, not in any sport.

A Bloodbath in Montreal

IF YOU THINK there's too much violence in modern-day hockey you wouldn't have enjoyed reading the headlines in all the papers after a game played in Montreal on January 12, 1907.

The front page of the *Montreal Star* called for six months in jail for the combatants in the Ottawa-Montreal donnybrook that had taken place the night before. One headline writer called it "the worst exhibition of butchery ever seen on ice."

Montreal's Hod Stuart, who for some reason played with bare knees, emerged from the game looking as if he'd been in a train wreck. Stuart had been nailed over the head by a hockey stick, a two-hander delivered by Ottawa's Alf Smith. For several minutes Stuart had lain on the ice like a corpse.

In another confrontation, Ottawa's Baldy Spittal smashed his stick over Cec Blatchford's head and Blatchford was carried off unconscious. Then Harry Smith, Alf's brother, whacked Ernie Johnston in the face with his stick, and blood gushed from Johnston's broken nose.

The next day, when the referee proposed to league officials that the chief culprits in the brawl, Alf Smith and Baldy Spittal, be suspended for the rest of the season, the motion was quickly voted down. The Ottawa boys weren't that unruly, the officials opined. In the heat of the game, they simply used poor judgment. The league president, who favored a lengthy suspension, was outraged at the decision and turned in his resignation.

Montreal police, meanwhile, shocked by the acts of violence on the ice, decided to prosecute. When the Ottawa team returned to Montreal two weeks later, the Smith brothers and Spittal were promptly arrested, charged with assault and released on bail. At their trial, Alf Smith and Spittal were convicted, fined $20 apiece and told to stay out of trouble in future. The evidence against Harry Smith apparently was less conclusive for he was found not guilty.

Was It Murder on Ice?

THE NHL IS celebrating its 80th anniversary, and in all that time the league has had only one fatality in a game. That occurred in 1968 when Bill Masterton of the Minnesota North Stars died after striking his head on the ice while playing against the California Seals.

But the death of star player Owen McCourt of the old Federal League in 1907 was no accident. In fact, throughout the country, it was called "murder on ice," and there were demands that the player causing the fatality be sent to jail for life.

Owen McCourt, who played for Cornwall, Ontario, was the leading scorer in the four-team Federal League, an ancestor of the NHL. During a game with the Ottawa Vics on March 6, 1907, McCourt became involved in a fight with Art Throop of Ottawa. Soon other players joined the scuffle, one being an Ottawa boy named Charlie Masson. During the battle, Masson smashed McCourt over the head with his hockey stick. Unconscious, McCourt was taken to hospital, blood streaming from his wound. Within a few hours he was dead.

Masson was immediately arrested and charged with the murder of Owen McCourt. At the trial in

Cornwall a few weeks later, witnesses gave conflicting testimony. While some indicated it was Masson's vicious attack that led to McCourt's death, others said McCourt had been struck on the head by another player just before Masson's stick creased his skull.

Judge Magee told a packed courtroom he was unable to determine which blow was the cause of McCourt's death — in fact, it could easily have been a combination of the two. As a result, he had no alternative but to acquit Charlie Masson of the murder charge.

The Ottawa team, distressed over the death of McCourt, cancelled all their remaining games, even though the league championship was within their grasp. One of the Ottawa players said, "I never want to see a hockey match again. The game in Cornwall was frightfully rough, and poor Charlie Masson kept telling us to play clean hockey or not at all. I firmly believe that if he struck McCourt at all, he did it in self-defence."

McGill Boys Organize Hockey

THE RECORDS SHOW that ice hockey has its origins in Europe. In France a crude form of hockey was called *hoquet*. In Ireland it was hurley and in Scotland it was called shinty or shinny on ice.

There's no doubt that British soldiers, posted to Canada in the 1800s, played games of hurley or shinny in places like Halifax and Kingston, for both claim to be hockey's birthplace. Kingston has long claimed that the British garrison stationed in that city played hockey on the ice in Kingston Harbour in 1855, while Maritime sports historians say games were played in Halifax even earlier. There's convincing evidence a form of hockey was played on Long Pond, in Windsor, Nova Scotia sometime before 1810. Montreal historians also make a claim concerning a game between the Dorchesters and the Uptown Club played there in 1837.

Most researchers agree that Montreal deserves to be recognized as the site of the first game played indoors. On March 3, 1875, a group of McGill students introduced what might legitimately be called "the first game of organized hockey played indoors." The game was organized by James Creighton, originally from Halifax and a graduate of Dalhousie University. Creighton, who was about to enroll at McGill for postgraduate studies, arranged for some Halifax friends to send a couple of dozen shinny sticks to Montreal. With the help of the eager McGill players, he drew up some rules and booked the Victoria rink for the big game.

Because the game was played on a rink surrounded by a low dasher, with an ice surface of 80 by 200 feet (outdoor games were played on much larger surfaces), Creighton decided to limit the number of players to nine per side. In outdoor shinny, any number could play, and games involving twenty to forty players were common.

For indoor play, the rubber lacrosse ball used for a puck was found to be unsuitable. It was either pared off on two sides to produce a flat rubber object that slid rather than bounced, or it was discarded and a flat, circular piece of wood was used instead.

Two poles or flags were planted in the ice to serve as a goal area. It's reported that two volunteers served as goalkeepers in this game, which may have been another hockey "first."

The first game, won by Creighton's team by a 2–1 score, ended on a sour note. In his book *Hockey's Captains, Colonels and Kings,* J.W. Fitsell, a noted Kingston hockey historian, states that "heads were bashed, benches smashed and lady spectators fled in confusion."

Later on, Creighton and the McGill students introduced colorful uniforms, team positions, more elaborate rules and referees to enforce them.

Others may argue, but Montreal's claim to be the site of the first organized hockey game played indoors appears to be pretty solid.

The First Goal Nets

WHAT WOULD HOCKEY be without goal nets? And yet, when goal nets were first introduced back in 1900, many critics said the game would be a lot better off without them.

Before goal nets were invented, two wooden poles stuck in the ice marked the goal area. And behind the goal stood a judge, handkerchief in hand, which he waved whenever the puck crossed the line.

Then some chaps substituted a pair of gas pipes for the wooden poles. The pipes were joined at the top by a curved metal crossbar over which some netting was draped. The idea was borrowed from the game of ice polo, which was popular at the time in places like Minnesota.

When the new goal nets were introduced in

1900, the *Montreal Gazette* said they helped turn an otherwise good goalkeeper into something resembling a wooden Indian outside a tobacco store. The poor goalie was practically nailed to his place, the paper stated. The possibility of his going in behind the goal area was reduced to a minimum, and if his skates got tangled in the netting, there was an excellent chance he'd break his neck. In short, he'd be worse off than an old Roman gladiator caught in the meshes.

The goal net was of no earthly use to the goal umpires, said the *Gazette*. The goal umpire couldn't possibly miss any goals unless he happened to be afflicted with some rare optical malfunction. There might be only one time in a hundred when the netting might be of use.

Meanwhile, the *Brooklyn Eagle* endorsed the nets and said they would revolutionize the game. They would eliminate frequent disputes, claimed the *Eagle,* and matches would then be won or lost on merit alone.

The American nets of the day differed from the Canadian model. American nets had posts made of rubber-covered iron pipes but fixed upon springs. When a player slammed into the post it bent right back to ice level, then sprang upright again.

With goalies nowadays griping about forwards who charge the net, without fear of personal injury because modern-day nets are easily dislodged, it's obvious that hockey still hasn't found the perfect goal net.

Some Teams Will Do Anything to Win

MANY YEARS AGO two small towns in Ontario developed a fierce hockey rivalry. Whenever Brantford played Preston, fan interest was at a peak. Winning was so important to the rivals that on at least one occasion an attempt was made to bribe the referee. Midway through one bitterly fought game, referee Jimmy Fraser was offered $10 if he would make sure Brantford won. When he declined the money and Preston squeezed out a one-goal victory, Fraser was approached again. This time he was offered $15 if he would report to the Ontario Hockey Association that the winning goal was scored after the expiration of time.

In 1895 in Quebec City, Ottawa edged Quebec 3–2 one night and the crowd became very hostile toward the referee, a man named Hamilton. After the game, a number of fans chased Hamilton and captured him just as he was about to board a train for Montreal. They dragged him back to the arena and, twisting his arm, tried to coerce him into declaring the match a draw. Fortunately police arrived just in time to rescue the badly shaken official and escort him back to the train station, from whence he happily fled the city.

A Special Train for Charlie

IN 1902 A MONTREAL TEAM left for Ottawa and a big game with the Senators. But there was one major problem: Montreal's star player, Charlie

Liffiton, was unable to get off work in time to catch the train and would have to be left behind. Montreal officials huddled and agreed their chances against Ottawa were slim without Liffiton. So they chartered a special train for the player.

When Liffiton was released from work, he raced to the station and hopped aboard the "special." Just Charlie, alone in a car, while up front the engineer and the fireman pushed the train to breakneck speeds. The train left Montreal at 6:20 p.m. and arrived in Ottawa at 8:40 — 20 minutes ahead of game time. A horse-drawn sleigh got the star player to the arena in time to throw on his uniform and be ready for the opening whistle. In order to have Liffiton in the Montreal lineup, team officials paid $114 to the CPR for the special train.

Was it worth it? Indeed it was, for Liffiton, who was averaging a goal a game, paced Montreal to a 4–2 victory.

Ballard Made Leaf Fans Boil

WHEN HAROLD BALLARD ran the Toronto Maple Leaf franchise in the seventies and eighties, he was constantly making headlines with his outrageous behavior and comments. Here are several things he did or said that caused many to call him names like "tyrant," "chauvinist," "racist," and "boor."

- Guesting on *As It Happens,* a CBC radio show, he called popular broadcaster Barbara Frum "a dumb broad," told her to "shut up," and further shocked listeners by telling Frum that "women are only good for lying on their backs." Ballard later told writer Earl McRae that he couldn't "stand feminist broads. They're a bunch of frustrated old maids. A lot of them phoned me after the Frum incident and complained. I said to them. 'What's the matter, honey, can't get a man? You want my body?' Boy, they went nuts. I loved it."

- Referring to gentlemanly Inge Hammerstrom, a Swedish forward who joined the Leafs at the same time as Borje Salming, Ballard commented: "Hammerstrom could go in the corners with half a dozen eggs in his pocket and not break one of them."
- He called Czech defector Vaclav Nedomansky "a traitor" for fleeing his homeland in order to play hockey in Canada with the Toronto Toros of the WHA. Ironically, a few months later, when Ballard signed two Czech players, Peter Ihnacek and Miroslav Frycer, he called them "brave young men for having the guts to leave their native land to start life anew in Canada."
- He refused to converse with *Toronto Star* hockey writer Frank Orr because he disliked some of Orr's columns. Behind Orr's back he called the heterosexual sportswriter "a queer."
- He threatened to bar Bobby Hull from Maple Leaf Gardens because Hull was thinking of removing some of his mementos from the Hockey Hall of Fame. When Hull was hired to do appearances for *Hockey Night in Canada* out of Toronto and

bluntly asked Ballard if the threat to keep him out of the Gardens was true, Ballard laughed and lied. "No way, Bobby. You're welcome in my rink anytime," he told the former scoring champ.

- During his early relationship with Leaf captain Darryl Sittler, he told reporters, "If I could have another son, I'd want one just like him." A few months later he was calling the popular Sittler a "cancer" on the team.
- When Gordie Howe scored his 1,000th career goal while playing in the WHA, Ballard refused to allow the news to be flashed on the scoreboard over center ice at the Gardens. "Why, that's not an accomplishment worthy or recognition," he scoffed. "A blind man can score goals in that league."
- When new private boxes were installed in Maple Leaf Gardens, Ballard had legendary broadcaster Foster Hewitt's famous broadcasting booth — the gondola — removed. It went to the incinerator instead of to the Hockey Hall of Fame. When there was a public outcry, Ballard said he would sell off Foster's favorite chair from the gondola and give the profits to charity. Then he acquired 25 chairs, painted Foster's name on the back of them, and sold them, as well. (In fact, Foster never did have one particular chair he used during his hundreds of Leaf broadcasts.)
- Ballard cut the salary of longtime scout Bob Davidson by two-thirds in order to

force him to quit the Leaf organization. The ploy worked because Davidson promptly turned in his resignation.

- When two of his players, Sittler and Salming, signed up to take part in the popular TV intermission feature "Showdown," a series approved by the league, Ballard sought a court order to prevent the Leaf stars from participating. When his request was turned down, he banned the "Showdown" tapes from all Leaf telecasts, virtually throwing the segment's producers into bankruptcy.

- When the NHL ordered all teams to put players' names on the backs of their game jerseys, Ballard balked at the edict, fearing it would hurt the sale of game-day programs, which contained the lineups. When pressured by NHL president John Ziegler to conform, Ballard had the players' names stitched on the jerseys — but in the same color as the jersey itself, making the names unrecognizable from any distance.

Well, Excuse Me!

WHEN PUNCH IMLACH was hired (for the second time) as general manager of the Toronto Maple Leafs in the seventies, he antagonized players and fans with his "let's clean house" approach. He dumped players he felt were still loyal to former general manager Jim Gregory. He traded players like Pat Boutette, Dave Hutchison, Tiger Williams, and others. And he infuriated everybody when he swapped popular Lanny Mc-

George "Punch" Imlach, the Maple Leafs' tough-as-nails coach and general manager.

Donald, a genuine Leaf hero, to Colorado. And he caused another ripple of anger to sweep through Toronto when he suggested he would get rid of captain Darryl Sittler, too, if Sittler didn't have a bothersome no-trade clause in his contract.

Meanwhile Imlach had hired Joe Crozier, an old friend, to coach the Leafs. When team owner Harold Ballard, never one to hide his emotions, expressed his disdain for Crozier, the players saw their opportunity to get back at Imlach. They simply didn't listen to or perform for Crozier. Their attitude infuriated the coach and general manager.

Crozier, sensing he was about to be fired by Ballard, called a team meeting and lectured the Leafs for their behavior. When he finished, there was silence in the Leaf dressing room. It was left up to free spirit Ian Turnbull to come up with an appropriate response. He lifted one leg and cut loose with a thunderous fart. That about said it all.

Was Hockey Invented by the British Royal Family?

IN MY RESEARCH into hockey's beginnings recently I came across an article written in 1937 by Ian Gordon, a British journalist who claims that hockey owes its life to the British Royal Family. In his astonishing claim Gordon writes:

> While it is true that the Dominion across the Atlantic [Canada] has nursed and developed ice hockey to the fine pitch of physical perfection and precision that has earned it the title of the fastest game on earth, the idea originated at Windsor Castle.
>
> The game is in modern times labelled "the national sport of Canada" but it owes its life to the Royal Family. Among its first players are included two King Emperors, and the first excited spectators were ladies of the Royal Household.
>
> In the hard winter of 1853 the house party at the country palace looked for diversion on the frozen lake on the grounds. The idea was born to play a game of field hockey on the ice; sides were chosen, sticks found, and the bung from a barrel acquired to take the place of the ball, which bounced too much for any accurate control.
>
> While Queen Victoria and her attendants stood by giving encouragement, officers of the guards skated over the surface trying to score into the net defended by the Prince Consort. The result was not recorded but history tells that the players were rewarded with a well-spiced rum punch.

It was more than 20 years later that the game crossed the ocean to Canada. On a visit to England, a student of McGill University came upon a game of field hockey. His versatile brain followed along the same lines as those pioneers at Windsor Castle, and on his return to his studies that winter he called together a band of enthusiasts, pointed out the natural playing resources of the severe Canadian winter, with its months of ice and snow, and promptly organized the first team at McGill University.

Support later came from an unexpected source; not a Canadian sportsman but from an Englishman. Lord Stanley, the Governor General, presented a handsome trophy, and from that time the success and ever-growing interest in the sport in Canada was assured.

Of course, Maritime historians such as Howard Dill and Dr. Garth Vaughn claim that some form of hockey had been played in Nova Scotia, notably on Windsor's Long Pond, in the early 1800s, or almost a half century before the games described above at Windsor Castle.

Bruins' Leading Scorer Suspended for Life

IT HAPPENED ALMOST half a century ago — in 1948. Hockey star Don Gallinger suddenly found himself banished from the game he loved.

Gallinger, a versatile athlete who turned down pro baseball offers from the Philadelphia Athletics and the Boston Red Sox, was summoned to the NHL at the age of 17. The shifty centerman was Boston's leading scorer when his career suddenly skidded to a halt at age 22. In the final month of the 1947–48 season, NHL president Clarence Campbell suspended Gallinger for life for gambling on hockey games.

"It was such a dreadful thing," Gallinger told *Toronto Sun* reporter Steve Simmons in 1989. "Nobody knows more about depression and despair than I do. I was just 22. I would never wish on people what I have gone through.

"Sure I bet on games. But I never fixed a game. When they called me in, I wasn't worried. I never thought they could pin anything on me."

But they did. Gallinger and Billy Taylor, then with the Rangers, were identified as having done business with a Detroit bookmaker and racketeer named James Tamer. Police taps on the former prison inmate's phone calls produced information about hockey bets, and the names Taylor and Gallinger surfaced.

The final bet Gallinger made was a $1,000 wager on a game between the Bruins and the Blackhawks. The Bruins won the game and Gallinger figured in the tying goal. He lost the bet.

At first, when called upon to explain his actions, Gallinger denied everything. He knew the charges against him would be difficult to prove. Only if Taylor confessed to any wrongdoing would Gallinger be implicated. Taylor decided to confess and was suspended for life.

A few months later, in a five-hour meeting with Campbell, Gallinger finally admitted his guilt. He, too, drew a lifetime suspension. Gallinger never forgave the league president for acting as judge and jury, and it always puzzled him why Babe Pratt, a third player who had confessed to gambling on hockey games two years earlier, had drawn a mere 16-game suspension. Incredibly neither Gallinger nor Taylor was represented by a lawyer, and some of the evidence — the wiretaps obtained by Detroit police — were obtained illegally.

All hockey avenues were closed to the banished stars. Gallinger applied for coaching and management positions with several teams but was shunned wherever he applied. He lost his 11-year-old daughter to cancer. His wife left him, taking two other children with her. The business he was in collapsed. "I was lost and afraid," he told Simmons. "I was ready to blow my brains out."

Some say it was an act of mercy when Campbell reinstated Gallinger and Taylor in 1970. Others say the NHL president feared a lawsuit from the banished pair. Taylor made a successful return to the fold, securing scouting jobs. But Gallinger's attempts to find hockey employment in the league that banished him met with failure at every turn.

Did Hockey Begin on Howard Dill's Pumpkin Farm?

IN THE *BOSTON GLOBE* of October 3, 1991, on the first page of the sports section, there is a color photo of Howard Dill, arms folded, sitting on a giant pumpkin. From under his peaked cap he gazes out over a small pond on his 250-acre farm near Windsor, Nova Scotia. The murky patch of water that attracts his wistful stare is known as

Long Pond or Steel Pond. The caption under the photo reads: "Howard Dill dreams of days when hockey, in possibly its earliest form, was played on the pond that sits on his property."

Writer Kevin Dupont of the *Globe* came all the way from Boston to see the pond and to interview Dill, a four-time world champion pumpkin grower, a hockey historian, and an assembler of a marvelous collection of hockey memorabilia. Although arguments abound as to when and where the game of hockey originated, Howard Dill, and the good people of Windsor, believe the nondescript patch of water on the Dill property should be recognized as hockey's birthplace.

To back his claim that his pond is historically significant, Dill points to an 1844 story in the London periodical *Attaché,* in which author Thomas Haliburton writes about hurley, a game closely resembling hockey, being played on Long Pond circa 1810. Haliburton recounts his boyhood school days at King's College, today known as King's Edgehill School, which stands a short distance from the small pond in question. Haliburton's words are possibly the oldest written evidence of hockey being played in Canada: ". . . and the boys let out racin', yellin', hollerin' and whoopin' like mad with pleasure . . . and the game at bass [*sic*] in the field, or hurley on the long pond on the ice . . ."

"The way I see it," Dill says, "the proof is right there in that story." The man who knows pumpkins (he grows 600-pounders and sells the seeds all over the world, advising clients to "plant 'em and jump back fast") also knows his hockey history.

As for the pond, in its heyday in the thirties and forties, kids played hockey on it all the time. School kids mingled with town kids. They would skate and play hockey on the pond all day. At night they would light bonfires and toast marshmallows. They had been doing it for generations. Why wouldn't they be doing it as far back as 1800?

Forty or fifty years ago, when Dill played hockey on the pond, it was close to 200 feet long and about 50 feet wide. Over the years the water level has dropped and now the pond is a third of its former size. Dill thinks the pond should be recognized as the cradle of hockey in North America — until someone steps forward with conclusive written proof that it isn't. "It should be preserved," Dill says. "Maybe a sign erected so people who come here can look at it and say, 'That's where hockey began, back in the early 1800s.'"

When Royalty Played Hockey

JOURNALIST IAN GORDON, writing about hockey in England, reveals that Lord Stanley, donor of the family trophy, actually played the game — at least on one occasion. And among his companions were the most famous bluebloods in the British Empire:

The [hockey] team spirit in England was encouraged in the 1890s in a very unexpected way. A Royal team was formed at Buckingham Palace in the winter of 1895, and when a hard frost — which gave sufficient ice on the lake behind the Palace — rewarded earnest desire, a challenge was issued to a team skippered by Lord Stanley, the Earl of Derby. Buckingham Palace included in their line-up the Prince of Wales, later to become King Edward VII, and the Duke of York, who afterwards became King George V.

The rival teams were six a side. Lord Stanley had four members of his family playing alongside him, and their Canadian experience gave them a big advantage. This resulted in numerous goals being chalked up to their credit, while the Palace combination could only score once.

Until the end of the century, hockey came in for considerable patronage from the Royal Family, and at most club games there was at least one supporter from Buckingham Palace to follow the play closely.

Hengler's Rink in London — now the Royal Palladium — was the favourite place, and many members of the European Royal Families, when visiting London, were escorted there to be initiated into the daring game.

Although England has thus played such a big part in giving a historical background to ice hockey, the sport had little public favour here. The main reason for this was the lack of opportunities for training boys to skate. Hard winters failed to materialize as they did in the "good old days" and the post-war youngster knew little of the joy of skimming over ice on two thin blades of steel.

Forward Passing
Opened Up the Game

PRIOR TO THE 1929–30 NHL season the league removed the shackles from the forward pass. Prior to that a player couldn't pass forward to a teammate in the attacking zone. What is more, a team was no longer permitted to keep more than three players (including the goalie) in the defensive zone while the play was up the ice. Laggards who didn't move up with the play could receive a minor penalty. Did the new rules lead to more scoring? You bet they did.

In the 1928–29 season, before the new rules were initiated, the trend toward defensive hockey was so great that little George Hainsworth, the Montreal goalie, recorded 22 shutouts in 44 games and yielded only 43 goals to opposing shooters. Boston, the highest-scoring team in hockey, managed only 89 goals all season, and Toronto's Ace Bailey won the NHL scoring championship with a mere 22 goals and 10 assists for 32 points.

Compare those statistics with the following season when the new forward pass rule was in place. Every team in the NHL topped 100 goals, the Bruins leading the way with 179 — 90 more than they had scored the previous year. Cooney Weiland of Boston went on a scoring spree that netted him the Art Ross Trophy with 43 goals and 73 points. The previous year he had scored 11 goals and 18 points. Two other players, Dit Clapper of the Bruins and Howie Morenz of Montreal, hit the 40-goal plateau. Clapper had scored nine goals one year earlier, while Morenz netted 17.

Defensively Tiny Thompson, the Bruin netminder, was the only goalie to give up fewer than 100 goals. He yielded 98 (55 more than Hainsworth had given up the previous season) in winning the Vezina Trophy.

There is no doubt that the introduction of the forward pass within all three zones on the ice contributed greatly to a huge increase in scoring in the NHL.

Moosomin First in Saskatchewan Hockey

THE PROVINCE OF SASKATCHEWAN was formed in 1905, but hockey was a fixture there long before that. Even so, it took a strange set of circumstances to bring the winter sport to that region of Canada.

It seems that a man involved with hockey equipment in Toronto received an order from Winnipeg one day. The request was for a couple of dozen hockey sticks, which were in short supply in the Manitoba capital. Somewhere en route west the address tag attached to the bundle was lost and the precious sticks never reached their destination. In time they surfaced in Birtle, Manitoba, where they were placed in a storage room by the station agent.

A traveling salesman stopped by one day to visit the agent, and the conversation turned to hockey. The agent showed the salesman the hockey sticks and said he had been having a lot of trouble locating the owner. Somehow a deal was made. The salesman, a resident of Moosomin, Saskatchewan, and obviously a smooth talker, left with the sticks.

Returning to Moosomin, the salesman recruited

some neighbors and distributed the sticks. A patch of nearby ice was cleared of snow and the first hockey game in that part of Saskatchewan was played — on a January day in 1895.

It was, of course, a makeshift game at best, with the players using a lacrosse ball for a puck. The participants were forced to play heads-up hockey right from the start, mainly because of a well casing in the center of the ice from which they drew water to flood the ice.

They Didn't Stay Around Very Long

WHEN THE NHL WAS FORMED in November 1917, there were five charter members. One of the five, the Quebec Bulldogs, decided to wait another season before joining the new circuit. That left the Montreal Canadiens, the Montreal Wanderers, the Ottawa Senators, and the Toronto Arenas.

The Wanderers not only hold the record for the shortest stay in the NHL, they recorded the fewest wins. Their season was only two weeks old when, on January 2, 1918, their arena burned to the ground. Homeless, the team ceased operations and never returned. The Wanderers' proudest moment came on December 19, 1917, when they edged Toronto 10–9 in their home opener before 700 fans. It was their one and only victory in the NHL.

The Wildest Stanley Cup Parade Ever

THE HEADLINES in the Philadelphia newspapers said it all: "Miracle Flyers Take the Cup. City Goes Wild with Joy." The date was Sunday, May 19, 1974. Our NBC telecast team (Tim Ryan, Ted Lindsay, and myself) had witnessed the incredible postgame explosion of noise the day before when we covered the Flyers' thrilling Cup victory over Boston on national television.

But the celebration in the arena that Saturday afternoon was just a squeak to the pandemonium that greeted the victors the following day. Over two million Philadelphians jammed Broad Street to honor their heroes with a ticker tape parade. It was a parade that far surpassed any other Cup-winning parade in history. The streets were so crowded that several of the Flyers had to abandon their cars and push their way through the mob just to reach the mall where the open convertibles awaited them.

The crowds were so thick that the parade proceeded at a turtle's pace. The players, most of whom had been imbibing liberally since the game had ended the previous afternoon, often had to make "pit stops" to relieve themselves. They simply hopped out of their convertibles, knocked on the nearest door, and were greeted like soldiers home from a war. "Of course, you can use our facilities" was the response to every request. "All we ask in return is an autograph."

Bernie Parent and captain Bobby Clarke came in for the loudest ovations. Parent had provided coach Fred Shero's team with miraculous goaltending, and the netminder had earned the Conn

Smythe Trophy as playoff MVP. Clarke's inspirational leadership was also a major reason the Flyers were able to become the first expansion team to capture Lord Stanley's old basin.

And while she declined an invitation to be part of the parade, singer Kate Smith was lauded for her role in the Flyer victory. In two playoff games Kate appeared "live" at the Spectrum to sing "God Bless America." On both occasions the opposing team failed to score a single goal. And Kate's record as a Flyer good luck charm was simply awesome. Whenever her famous song was heard prior to a home game, the Flyers were almost unbeatable. By the end of the 1974 playoffs her mark was 37–3–1.

Home of the Face-off

THE LITTLE TOWN OF PARIS, ONTARIO, is credited with being the birthplace of hockey's face-off, while referee Fred Waghorne is recorded as its inventor. Waghorne, born in England in 1866, was a highly respected hockey referee in Canada for more than 50 years.

The distinguished official was handling a particularly difficult game in Paris one night in the early 1900s. Throughout the contest the fans supporting the teams involved screamed for their centermen to beat rival pivots to the puck. In those days, when face-offs were required, it was customary for the referee to place the puck between the sticks of the centermen, shout "Play," and jump quickly out of the way.

During the game, the opposing centermen were so eager to win the draw that Waghorne's hands, arms, and legs took a frightful beating. By the half-way mark he was bruised and bloody and he had had enough.

He told the centers before the next face-off, "You boys put your sticks on the ice and keep them 18 inches apart. And be ready for what happens next." He stood back and threw the puck between the poised sticks — like a man throwing a dog a bone. Instinctively the two players clashed their sticks together in an effort to control the puck, and the modern-day face-off was born.

Waghorne was so pleased with the results of his face-off invention that he proceeded to add another innovation to refereeing. He threw away the large handbell he'd been using to signal stoppages in play and introduced a whistle. Soon all hockey officials followed suit and began using whistles, but some of them had lingering regrets over the phasing out of the handbells.

"They were very effective for keeping obnoxious fans at bay," Waghorne said. "If a fan reached out from rinkside and grabbed a player or a referee, you could wallop him over the head with the bell. He'd see stars and hear bells ringing — all at the same time."

Richard Suspension Leads to Hockey's Biggest Riot

LATE IN THE 1954–55 SEASON the Montreal Canadiens were playing the Boston Bruins at the Boston Garden. With the Bruins leading by two goals, Montreal coach Dick Irvin pulled goalie Jacques Plante and threw an extra attacker

The man who touched off a riot: the Canadiens' Rocket Richard in full throttle.

onto the ice. Rocket Richard, the Habs' ace scorer, was racing over the Bruin blue line when Boston defenseman Hal Laycoe clipped him across the head with his stick. Referee Frank Udvari signaled a delayed penalty, and when the official blew his whistle, Richard sought immediate vengeance. He rushed over to Laycoe, raised his stick, and lashed out at him.

Linesman Cliff Thompson grabbed Richard and wrestled his stick away. But Richard broke free, picked up a loose stick lying on the ice, and attacked Laycoe a second time. He was held momentarily by Thompson, then broke loose again, grabbed yet another stick, and went right back after the Boston player. In the melee Richard punched linesman Thompson, giving him a black eye, and moments later he threw a blood-soaked towel at referee Udvari. Richard was thrown out of the game and fined $100. Any further punishment would be doled out by NHL president Clarence Campbell.

On March 16 Campbell stunned Richard by suspending him for the rest of the season and for all playoff games. Richard was outraged and so were his countless loyal fans. Callers phoned the NHL offices in Montreal, and many were so furious that they threatened Campbell's life.

The following night, March 17, the Canadiens hosted the Detroit Red Wings at the Forum. Campbell stubbornly insisted on occupying his regular place in the stands, accompanied by his secretary (and future wife) Phyllis King.

Perhaps if Montreal, battling Detroit for first place, had grabbed an early lead over the Red Wings, the crowd would have settled down and ignored Campbell. But Montreal fell behind 4–2, and with each Red Wing goal Campbell and Miss King were subjected to much verbal abuse. Then programs, paper cups, and other garbage were thrown at them. Suddenly a tear gas bomb went off and people panicked. They scrambled over seats and into the aisles, seeking the nearest exits. Police moved in and their quick action probably averted a major disaster. The game was stopped and later forfeited to Detroit. Campbell and Miss King were escorted to a nearby dressing room where they were temporarily safe.

Outside the Forum the mood of the fans, ugly to begin with, turned vicious. A mob spirit was unleashed that led to vandalism and violence. Cars were damaged, store windows were broken, and shops were looted.

Campbell would say later, "I'm convinced the riot that night marked the initial indication of the resurgence of French nationalism in Quebec. The majority of those involved were not even hockey fans but thugs who seized the Richard incident to vent their unrest against the Anglos of which I was polarized as leader."

Jack Adams, outspoken manager of Detroit, said, "It's the reporters who've turned Richard into an idol, a player whose suspension can transform hockey fans into shrieking idiots. Well, Richard is no hero. He let his team down, he let hockey down, he let the public down."

Richard, who had slipped into the game that night almost unnoticed, felt deep regret over the incident. "I wanted to go in the streets and use a loudspeaker to tell the fans to stop their nonsense. But it wouldn't have done any good. They would have paraded me around on their shoulders."

Aside from the suspension, Richard suffered the loss of a long-sought prize — the 1955 NHL scoring crown. While he sat out the final three games of the season, teammate Boom Boom Geoffrion slipped ahead of him in the scoring race and captured the Art Ross Trophy by a single point, 75–74. Richard fans, perhaps sensing that the Rocket would never again come close to a scoring title, booed Geoffrion unmercifully when he swept the crown from the head of their hero.